D1563961

Ovid and the Politics of Emotion
in Elizabethan England

Ovid and the Politics of Emotion in Elizabethan England

Cora Fox

palgrave
macmillan

OVID AND THE POLITICS OF EMOTION IN ELIZABETHAN ENGLAND
Copyright © Cora Fox, 2009.

First published in 2009 by PALGRAVE MACMILLAN®
in the United States—a division of St. Martin's Press LLC,
175 Fifth Avenue, New York, NY 10010.

Where this book is distributed in the UK, Europe and the rest of
the world, this is by Palgrave Macmillan, a division of Macmillan
Publishers Limited, registered in England, company number 785998,
of Houndmills, Basingstoke, Hampshire RG21 6XS.

Palgrave Macmillan is the global academic imprint of the above
companies and has companies and representatives throughout the
world.

Palgrave® and Macmillan® are registered trademarks in the United
States, the United Kingdom, Europe and other countries.

ISBN: 978-0-230-61704-9

Library of Congress Cataloging-in-Publication Data

Fox, Cora, 1968–
    Ovid and the politics of emotion in Elizabethan England / Cora
Fox.
        p. cm.
    Includes bibliographical references.
    ISBN 978-0-230-61704-9 (alk. paper)
    1. English literature—Early modern, 1500–1700—History and
criticism. 2. Emotions in literature. 3. Self in literature. 4. Ovid,
43 B.C.–17 or 18 A.D.—Influence. 5. English literature—Roman
influences. 6. Allusions in literature. 7. Intertextuality. I. Title.

PR428.E56F69 2009
820.9'353—dc22   2009009734

A catalogue record of the book is available from the British Library.

Design by Scribe Inc.

First edition: December 2009

10 9 8 7 6 5 4 3 2 1

Printed in the United States of America.

CONTENTS

ACKNOWLEDGMENTS

This project has been through many metamorphoses to reach its present state of relative stability. It would not have been possible without junior leaves and summer support provided by the Arizona State University (ASU) Department of English, the ASU College of Liberal Arts and Sciences, the Arizona Center for Medieval and Renaissance Studies (ACMRS), and the ASU Women's Studies program. In particular, the faculty fellows program though the ACMRS gave me not just time but intellectual support and encouragement from my excellent medieval and Renaissance colleagues across the campus of ASU.

A section of Chapter 2 on Adicia's transformation was originally published as "Spenser's Grieving Adicia and the Gender Politics of Renaissance Ovidianism" in *ELH* in 2002, and some of the material of Chapter 4 on Reginald Scot was published in 2007 as "Authorizing the Metamorphic Witch: Ovid in Reginald Scot's *Discoverie of Witchcraft*" in *Metamorphoses: The Changing Face of Ovid in Medieval and Early Modern Europe*, edited by Alison Keith and Stephen Rupp. Thanks to the editors and anonymous reviewers of this journal and this collection for their feedback on my work and to the presses for permissions to reprint these pieces within this book. I would also like to thank Suzan Griffiths, librarian at St. Catharine's College, Cambridge, for providing such helpful access to Reginald Scot's *Discoverie of Witchcraft* and to Jerry Linstead, porter at St. Catharine's, who cheerfully helped us take the digital images that appear in this book. Brigitte Shull, my editor; Lee Norton at Palgrave; and Jennifer Kepler, my copyeditor at Scribe, Inc., have been amazingly efficient and helpful. I feel lucky to have had them to help me produce this book.

At ASU, I have been surrounded by Renaissance colleagues over the years who not only have been generous with their time and comments but have also inspired me with their excellent scholarship to reach greater insights in my own. Ayanna Thompson, Bradley Ryner, David Hawkes, Curtis Perry, Ian Moulton, and Melissa Walter have all at various times helped me develop whatever insights I achieve in this book. Ayanna and Curtis in particular have commented, sometimes repeatedly, on my writing, and I have benefited from their now well-acknowledged excellence as scholars and their friendships. I was also very fortunate to have the advice and friendship of Tom Roche for a brief period when he visited the ACMRS on the fellowship program that allowed my sponsored junior leave. I have tried to limit all references to "levels" of allegory in Spenser based on his wise arguments, and I hope he will be pleased.

My community of friendship at ASU is too wide to record here, but there have been many who have also helped me clarify and broaden my ideas, especially Taylor Corse, Mark Lussier, Keith Miller, Jennifer Parchesky, Claudia Sadowski-Smith, Bob Sturges, Beth Tobin, and Rosalynn Voaden in the Department of English; Holly Cashman, Markus Cruse, Daniel Gilfillan, and Juliann Vitullo in the School of International of International Letters and Cultures, and Diane Wolfthal in the School of Art. I am so grateful to have worked with such brilliant people. I have also had terrific students who have discussed ideas from this book in many different classes and contexts, and I had the capable and enthusiastic help of Megan Sawyer as a research assistant for one particularly productive summer.

When I started the project that would lead to this book as a graduate student, the group of those working on Ovid in Renaissance literature was small, and it has been a pleasure to watch it grow over the last decade. I have presented many of the ideas in this book at the annual conferences of the Shakespeare Association of America, the Renaissance Society of America, and the Modern Language Association, and I am particularly grateful for the feedback and encouragement of Lynn Enterline, Heather James, Theresa Krier, and Mihoko Suzuki at those conferences and beyond. The conference "Metamorphosis: The Changing Face of Ovid in Medieval and Early Modern Europe" in 2005, sponsored by the University of Toronto's Center for Renaissance and Reformation Studies and organized by Alison Keith, was of particular importance as my final chapter took shape and discussions that weekend changed the frame of reference for my analyses. I would like particularly to thank the organizers and attendees of that conference for their stimulating insights. In the last few years, I have also had the good fortune to work on an edited book project with Barbara Weiden Boyd, whose intellectual intensity and remarkably broad learning helped me refine and rethink the project in its final stages.

I am also fortunate to have been guided into the field by a group of outstanding and generous scholars at the University of Wisconsin–Madison, including Heather Dubrow, David Loewenstein, Jane Tylus, and Susanne Wofford. With the greater perspective I have gained in my own career, I only now fully appreciate how remarkable this group of faculty members was for those of us lucky enough to have been their students, and I want particularly to thank Heather for continuing to mentor and support me through the tenure process at ASU. Susanne's influence on my work and career is so deep that I will never feel I have fully repaid her, although I hope our friendship will continue to grow in ways that might make such a thing possible.

My personal debts to friends are too many to record, but I would like to mention those who have more immediately supported my many years of writing and rewriting this project: Kim Blockett, Celina Chelala, Christian Flaugh, and Everett Fox (my friend and brother). I need also to acknowledge in particular the influence and support of my father, Everett Allen Fox. I dedicated my doctoral dissertation on Ovid in the Renaissance to my mother, Suzanne Jones Fox, who died when I was eighteen and who was the first to tell me Ovid's stories. It is with particular pride, then, that I dedicate this book to my daughter, Lily Suzanne Fox, whose first three years of life were the last three years that I worked on this project. I would also like to publicly acknowledge my debts to her wonderful daycare and preschool teachers, who facilitated her days of play while I worked, and her beloved "aunt" Holly Cashman, who was in the hospital when she was born and has never stopped being there for both of us. This book would not exist without these people who have helped me raise my daughter. Lily will be surprised one day when she realizes that all those books without pictures in the house helped her mom work on such interesting characters as queens and witches. Becoming a mother has made me more aware of the high stakes involved in analyzing these figures in our history, and I am so grateful for Lily, whose daily joy and humor ground me when I find that history hard to embrace.

INTRODUCTION

> *Without the—always anterior—Book and Code, no desire, no*
> *jealousy: Pygmalion is in love with a link in the code of statuary;*
> *Paolo and Francesca love each other according to the passion of*
> *Lancelot and Guinevere (Dante, Inferno, V): itself a lost origin,*
> *writing becomes the origin of emotion.*

—Barthes, *S/Z*

In a well-known origin story from Ovid's *Metamorphoses*, Philomela is abducted and raped by her brother-in-law, Tereus, who cuts out her tongue to prevent her from revealing his crime. She communicates the truth to her sister by weaving the story into a tapestry and is eventually metamorphosed into a bird (a nightingale or swallow in Ovid's retelling), singing her song perpetually. In 1592, during Queen Elizabeth's later reign, Lavinia, on stage in Shakespeare's *Titus Andronicus*, is raped by two male characters who "outdo" Tereus by cutting off her hands as well as her tongue to prevent that old Ovidian trick. Lavinia, however, reveals the rape to her family by paging through to Philomela's story in a volume of Ovid's *Metamorphoses* physically brought on to the stage. This famous episode of self-conscious Ovidian allusion has become a touchstone for critics working on the play and its relation to the classical tradition in the English Renaissance.[1] In Shakespeare's evocation of this Ovidian tale, we witness not only the insistent "literariness" of Ovidian intertextuality in this period but also its explicit association with the representation of a female subject, one who finds her "self" in Ovid's book. The self she finds is a grieving self—a figure whose subjective response to violence is marked by her expression (in this case a silent representation) of a distinctly Ovidian emotional state. In the end, in both Ovid and Shakespeare, Philomela and Lavinia both participate in the story's concluding violence, a bloody revenge, and immediately following the revelation of her double in Ovid's poem, Lavinia takes a staff in her mouth and writes the names of her rapists in the dust, recalling Ovid's Io, another figure who has been raped in the same poem. Her father and uncle, relieved to uncover this "treason" (4.1.47, 66) twice compare her rape to Tarquin's of Lucrece and vow to revenge themselves on "these traitorous Goths" (4.1. 92).[2] Ensnared in overdetermined intertextuality, the characters of the play unravel from this scene, modeling both the private grief of Titus and his family as well as the political dismemberment of Rome on the "Book and Code" of Ovid's *Metamorphoses*. Because Lavinia is so conspicuously more than the product of an unmediated text and is instead defined through Ovidian intertextuality, her character gains a discursive significance that enables her to "speak" even as she remains silent for the resolution of the play. The emotion defined by her very "Ovidianness" is strategic and has political consequences, as she motivates and participates in the bloody revenge and reestablishment of political order that conclude the play.[3]

This dramatic moment in *Titus Andronicus* offers a window onto the central role of Ovidian writings in constructing emotion in relation to politics in late Elizabethan England. Ovid's *Metamorphoses* was one of the most influential of the "reborn" classical texts of the Renaissance, and the discourse its imitations produced, Ovidianism, played a crucial ideological role in sixteenth- and seventeenth-century European culture on the Continent and in England.[4] Within this particular period in England's history—a period of marked political instability as well as the culmination of a century that saw surprising renegotiations of ideas surrounding the experience of emotion—Ovidianism intervenes repeatedly and in many different cultural realms to represent (and therefore define) certain kinds of affective states: emotions such as rage, grief, and excessive or impotent desire. These emotions are often feminized and are associated with women in Western culture before and after the Renaissance, but they take on particular resonances in the context of Renaissance England's redefinition of the private and public aspects of the self. Ovidianism served as a code for emotional expression in the period, and it participated in scripting not just private experiences of the self but public uses of emotional rhetoric.

Classical literary intertexts in general, bringing as they did the cultural values of an ancient society into Renaissance England, helped shape English social identity in fundamental ways, and Ovidian texts, which flourished in the final years of Elizabeth's reign, are central loci for redefinitions of emotional life. Literary intertexts are, in fact, arguably the most important, while the least perceptible, influences on a culture's evaluations and experiences of emotion. As Barthes tellingly suggests in the epigraph to this introduction, literature is the (always already lost) source of emotional codes of behavior—Paolo and Francesca love according to the narrative model of Lancelot and Guinevere, Lavinia grieves (to cite our pressing Elizabethan example) according to the literary precedent of Ovid's Philomela. This fundamental facet of the human experience of narrative means that in order to understand an individual or a society, and particularly such subtle but foundational aspects of everyday life as emotion, we need to turn to texts, and particularly to intertexts. Existing as the shifting ground behind artistic, and particularly literary, expression, intertexts are the sites of powerful negotiations between past and present, local and distant, subjective and intersubjective forms of emotional experience.[5]

Since 1986, when Leonard Barkan characterized Ovidianism as "a world where female emotions, themselves associated with change, are given special prominence," there have still been only a few studies that theorize the relation of this discourse to gendered subjectivity, or to the subaltern and antiauthoritarian positions that female figures often occupy.[6] Ovid's works, especially *Metamorphoses* and *Heroides*, so insistently explore the ways those in subjugated or impotent positions respond to authoritative kinds of power that the legacy of Ovidianism is intimately bound up with precisely these cultural questions surrounding individual and collective power. This book argues that Ovidianism functioned in English Renaissance culture to interrogate and revise cultural codes associated with the politics of emotional self-expression but at the same time, the Ovidian use of emotion as a political tool to challenge authority also legitimized a set of texts and values that allowed for subordinate, often female, voices to promote political investments outside of mainstream culture (whatever that culture was, depending upon the context). As both Heather James and Georgia Brown have convincingly argued from different perspectives, Ovidianism operated in, and in fact helped define, marginalized political contexts in the period. As James puts it, Ovidian texts are often the sites where "occasional" if not "unspeakable" thoughts arise in the Renaissance.[7] One cultural area where thoughts can be particularly unspeakable is the experience of emotion, and Ovidianism constituted politically enfranchised subjects who otherwise might not have been recognized or recognized themselves as such.

To define my matter of study as "Ovidianism" is to enter into a long and rich debate in Renaissance studies about how to accommodate poststructuralist and other theoretical insights about language processes into our study of this insistently intertextual period. Intertextuality is at the core of our construction of the period we call the Renaissance, and while intertextuality may be the central term and idea underlying all poststructuralist theory, grappling with its consequences is a particular pursuit of Renaissance critics.[8] This is, after all, the period in which humanism made all uses of language self-conscious and dialectical relationships between contemporary and ancient texts particularly so.[9] While it is granted and assumed that all textual representations have cultural effects, the effects themselves are harder to trace, especially when we are lacking so much of the material and textual evidence that might give us insight into how everyday Renaissance English citizens negotiated their lives with classical models serving as mainstays of their artistic and literary production. But while such study will always be speculative and is bound to be partially defeated by the scope of its aims, it is essential if we want our theorized readings of texts to engage the crucial questions of culture that make study of a previous period important and relevant.

This book, therefore, is also a case study in this kind of combined intertextual and cultural reading: it draws together particular close analyses of texts from various cultural and institutional realms to construct a picture of the consequences of intertextuality, and in this specific case, Ovidian intertextuality, which is arguably the most vacillating and controversial intertextual force in the period. Seeking to trace the influence of Ovid in various texts and discourses, the following study more broadly analyzes the ideologies of the Elizabethan subcultures within which these Ovidian texts were produced and that they subsequently construct. In each chapter, focused on a cultural milieu and a text that helps to define it, the book furthers the central argument I have suggested above: the most important cultural work Ovidian intertextuality performed in the period was to define certain kinds of emotional experience as politically legitimate and central to an individual's construction of his or her autonomous self. As Steven Mullaney and others have recently argued, Renaissance England was a culture in the throes of a major crisis in the everyday experience of emotion.[10] Having lived through Reformation England's fraught shifts between Catholicism and Protestantism as the state religion, as well as the many other ideological shifts that characterized England's emergence as a true European capital and the center of a nascent empire, English citizens at this time experienced a redefinition and reevaluation of emotion and in particular its public and political effects. Such rapid and marked cultural renegotiations opened up new possibilities for understanding emotional experience and the role of emotion in the experience of subjectivity, a Renaissance concern that has been at the center of critical debates about the period, especially in the last two decades.

Recent scholarly work on humoral and other competing cultural conceptions of emotion in the Renaissance has changed the ways we read references to emotional experience, the body, and subjectivity in literature as well as other textual productions of English Renaissance culture.[11] Primarily historicist and materialist, these studies of Renaissance humoralism have revised our readings of the complexities of emotional experience in the period, and they have provided convincing evidence for the centrality of humoral understandings of the self and its affects. Literature, however, is often informed by conflicting epistemological systems and varying cultural narratives, and critics such as Jacqueline Miller have traced understandings of emotion based not on philosophical or protomedical discourse but on rhetorical theories of imitation. Miller traces, for example, an alternate theorization of mimetic emotion, the kind of feeling Renaissance rhetors seek to elicit in their audiences when they make pathetic appeals, where the audience is "infected" by the emotion experienced or imitated by the rhetor.[12] Her work illustrates a cultural self-consciousness about imitated emotion that should inform our readings of the many lamenting, raging Ovidian figures in Renaissance literature. Just as Neoplatonism and Neo-Stoicism offered conflicting models of the relation between reason and the passions, a perhaps less codified but no less pervasive Ovidianism did similar cultural work. Unlike the philosophers Plato and Seneca, Ovid is insistently literary and in fact nonsystematizing, which makes the mechanisms of his cultural influence uniquely tied to narrative structures, plotting, and imagery, sites of reading that may be less clearly marked as engaged in intellectual or ideational negotiations but that are equally central to the constructions of culture.

Although influenced by these current critical discussions, the readings of Ovidianism that are the focus of this book also reflect the recent resurgence of interest in many fields of the social sciences in analyzing emotion in cultural terms. I draw broadly on a body of writings in the social sciences, particularly in the field of cultural anthropology, that seek to deconstruct naturalized ideas about emotional experience and uncover the cultural processes that determine which emotions are privileged or even experienced as part of the experience of the self. Building on Clifford Geertz' semiotic definition of culture, social scientists in the last three decades have turned toward theorizing emotion, or variously the part of human experience called "the passions" or "affect," in cultural, rather than purely psychological terms.

Catherine Lutz' important anthropological study of the cultural construction of affect, *Unnatural Emotions: Everyday Sentiments on a Micronesian Atoll and Their Challenge to Western Theory*, for instance, was the seminal book to outline the ways emotion has been naturalized in Western culture and how the relations of power that preserve its constructions have been effaced. Her third chapter, which traces the history of emotion as both a positively and negatively charged concept in Western culture, has become a classic text for those interested in analyzing the significances of emotion. She articulates a way of understanding Western emotion as enmeshed in ideological systems of power that helps shed light on the emotional politics of Ovidianism. As she explains, the aim of her work is "to deconstruct an overly naturalized and rigidly bounded concept of emotion, to treat emotion as an ideological practice rather than as a thing to be discovered or an essence to be distilled."[13] My work is influenced by this reconceptualization of emotion, and it contributes to writing the history of emotion Lutz undertakes by theorizing literary representation as a major site for constructions of the self as defined in emotional terms.

As Lutz points out, in current Western culture, emotion is often simultaneously valued negatively when opposed to rationality and positively when opposed to cultural estrangement: "To say that someone is 'unemotional' is either to praise that person as calm, rational, and deliberate or to accuse them of being withdrawn or uninvolved, alienated, or even catatonic. Emotion is, at one time, a residual category of almost-defective personal process; at others, it is the seat of the true and glorified self."[14] Lutz goes on to argue that the more positive associations with emotion are formed in the Romantic period of the nineteenth century, and while her attempt to historicize her theory begins to explain emotion's history, a reading of Ovidianism in the Renaissance reveals just such a dual role for emotion before the period Lutz cites. One sees an especially potent example of this kind of doubled value in the male figure of the Renaissance melancholic, who, as Juliana Schiesari has shown, was both pathologized as humorally imbalanced and celebrated as intellectually or artistically inspired or authentic beginning in this early period.[15] The accumulation of laments and the highlighting of grief that are characteristic of Renaissance Ovidianism represent a pre-Romantic concept of emotion that is shaped by the Renaissance focus on interiority as the site of agency, and Ovidian irony accomplishes this complex dual valuing of emotion by representing female emotion especially as excessive and sometimes humorous but at the same time insisting on its legitimacy as a location for authentic interpersonal and political critique.

To argue that expressions of grief are politically powerful is to qualify some feminist criticism and contemporary popular discourse that constructs grief as the typical emotion associated with female weakness and rage as a sign of the excessive or unreasonable nature of the female self. This tendency to read emotion in these terms is ubiquitous, but feminists such as philosopher Elizabeth Spelman helpfully reorient this discourse. In her classic article "Anger and Insubordination," Spelman points out that anger as an expressed emotion in women and other subordinate groups is a political act. To be angry is to assume that one has the right to be angry and that the subordinate group is entitled to equal standing with the dominant group. Repoliticizing emotional expression, countering the associations of it with feminine weakness and irrationality, is, I believe, important for current feminism, and it is essential for reading culture.[16] As this study repeatedly reveals, emotive rhetoric is perceived in the Renaissance to have even more potency than it does in our own twenty-first-century cultural moment, and even excessive emotions like grief and rage both have their place in moments of political engagement.[17]

As I noted above, the early modern humoral (i.e., emotional) body has recently been the focus of intense critical interest, and two scholars, Gail Paster and Michael Schoenfeldt, have between them retheorized our understanding of the consequences of this bodily model for understanding Renaissance subjectivity. While both Paster and Schoenfeldt have shown that identity was experienced as supremely bodily in the period, their differing points of view on the nature of that body reveal instability, rather than certainty, in cultural understandings of this element of the self. Both point to the ways the Galenic body is seen as coextensive with the outside world, operating through a system of humoral regulation, but they explain the consequences of this model of identity in opposite ways. In Paster's description, the body is leaky and sometimes uncontrollable, and it is constantly the site of the disciplining social experience of shame. Schoenfeldt also analyzes the system of bodily regulation central to the Galenists, but he focuses on the ways Renaissance writers seem to emphasize the order and balance required to regulate that system and argues that the control of the body facilitated a kind of individual agency. While Ovidian representations of the body would seem to have more in common with Paster's threatening model of bodily fluidity, and metamorphic and metamorphosed bodies are not sites of agency in the material sense, in Ovid the unstable body that can be instantly transformed becomes a site of symbolic power and agency. Ovidianism also models subjectivity that is not determined by the body (and in the case of Echo, is finally without a body at all) but that depends upon the metamorphosis of the body as a moment of symbolic power. Metamorphosis often occurs in Ovid, for instance, when characters reach the limits of endurable emotion, as when Procne, Philomela, and Tereus are transformed into birds at the end of their tale. It can also occur when a character is robbed of agency, such as when Actaeon becomes a hunted stag; when one is punished, such as when Arachne becomes a spider; or when one escapes, such as when Daphne becomes a laurel or Arethusa becomes a spring to prevent the bodily violation of rape. Each of these transformations draws attention to the bodily constituent of the self and symbolically marks agency, and therefore subjectivity, at the moment of bodily change, but in most of these examples, some essence of the self survives the bodily metamorphosis, suggesting another model of a less Galenic self that is at play throughout Ovid's poem. In dialogue with humoral conceptions of the body, Ovidianism registers the interdependence of body and self, but it also reveals the way the self can outlive the body, even as it aestheticizes and attaches symbolic value to the body as the site of metamorphosis.[18]

Interestingly, the critical strain in Renaissance studies that has focused on metamorphosis as the central idea and structuring principle of Ovid's antiepic has often not fully attended to the implications of this trope for theorizations of bodily experience.[19] Bodily change is the foundational thematic device of *Metamorphoses*, and it is also the imaginative force behind the poem's challenges to models of subjectivity itself. The mysterious ways in which figures with agency are transformed to vegetable, inanimate, or other forms of animate matter throughout the poem offer challenges to modern conceptions of identity and may explain on a profound level the poem's popularity during this time of such self-consciousness about the nature of the self. While Ovidian conceptions of the body do not necessarily reflect material culture, it is not safe to assume that metamorphosis is perceived primarily as a metaphor for types of psychic change.[20] My final chapter will reveal, in fact, the way Ovidianism served to model actual bodily transformation in the witchcraft debates and participated in politicizing these transformations. Because the subject in the *Metamorphoses* and texts for which it is an intertext is so self-consciously and so temporarily embodied, Ovidianism is more conspicuously engaged in negotiating the link between the body and the emotive self than any other Renaissance discourse.

In addition, the Ovidian body reflects and reciprocally constructs Renaissance conceptions of sexual difference in multiple ways. Especially in the few tales where figures actually assume the bodily characteristics of the opposite sex (such as Tiresias and Iphis and Ianthe), biological differentiation is insistently eroded, and it might be tempting to equate such representations with the Galenic one-sex model, in which male and female anatomy are homologous and therefore perhaps more easily interchanged in everyday thought. There were, however, multiple and competing conceptions of sexual difference in the period, and the poem actually enacts many different formulations in its pages.[21] All types of biological specificity are continuously undermined by the poem's imagery of bodily change, but the sex one is has important and sometimes deadly consequences. The possibility that bodies can change, combined with the eroticism of the many narrators' descriptions of bodies in the poem, in fact, draws attention to the biological conditions of gendered identity. In addition, the poem does not represent the female body as a defective male, which is common in Galenism—in the *Metamorphoses* all bodies are similarly defective in that they are unstable and constantly prone to changes of great magnitude. As one of the many discourses for representing sexual difference in the period, Ovidianism asserts the instability of all bodies—of all matter, in fact—but insists that gender is linked in specific and politicized ways to biological sex.

Ovidianism, therefore, provides a challenge to some of the central dualistic emphases of Western thought on bodies and subjects. In *Volatile Bodies: Toward a Corporeal Feminism*, Elizabeth Grosz traces the history of the Cartesian dualism of mind and body and its disabling effects on attempts to reimagine the female body as a site not effectively always secondary to mind, thought, or other types of privileged bodies. Drawing on, but also pointing to, the limitations of Spinoza's attempts to articulate a universal substance that encompasses both mind and body, Grosz suggests a reconceptualization of the body as truly integrated and interdependent with the mind or consciousness. Using the model of the body and mind as substance in process, like a flame, she seeks a way out of the limiting conceptions of the two as mutually exclusive or in struggle.[22] For my study, what is important in her feminist critique of the dualism and hierarchy of mind over body is that hers resembles the challenge *Metamorphoses* and later Ovidianism offer to that same dualism. While clearly not interested in rescuing specifically or exclusively female bodies from limiting philosophical conceptualization, Ovid's pre-Cartesian poem is the site of a similar elision of the mind–body divide, which of course has its roots in the writings of Plato and Aristotle. As figures with agency are transformed, they do not just retain an essential mind unaffected by bodily change; nor, conversely, do they lose the consciousness of their previous state of bodily being. Rather, bodily metamorphosis and psychic transformations are interrelated, mutually constituted, dependent upon each other in ways that suggest that the dualism is itself a false one. One of the broad secondary assertions of this project, therefore, is that the cultural work of Ovidianism is partially occurring in its refigurations of the emotive subject as "in process" and not neatly divided between body and mind.

Because Ovid's works, especially *Metamorphoses*, are so filled with images of strong emotional states, it is surprising that little cultural analysis of Ovidianism in these terms has been done. There has been some very exciting research on Ovidianism in the Renaissance in the last two decades, and yet the author of each new work still claims that we have much further to go in understanding the depth of this period's engagement with this crucial classical source.[23] I make the same claim, and this book proudly participates in what Valerie Traub has called the New Ovidianism in studies of the Renaissance.[24] It is worth stopping, however, to consider why the study of Renaissance Ovidianism seems so central and pervasive and at the same time so nascent. Although there have always been scholars, since the Renaissance itself, to point out the ubiquitous Ovidian allusions and references in the period, there has recently been a turn toward more culturally engaged analysis that has gathered steam in the last few years. This reexploration began around the same time that Renaissance scholars embraced New Historicism, with its focus on dominant and subordinate texts and textual processes, and it came of age with the turn toward the marginal in historical and cultural studies. It might be argued, therefore, that while Ovid was always acknowledged as a crucial source for Renaissance writers, it took such critical turns, and the theoretical paradigms that underlay them, to fully engage with the significance of this intertext in the period. Unlike Virgil, whose subversions are enclosed within the grander sweep of epic form and ideology, Ovid needed an altered critical attention to be reestablished as a fundamental and definitional author for Renaissance England. Occupying as it did the position in many Renaissance contexts of a counter- or marginal discourse, Ovidianism's time has come because we are now armed with the appropriate theoretical and historical tools to read it, as well as, it must be noted, the critical interest in uncovering the oppositional in our readings of previous cultures.

The recent explosion of criticism on Ovidianism in the development of Renaissance European cultures is also partly the result of the fact that Ovid's works themselves experienced a disciplinary renaissance in classical studies in the last few decades. Considered by many modern academics a stylistically ingenious but ultimately politically neutral teller of pretty (!) stories, Ovid moved into center stage in the second half of the twentieth century and especially in recent evaluations of the politically charged literature of the Augustan age.[25] Even in some recent work, however, Ovid's writings are sometimes dismissed or excused as beautiful but unserious texts—Ovid's rhetorical skills having apparently worked against him to create his reputation as an ornamental but ultimately frivolous poet. All of Ovid's major works (the *Ars Amatoria, Remedia Amoris, Fasti, Heroides, Amores,* and *Tristia*) represent significant and often foundational contributions to generic traditions in Western literature, and the works have not received as much critical attention from classicists as their historically influential and artistically beloved status might warrant. The place of all of Ovid's works, which have widely circulated throughout Western history, in Roman literature has begun to be more thoroughly investigated, and further work by classicists will open new directions for those interested in the cultural status of the original texts and their legacies.[26]

In addition, the tradition of scholarship on *Metamorphoses* that subordinated it to *Aeneid* may reflect what appears to have been Ovid's original purpose: to offer a countertraditional, antiauthoritarian poem to match the nationalistic, imperialistic, and, Ovid might argue, morally narrow, *Aeneid*, written by Virgil about twenty years before Ovid's own antiepic. As anyone who reads *Aeneid* acknowledges, Virgil's epic is propagandistic, but it is also a complex, imaginative construction filled with considerable ambivalences about epic and heroic narrative.[27] Set a thousand years before the time it was written, it tells the story of Rome's founding in a glorious tale of imperialism and therefore supports the Emperor Augustus' political purposes at the time the poem was written. It also contains direct allusions to the glory of Augustus' reign through predictions and visions of the future that are set pieces in the action of the poem. It is, most insistently, a political text, filled with topical significances that place it firmly within the political culture of its time, and while many of its political resonances are ambiguous and even potentially subversive of the poem's nationalistic claims, its overall political purpose is celebration rather than critique. Ovid's response to Virgil's great epic of empire, *Metamorphoses*, must also be read as political, and it is the more broadly oppositional nature of Ovidianism, clearly known to Renaissance writers who had been raised on the Roman literature of this period that has not received enough attention in our evaluations of the cultural resonances of Ovidianism.[28]

When *Aeneid* is read through the lens of Ovid's *Metamorphoses*, its subtle literary and political negotiations are overshadowed by Ovid's insistent parody and critique of its central epic narrative. Ovid's poem also announces its ambitions to praise Augustus, but it does so in complex and often ironic ways. For instance, Ovid first compares

Augustus in book 1 to Jove—a flattering comparison, but the context for this praise is the tale of Lycaon, which brings on the wrath of the gods against sinful human nature and the flood that destroys the first race of men. Augustus was engaged in a program of moral reform in Rome at the time this poem was written, and if Jupiter does stand in for him, he is an excessively angry god. While Ovid's poem had additional literary purposes and influences—it announces, for instance, its hybridization of Callimachean lightness and epic grandeur in the opening lines—*Metamorphoses* responds radically to Virgil; that is, it responds by questioning the prior poem's foundational assumptions.[29] *Metamorphoses* is nonlinear to counter Virgil's historical and epic linearity; it is decidedly, often humorously, unheroic to respond to Virgil's celebrations of Roman heroism; it demystifies and often degrades most figures of authority, including the gods, to subtly mock Virgil's emphasis on the virtuous Roman life.[30] While such direct dialogue between the two texts is, of course, in many respects a way of paying homage to Virgil, *Metamorphoses* critiques, in its matter and style, the very essence of Virgilian poetic authority and, by extension, Augustan political authority. It is this antiauthoritarian nature of Ovid's poem that carved out a distinct space for an Ovidian tradition that would survive into the late Middle Ages and flourish in the Renaissance, and that continues to thrive through the works of writers and artists to this day. Ovid is the great poet of the "counter-" and the "anti-," and in the Renaissance, this political persuasion would make his works important for writers interested in critiquing or conceptualizing alternatives to traditional forms of poetry.[31] It also made the poem a rich source for alternative representations of subjectivity and, as I have begun to argue above, for alternate, marginal, or subversive models of emotional and political expression.

When read with a knowledge of its Augustan context (which is certainly how Renaissance readers would have come to the poem), it is difficult to understate the critique of abuses of power to which the poem obsessively returns. This foregrounding of absolutist forms of power and its consequences for individuals must also reflect Ovid's own situation as an author experiencing the emperor's displeasure. What we know about Ovid's life, sketched mainly in his own writings, is that he was exiled by Augustus in 8 AD for what he describes as "*carmen et error*," a poem and a mistake.[32] The poem was most likely his *Ars Amatoria*, which would have offended the emperor in its representation, and in fact, celebration, of adultery, since Augustus had made adultery a crime in 18 BC. The mistake has not been fully identified, but Ovid seems to have been at least indirectly involved in an affair of the emperor's granddaughter, Julia, that resulted in her own banishment the same year and other punishments for those of the same political circle. While we are destined to have only sketchy access to his life, just the fact that Ovid constructs himself as an exile in his later writings, physically outside the central systems of power, situates his writings, and particularly *Metamorphoses*, as politically unauthorized texts. *Metamorphoses*, in fact, seems to have been published from exile, so the book physically negotiated the subtle power relationship between poetic authority and political authority. The relation between artistic expression and statelike systems of power is repeatedly scrutinized in the poem, for example in the tale of Arachne, which is essentially an allegory of an artist's confrontation with an all-powerful, jealous, and violent figure of authority. The poem was supremely political from its beginnings, embroiled in the struggle between poet and prince, and its political critique is a central facet of Renaissance Ovidianism.

As the example of Arachne reminds us, power is also defined insistently and repeatedly within *Metamorphoses* in gendered terms. Although not all figures with power are male (far from it! Venus, Minerva and Diana are responsible for many of the most resonant and violent interventions into human society represented in the poem) and many figures who are conspicuously robbed of agency are male (Actaeon, Orpheus, Narcissus, and Marsyas are only some of the most famous for Renaissance audiences), the most repeated and exemplary structure for a tale in the poem, especially in its middle books, is the narrative of rape, usually of a female by a male figure. As Amy Richlin rightly points out, it is politically dangerous to ignore or downplay rape as the central, and sometimes not-so-ironically eroticized content of so many Ovidian tales. My study focuses, in fact, on many of the most troubling rape narratives in the poem, but I and many other critics disagree with Richlin's evaluation of Ovid's work as functioning, like pornography, to un-self-consciously suppress or objectify its female figures through these violent representations.[33] Ovid's narrative quite explicitly lingers on articulating sympathy for female figures as victims of not only specifically sexual but also other forms of oppressive violence. However much that sympathy may be dictated by patriarchal assumptions about the nature of women, the poem attempts to articulate a feminine response to violence and an interior life in the female figures who grieve, lament, or rage throughout the poem.[34] In the later intertextual encounters I analyze here, that struggle to represent a marginalized subjectivity is often highlighted and even more pronounced.

In addition, the poem's scrutiny of social gender roles is different from, and subversive of, previous treatments of gender in relations of love and war in the epic tradition. The world of political power struggles, sketched as sweeping history by Virgil, is replaced in Ovid with stories of more intimate wars, often between male and female figures. Especially in the first two-thirds of the poem, before Ovid turns in later books toward actual retellings of Homeric and Virgilian poetic history, the narrative scope of the poem tends toward the individual, quasi-domestic scale. Although the poem opens by wittily announcing its universal significance, retelling the creation of the world and the ages of man, it quickly moves to the stories of individuals caught up in these geohistorical changes. The wolfish nature of human beings as a race is described through the tale of Lycaon, for instance, and then the creation of a second stony race of human beings after the flood is described through the story of Deucalion and Pyrrha. *Metamorphoses* is not the epic of national history but of individual histories invested with crucial cultural significance.[35] In the encounters of individual mortals and nymphs with the Olympian gods and similarly powerful mortal authority figures, Ovid argues through example for the centrality of such encounters to human life and suggests that the formation of individual identity in response to the powers aligned to obliterate it might be the essential heroic activity. The poem highlights the fact that individual politics prefigure national politics, and in fact that they are insistently intertwined.[36]

This focus in Ovid on intimate struggles for supremacy or agency ends up producing complex articulations of certain emotions as politically charged and often important forms of resistance, and it is often female figures who preside over or are powerless within these private but political spheres. Daphne, for example, becomes the laurel not just to signify her ambiguous but violent subjection to Apollo, her would-be rapist, but to all poets and conquering military heroes, and in fact to Augustus himself, whose gates will be guarded by laurel trees. Ceres, in contrast, whose laments over her private loss are given considerable weight in the narrative, is also aligned with and supported by two other nymphs who attempt to escape male violence—Cyane and Arethusa—and she is so powerful that she will continue to bring dearth and winter to the world because she has lost her daughter Proserina to Pluto for half the year. The female figures in Ovid's poem, however, cannot really be read as protofeminist examples indicating social concern for actual Roman women; they are representations that attempt to account for experience left out of other, notably epic, descriptions of social relations. In fact, because the poem destabilizes conceptions of bodily sexual identity through the trope of metamorphosis, gender distinctions are always on the verge of breaking down. So, while it is useful to highlight a female subject position in the discourse, and the femininity of this position is asserted by the poem's insistence on rape as a foundational narrative structure, femininity itself is not stable. Figures like Orpheus, for instance, who grieve and represent social impotence in ways similar to most female figures in the poem, are accommodated as not necessarily effeminized, but perhaps analogous figures in the poem's definitions of the subject. While the poem is firmly invested in articulating a feminized subject position, it simultaneously challenges what it means to be feminized at all.

In addition to privileging the interior psychological experiences of female figures, the *Metamorphoses* is filled with representations of female speech—embodied, disembodied, powerful, and powerless. This fundamental fact is the starting point for Lynn Enterline's important analyses of both Ovid's poem and Renaissance Ovidianism in *The Rhetoric of the Body from Ovid to Shakespeare*. Enterline argues that Ovidianism influenced Renaissance conceptions of the relationship between the body and voice in fundamental ways, and she points out that it is often a female body that is the site of the shifting interpretation of that relationship throughout Ovidian writings.[37] As my specific readings of Ovidian female figures in the Renaissance will reveal, some of the narratives most commonly referred to are those that involve extensive female laments, such as the tales of Philomela, Daphne, Proserpina, and Arachne. Female lament as a mode becomes characteristic of Renaissance Ovidianism in general, and is, in fact, one of the defining characteristics of that most Ovidian genre of this period, the minor epic. The effects of the representations of this kind of grief are central concerns of both Ovid and the Elizabethan writers who deploy Ovidianism to negotiate their own cultural encounters with the significances of grief itself, and this is perhaps the most notable emotion under scrutiny in Renaissance Ovidian texts.

Ovidian grief differs from, and comments on, the loss and lament that characterize the epic tradition more generally, especially as it is consolidated in *Aeneid*. As Thomas Greene puts it, "participation in heroic sorrow" is the goal of primary epic, and it is characteristic of most epics in the later tradition.[38] *Aeneid*, influenced by Greek and especially Homeric traditions of lament, is filled with examples of grieving women, but most of this lament is set in the context of war and represents a ritual response to the death or destruction of male heroes. *Aeneid* is, however, particularly interested in female grief in its most famous episode, the abandonment of Dido by Aeneas. Dido's grief has had such an influential afterlife that its significances are well known, but it is worth stating the most obvious—this is a tale of abandonment, and it represents the consequences of grief as dangerous primarily for Dido herself, resulting in her suicide, and Carthage, the society her person represents and in some sense embodies. While Aeneas' denial of Dido's pleas to stay is evaluated by the poem's rhetoric as tragic, the text explicitly asserts that this abandonment is the great test and affirmation of Aeneas' heroism. While the rest of the poem will contain female figures who perform ritual laments for the dead, the structure of the work emphasizes the Dido episode as what its glorified heroic narrative must leave behind. In contrast, in *Metamorphoses*, female grief is the main matter of many of the tales, so it is repeatedly emphasized and legitimized. While most of the female figures in the poem suffer injustices, not many are abandoned (Dido's abandonment is narrated, but only in passing); most, instead, are grieving as a response to more aggressive, usually violent, forms of mistreatment—the threat of rape, murder, mutilation or, in more complex ways, shame. They are not performing ritualized lament over war dead but are protesting the social structures that leave them in positions of vulnerability or impotence. Unlike Dido, whose grief is evaluated as necessary for the heroic endeavor that is the central matter of the poem but who is explicitly represented as a passive sufferer, Ovidian heroines often commit acts of violence or vengeance themselves. They are not left behind by Ovid's poem but are instead central to the poem's plots as protagonists, even when their agency is ultimately eroded or erased through metamorphosis. Ovid is writing his excessively grieving poem (as well as his *Heroides*) from Dido's point of view, and later English Ovidianism will continue this interest in the many causes, valences, and significances of this grief.

The defining characteristics of Ovid's *Metamorphoses*, outlined above, ensured that the survival of this text would always be at least a subtle challenge to authoritative artistic and political institutions. That the text survived at all is testament to the power of the poem to articulate fundamental Western concerns. In the Middle Ages Ovid was preserved in monasteries, and it took on a very different set of cultural associations when it became the basis of the *Ovide Moralisé*, an edition of *Metamorphoses* that included heavy moralizations of the tales on the same page as Ovid's narrative. As Ovid's works were incorporated into the allegorical reading systems of the medieval church, a new strain of Ovidianism was born. Instead of the licentious, politically rebellious poet, Ovid became in these moralizations the pagan predecessor to Christian typological truth. The narratives, filled with irony and ambiguity in their telling in *Metamorphoses*, became in this cultural milieu moralistic and religious exempla, redirecting the tradition's antiauthoritarian potential. At the same time, Ovid's less moralized writings, such as his *Ars Amatoria* and *Heroides*, were also extremely important as rhetorical sources for medieval writers, and the twelfth and thirteenth centuries have been termed the *aetas Ovidiana* for the strong influence Ovidian writings had on literary culture of this time.[39] In the writings of such important figures as Dante, Chaucer, Boccaccio, and Petrarch, as well as Ariosto and Tasso, the licentious Ovid, preceptor of love, existed alongside the moralized Ovid, and these two sets of associations competed with and complicated each other into the Renaissance. While a survey of these various Ovidianisms is beyond the scope of this book, many of the readings that follow will account for traces of Continental Ovidianisms in English texts. It is particularly important to recognize that while Renaissance writers were certainly familiar with Ovid first through the original Latin school text, possibly as mediated through moralization and the allegorical tradition, they also received Ovidianism secondhand, following this general explosion of European Ovidian writing.[40]

The second resurgence of Ovidianism in England reached its peak in the decade of roughly the 1590s, and debate about why this should be so has resulted recently in a number of theories that attempt to account for the discourse's cultural relevance. I will briefly explore some of these theories here, mainly to highlight the fact that this scholarly work reveals most profoundly that Ovidianism did many different kinds of cultural work, that there were, in fact, a number of different Ovidianisms. As I have argued above, Renaissance writers in England and on the Continent seem to have been particularly drawn to Ovid as a metamorphic writer at precisely the period when philosophizing about the experience of emotions was also a central cultural pursuit, but there are clearly other cultural codes, many of them related to redefining the social self, that were also negotiated through English Ovidianisms.

Leonard Barkan's *The Gods Made Flesh*, for example, traces Ovidianism as a way for Renaissance writers to engage with the great mystery of paganism—the religious significance of deity as a component of the familiar and natural in human experience. He argues that metamorphosis figured the liminal space in which human and divine meet and became the marker of an engagement with antiquity itself. He writes, "For postclassical civilization . . . metamorphosis is an essential metonym for the classical civilization that gave it birth. Through the repeated reinterpretation and reimagination of metamorphic myths, the cluster of beliefs associated with them comes to define the heritage of antiquity, whether that is viewed through a positive or a negative glass."[41] Jonathan Bate makes a similar claim when he argues that Shakespeare's use of Ovid was primarily a way of asserting a central tenet of Renaissance humanism, the universal importance and applicability of classical culture: "To think of Shakespeare as an Elizabethan Ovid is to see him as a typical, if exceptionally gifted, product of his age. Renaissance thinkers believed passionately that the present could learn from the past; the belief was the starting point of education and a formative influence upon writing in the period. It was the essence of what we now call Renaissance humanism."[42] Ovid's self-consciousness made him especially appropriate as a classical author for these humanists, who were themselves engaged in highlighting the artifice of language, and Bate argues convincingly that Ovidianism responded well to Erasmus' humanist dictum to produce copious texts, those which offer more than one perspective and engage the faculties of the reader or audience in more than one way.[43] In addition, Bate and Enterline have focused on the ways Ovid's use in both scholastic and humanist grammar schools to teach Latin and rhetoric filled the heads of future writers with tales from *Metamorphoses* as well as Ovid's other works (especially *Fasti*, *Heroides*, and *Tristia*). The humanist system of education created naturalized associations between good rhetoric, imaginative production, and Ovidian narrative style. At the same time, the perceived immorality of much of Ovid's highly ironic and explicitly sexual material caused anxiety and always ensured that Ovidian imitation would be culturally charged with the riskiness of sexual, and by extension other kinds of, transgression.

Georgia Brown has argued for an even more radical and pervasive function for Ovidianism specifically in the 1590s, the period that is the focus of my own study. She outlines the ways Ovidianism participated in and enabled literary, and therefore cultural, change. She argues that Ovid served in the period as a discourse of marginality and provided a site for resistance to formulaic and traditional modes of writing and thought: "[Ovid's] luxuriant wantonness challenged the simplicity of conventional moral judgments based on the denial of sensual experience, by insinuating a connection between poetic creativity and sexual desire which made literary morality a chimerical goal and eventually freed literature from the necessity to be didactic." Metamorphosis itself as a trope worked to break apart existing categories and suggest new ways of thinking.[44] Her study interestingly focuses on different texts (primarily Thomas Nashe and the generic tradition of the epyllion) and therefore different cultural sites from those highlighted in this book, and this fact alone supports her over-all point, as it suggests the widely subversive nature of the discourse in the period. A pervasive intertext, influencing cultural production from a number of different artistic, literary, and broadly institutional realms, Ovidianism had wide-ranging consequences for many overlapping ideological systems.

The place of *Metamorphoses* as a primary literary influence on the English Renaissance was solidified when it was translated in its entirety into English verse by Arthur Golding in 1567, and it is this translation that helped launch the later sixteenth century as an Ovidian age. Golding's translation, which Ezra Pound repeatedly praised and called "the most beautiful book in the language," was for years difficult to find in print, surviving mainly in a 1961 edition called *Shakespeare's Ovid*.[45] Recently, however, Golding's translation has resurfaced, with two new editions printed in 2000 and 2002,[46] most likely meeting the demand of new readers focusing on Renaissance Ovidianism. Golding's transla-tion presents itself as a unified text with broader meanings not to be found in previous piecemeal translations. Golding says in his epistle,

> This [book] I present
> too your good Lordship once ageine not as a member rent
> Or parted from the resdew of the body any more:
> But fully now accomplished.[47]

Golding had translated a few books of *Metamorphoses* before for his patron, the Earl of Essex, but he is clearly proud here of the complete-ness of his work and presents it as the superior fruit of his labors. Pre-senting the text as a body that can be dismembered plays, of course, on the work's central trope and organizing principle—bodies and the ways they can physically change—and Golding uses this trope to vali-date the reading of the full body over the reading of its parts. It is true that Ovid's episodic and historically moralized narrative was ripe for dismemberment, and we find many instances of tales abstracted for their own inherent meanings in Renaissance art and literature, but other artists, like those who are the focus of this study, clearly had a more profound engagement with the thematics and politics of Ovid's antiepic. As Joseph Loewenstein has pointed out, since Lactantius' prose summary of the fifth or sixth century, Ovid's tales were pre-served and transmitted in fragmentary form, but Golding's complete translation of Ovid's poem must have generated or reinvigorated an interest in Ovid's cumulative poetic and political representations.[48]

Golding's epistle, dedicating the translation to Essex, and his preface, in addition to offering excellent examples of the dual visions of Ovid as pre-Christian moralist or wanton pagan in the period, also address pressing cultural anxieties about the excessive emotion represented in the tales. In the epistle he gives examples of the traditional moralizations of a few tales from each book. For example, he writes that

> in the Tale of Daphnee turnd to Bay,
> A mirror of virginitie appeere unto us may,
> Which yielding neyhter unto feare, nor force, nor flatterye,
> Doth purchace everlasting fame and immortalitye.
> (67–70)

And

> all as doo in flattring freaks, and hawks, and hownds delight,
> And dyce, and cards, and for to spend the tyme both day and nyght
> In foule excesse of chemberworke, or too much meate and drink:
> Uppon the piteous storie of Acteon ought to think.
> For their and thyr adherents used, excessive are in deed
> The dogs that dayly doo devour theyr followers on with speede.
> (97–102)

As both of these examples reveal, most of Golding's professed moralizations are highly unsatisfying, and he admits this himself when he ends his summary of readings with a plea of humility before the task of interpreting for his lord and other readers:

> Theis fables out of every booke I have interpreted,
> To shew how they and all the rest may stand a man in sted.
> Not adding over curiously the meaning of them all,
> For that were labor infinite, and tediousnesse not small
> Boothe unto your good Lordship and the rest that should them reede.
> Who well might thinke I did the boundes of modestie exceed,
> If I thise one epistle should with matters overcharge
> Which scarce a booke of many quyres can well conteyne at large.
> (298–306)

The sly wittiness of this stance at once assures his possible detractors that there is commonly accepted moral truth in the poem, while at the same time inviting his aristocratic readers especially to interpret beyond such moralizations, which are a tiny fragment of the meanings that would fill the prodigious book he describes. Golding also spends some time defending the paganism of the book, in the epistle asking his readers to excuse the references to the gods, which reflect pre-Christian ignorance, and outlining topological readings of Ovid's creation stories, in which, for example, the flood in the story of Deucalion and Pyrrha is analogous to Noah's flood (492–510). Golding explains these topological readings as "colorings":

> All these things the Poet here dooth show
> In colour, altring both the names of persons, tyme and place.
> (490–91)

Through the epistle, Golding both excuses and makes claims for the poem's morality and relation to scriptural truth, while subtly implying the instability and insufficiency of such readings.

The anxiety about the poem's morality that the epistle's irony reveals is even more strongly felt in the preface, where Golding makes the related argument that the interpretations of the poet's representations of virtue and vice are the responsibility of the reader:

> For as there bee most wholesome hestes and precepts to be found,
> So are theyr rockes and shallowe shelves to ronne the ship aground.
> (141–43)

In fact, after asserting the wealth of both instruction and delight to be found in the poem, in the final few lines of the preface, he likens some readers to Odysseus' men enchanted by the sirens:

> If any stomacke be so weake as that it cannot brooke,
> The lively setting forth of things described in this booke,
> I give him counsell to absteine until he bee more strong,
> And for to use Ulysses feat ageinst the Meremayds song.
> (215–18)

Ultimately acknowledging that the poem might be the siren's song, Golding reveals that even with all of the accumulated allegory of tradition accompanying it, the poem is still erotically powerful and dangerous. While straightforwardly absolving himself of blame for the poem's immorality, he hints at the more lascivious aspects of the poetry, tempting readers to the pleasures of his translation. This balancing act, coping with the potentially transgressive elements of Ovidian matter while at the same time celebrating its themes, characterizes not just this translation but Ovidianism as a whole in this period.

In addition to addressing the possibility that his work might lead readers to vice, Golding also worries that it might lead them to excessive states of emotion. In fact he makes the argument in the epistle that what is "meant" by these "fables" is not "to further or allure to vice," but rather

> that men beholding what they bee when vyce dooth raigne in
> stead
> Of verture, should not let their lewd affections have the lead.
> For as there is no creature more divine than man as long
> As reason hath the sovereintie and standeth firme and strong:
> So is there none more beastly, vyle, and develish, than is hee,
> If reason giving over, by affection mated bee.
> (Epistle, 562–69)

While it may be difficult for modern readers to approach most of Ovid's tales as moral exempla, Golding here makes use of the tradition of the moralized Ovid, highlighting the tales as they are weighted with the allegorizations of medieval commentary. In fact, most of the interpretations of the Ovidian tales he references come directly from this tradition, so it is fitting that he sees the work (perhaps unironically) as functioning primarily as a caution against sinful emotional behavior. Reason is repeatedly "mated" (overcome, but also matched, sometimes equally) by affection in these tales, however, and Golding is at pains to justify his work as more than immoral entertainment.

He furthers his arguments for the value of the work for training readers in emotional regulation with direct allusions to the Neoplatonic conceptualization of reason as the bridle of the charioteer:

> The use of this same booke therefore is this: that every man
> (Endevoring for to know himself as nearly as he can,)
> (As though he in a chariot sate well ordered,) should direct
> His mynd by reason in the way of vertue, and correct
> His feerce affections with the bit of temprance, lest perchaunce
> They taking bridle in the teeth lyke wilfull jades doo praunce
> Away, and headlong carrie him to every filthy pit
> Of vyce, and drinking of the same defile his soule with it:
> Or else doo headlong harrie him upon the rockes of sin,
> And overthrowing forcibly the chariot he sits in,
> Doo teare him worse than ever was Hippolytus the sonne
> Of Theseus when he went about his fathers wrath to shun.

Golding's reference to the Hippolytus tale again draws on the tale's moralizations and emphasizes the book's almost medicinal use as an aid to reason. By setting the chariot of Hippolytus in contrast to the chariot of the well-governed Neoplatonic soul, however, Golding is slyly acknowledging the riskiness of the book itself, which provides the dramatic and violent image used in his example. By suggesting that every man who reads the book should not become a Hippolytus, he is overtly creating the work as the source of sinful emotional behavior, but this is a particularly ironic use of the tale, since in Ovid's telling Hippolytus is innocent, the victim of his mother's incestuous desires.

In addition, the famous ancient Greek admonition, "Know thyself" (inscribed at the Delphic oracle), which Golding celebrates as the main "use" of the book, comes under pointedly humorous scrutiny in Ovid's poem. In his retelling of the tale of Narcissus, Tiresias accurately predicts that the boy will only live so long as he doesn't know himself. In Golding's own translation,

> Narcissus did she call his name. Of whome the Prophet sage,
> Demaunded if the childe should live to many yeares of age,
> Made aunswere: Yea full long, so that him selfe he doe not know.
> The Soothsayers wordes seemed long but vaine, until the end did show
> His saying to be true in deede by straungeness of the rage,
> And straungenesse of the kind of death that did abridge his age.
> (3.431–36)

Golding again achieves a subtle irony, suggesting that a text that is quite skeptical about the value of truly knowing oneself, and in fact is skeptical about the nature of that self at all, will provide its readers with that specific kind of knowledge and achieve the desired result—a self governed by reason. As these examples suggest, Golding's position as translator of the *Metamorphoses* forces him to address what he perceives as its most transgressive or dangerous elements, and it is repeatedly emotional behavior or expression that he worries over. And he is not alone in identifying the potency of this discourse for modeling emotion in the period; other writers and artists also perceived the *Metamorphoses* as a siren song, filled with passionate, compelling, and dangerous representations of emotion.

In each chapter that follows, close analysis of a text or writer will ground a wider discussion of Ovidianism's participation in redefining the conceptualization and experience of emotion (or in the case of the chapter on Elizabeth, desire) in relation to power in a particular cultural arena. Chapter 1 turns to the overtly and insistently political sphere of Elizabethan court propaganda. While many representations in the later "cult" of Elizabeth figure her body as transcendently stable and enclosed in virginity, a whole world of Ovidian writings represent a counterdiscourse that has been largely absent from critical accounts of her self-fashioning. Rather than offering praise to the distant, unchanging, and unemotional body of the ruler, John Lyly's Ovidian plays, such as *Love's Metamorphosis*, and the Ovidian entertainments that were performed for the queen as she traveled on summer progresses, overall tend to celebrate Elizabeth's politically charged emotional statements and manipulations and associate them with her metamorphoses of her gendered royal person. These theatrical productions often celebrate the queen's transcendence of the limiting gender roles of other discursive systems of courtly literature, especially the Petrarchism that characterized her earlier court writings, and they repeatedly represent the body as the site of instability and metamorphosis. While the queen is sometimes idealized as ruler over the excessive laments and bodily transformations of the characters in these entertainments, she is also always linked through her gender to the nymphs and female characters who undergo these bodily changes and grieve for them. Ovidianism offered Elizabeth's courtly propagandists a way to celebrate the emotionality that was assumed to be her female nature and at the same time positively value her challenges to the stability of her gendered self.

In Spenser's *Faerie Queene*, the textual focus of Chapter 2 and an epic written by an author self-consciously on the margins of court life, Ovidianism serves to examine and critique the constructions of emotion encoded in the traditions of heroic epic and therefore at the center of the Western tradition. Written explicitly for the queen and thus engaged in imagining a powerful female reader and point of view, Spenser's poem becomes most Ovidian (retelling Ovidian tales, alluding to Ovidian characters or constructing new Ovidianisms of its own) when it is analyzing the relationship between authority and interiorized, often feminized, constructions of emotional life. *Metamorphoses* serves to construct an alternative kind of emotion that is pagan and unheroic to contrast with the emotional symbolism of Christian allegory occurring at one level in the narrative. Ovidian emotion, which is often constructed through digressions or similes, repeatedly destabilizes the heroic narrative by emphasizing the complexities of interior experience that are either not captured, in the case of a figure like Sylvanus who remembers Ovid's Cyparissus, or demonized, in a character like Adicia who is a textual repetition of Ovid's Hecuba. In addition, Spenser turns to Ovid for sympathetic, although sometimes ironic, treatments of emotion in general, and in doing so, he redefines the heroic tradition for his own culture. Sometimes emphatically valorized and at other times ridiculed and parodied, Spenser's Ovidianism repeatedly investigates the intense cultural anxiety about the emotions of powerful women in the period and the role of emotion itself in political and social life.

Chapter 3 examines Ovidianism in Shakespeare's plays. Outside the province of the court and exploiting the already strategically separate space of a cross-dressed public theater, Shakespeare repeatedly interrogates the repetitions of sexual violence that are implicit in Ovidian narrative. While the stage did not allow female bodies, I argue that it was politically invested in representing female experience as its most self-conscious exclusion, and it found the language for articulating the feminized experience of social impotence in Ovidian rape and revenge. Rapes in Shakespeare are almost always coded as Ovidian, and in a play like *Titus Andronicus,* the intertextual dialogue produced between the play and the ancient poem focuses on the questions of agency that are urgently investigated by Ovid's rape narratives. As Titus excessively laments his suffering at the hands of the evil Tamora and then eventually assumes the role of revenger, for instance, his character is defined through allusions to Hecuba and Procne, two Ovidian heroines. Titus therefore regenders the agency associated with revenge, and in doing so symbolically emphasizes the play's sacrifice of its female characters and the misuse of their emotional experiences. Highlighting at the same time that it destroys feminized and Ovidian forms of emotive expression as well as agency, the play comments in explicitly political terms on the model of female victimization that lies at the heart of the English literary tradition and the Western cultural tradition dominated by Rome, as Lavinia, who has been raped in the play, points to the source of her story in Ovid's *Metamorphoses.*

The final chapter focuses on Reginald Scot's *Discoverie of Witchcraft,* a text that, in addition to offering fascinating commentary on contemporary beliefs in magical transformation, includes citations from and commentaries on *Metamorphoses* itself. Exploring this text as a window onto the witchcraft controversies in the period, I contrast Ovidianism's constructions of emotion in literature with its deployment in writings with explicit interests in the lived experience of actual women. Scot argues that the witches being burned on the Continent and intermittently in English villages are victims of social rather than devilish forces. Outraged by what he sees as blasphemous beliefs in extrabiblical occurrences and powers, and sympathetic to the silly old women he constructs as victims of their own and their neighbors' errors, Scot writes a text that sets out to debunk every accusation and description of witchcraft that has authority in his period. What he produces is a protoanthropological account of witchcraft practices and the beliefs surrounding them. Within this account, Ovid's poem functions paradoxically as both an example of the fictionality of witchcraft as it exists in poetry and an authoritative text on witchcraft's incantations and spells. While it is often assumed that Ovidian metamorphosis was understood only metaphorically, Scot's treatise reveals a pervasive cultural belief in and controversy over actual bodily transformation, a fact that has serious implications for understanding the literary and artistic works that employ this imagery. Ovidian female figures were always potentially connected to fears of actual witches, and I develop my argument that they occupy a similarly transgressive and politically powerful place in Renaissance experience. In addition, the Ovidianism of the witchcraft controversies recorded cultural ambivalences about emotions such as sympathy and feminized expressions of desire. Occupying an imagined cultural space where female figures might potentially have dangerous kinds of agency, Ovidian witches are a female community where emotional states are feared to have deadly consequences.

The diversity of these texts is intentional, as I have suggested that this project seeks to trace a "Book and Code" of the variety Barthes describes in the period of its greatest resurgence, the end of Elizabeth's reign. But while the issues and ideological negotiations in each cultural realm are often widely different, and in fact Ovidianism serves multiple and sometimes contradictory cultural purposes in each literary and cultural location, what are striking are the similarities in the functions of this discourse. The fact that Ovidianism repeatedly serves to represent transgressive emotional states and negotiate the politics of emotional expression itself argues for a deeper cultural influence than we have yet uncovered in our readings of Elizabethan Ovidian texts. It is not just Lavinia, or Titus' family, or even Shakespeare searching for a pattern of female grief, who find themselves in Ovid's book, but a whole culture in the midst of redefining the politics of emotion.

Chapter 1

Elizabeth I's Metamorphic Body and the Politics of Ovidian Desire

John Knox's *The First Blast of the Trumpet against the Monstrous Regiment of Women* is often cited as evidence of the hostility to female rule that Elizabeth I faced when she took the throne in 1558, the same year his pamphlet was published:

> A woman sitting in judgment, or riding from parliament in the midst of men, having the royal crown upon her head, the sword and scepter borne before her, in sign that the administration of justice was in her power: I am assuredly persuaded, I say, that such a sight should so astonish [ancient writers like Aristotle] that they should judge the whole world to be transformed into Amazons, and that such a metamorphosis and change was made of all the men of that country, as poets do feign was made of the companions of Vlisses, or at least, that albeit the outward form of men remained, yet should they judge that their hearts were changed from the wisdom, understanding, and courage of men, to the foolish fondness and cowardice of women.[1]

Although Knox was not referring to Elizabeth (this was before the surprise of her ascension to the throne) and his view from within his radical Protestant community represents only an extreme one, his disgust is certainly evidence of more pervasive concern, and this anxiety is expressed using the language of metamorphosis.[2] Knox's misogynistic repulsion to the inversion of gender roles that he sees in the powerful female rulers around him is troped in his rant by bodily sex change. His vision of female power—a vision that comes remarkably close to a description of Elizabeth in one of her progresses through the city of London or her mythical moment of cross-dressed glory as the military leader of the troops at Tilbury—reveals an anxiety most urgently expressed by Knox, and so presumably felt by other subjects at the beginning of Elizabeth's reign, that the male multitudes watching the powerful civic figurehead who has become a woman will suffer the same fate themselves.[3] Knox makes explicit the cultural associations that link the idea of metamorphosis to uncontrolled femininity as well as corrupted state power, civic upset, and misrule.

Given the rhetorical use of metamorphosis in this passage, it might seem surprising that Ovidian metamorphosis was a major trope in so much of the dramatic literature of the Elizabethan court, but many of the plays and entertainments performed for Elizabeth were in explicit intertextual dialogue with *Metamorphoses*. This chapter will explore the question of how Ovidianism—associated as it was with paganism, witchcraft, and dangerous forms of feminized sexual power—became a characteristic Elizabethan political discourse. In the queen's later entertainments and in the many plays produced for her court by John Lyly in the later part of her reign, the queen is associated with the power to effect metamorphosis in others and, even more surprisingly, is implicated as a female figure in bodily changes themselves. How could Elizabeth's propagandists harness the cultural power of Ovidian metamorphosis for their own purposes in the face of such frightening gender associations? Given the way that gender role transgression is dangerously associated with bodily change in Knox's rhetoric, what cultural work was accomplished by this overtly political deployment of Ovidian metamorphosis?

To return briefly to Knox, his vision is terrifying specifically because it involves the metamorphosis (presumably) of regular women into Amazons and of men into regular women. He brings home his point by comparing the men of this womanish country to the men enchanted by Circe in *Odyssey* (and later *Aeneid* and *Metamorphoses*), implying that their transformations are the result of a misdirected and beastly perversion of desire. In book 10 of *Odyssey*, Circe famously lures half of Odysseus' crew into her hall and then turns them into swine. They are only released when Odysseus, with a magic herb from Hermes, resists her charms and demands that his men be retransformed before he agrees to be her sexual partner. In *Metamorphoses*, Circe is a figure in a number of tales, including a retelling of her encounter with Odysseus, and in each case she is a witch with the power to metamorphose both men and women caught up in various kinds of unrequited or thwarted desire. The allusion to this familiar classical figure highlights her power to effect unnatural transformations of human beings into forms of lower animal life and emphasizes the figural power of the myth as a tale of the transformative effects of excessive desire. Circe figures the destabilizations of gender roles that occur when feminized authority wields the power of metamorphosis specifically over men, as well as the corrupting influence of an emotional state that is overtly feminized. She stands as an exemplar of the destabilizing threat that lies at the heart of Ovid's poem and the antiauthoritarian sensibility it represents in ancient literature.

But Knox's metamorphosis is only ambiguously bodily. It is the hearts of the men that have been changed into those of women, and the bodily change is, he implies, figurative. He accuses the men of his country of monstrous gender-inversion in their interior natures but also ambiguously distances the animalistic horrors of Circean bodily change. In doing so, he draws a connection between the excessive movements of the heart—the passions, but more generally, that part of the self that some in the Renaissance characterize as interior— and unnatural, frightening bodily transformations. Metamorphosis can take place both in the body and the heart, and in both cases the change is feminized and decried, leading to beastliness when the metamorphosis is bodily and "fondness" when it occurs within the heart. Knox's subtle distancing in this passage from a conception of actual bodily transformation reflects larger cultural concerns about the possibility that bodies might be changeable, and it also registers concern about female desire arising from excessive emotion—"foolish fondness"—that is apparently an essential part of biological femininity. Unreasonable emotion seems to be the true danger of turning into a woman in this ideological system.

This set of concerns is similarly registered in the preface to Arthur Golding's translation of *Metamorphoses*, which I have addressed at some length in the Introduction. As the writer introducing this metamorphic poem into England in its complete form for the first time, Golding's prefatory material takes pains to bring the poem in line with mainstream Protestant theology on a number of issues, and the question of metamorphosis itself is one of his central concerns. In the preface he emphasizes that the metamorphosing figures in the tales should be mirrors, or figures, for transformations of the soul:

> For if the States that on the earth the roome of God supply,
> Declyne from vertue unto vice and live disorderly,
> To Eagles, Tygres, Bulles, and Beares, and other figures straunge
> Both to theyr people and themselves most hurtfull doo they chaunge,
>   . . .
> But if we suffer fleshly lustes as lawlesse Lordes to reigne,
> Than are we beastes, wee are no men, wee have our name in vaine.

> And if we be so drowned in vice that feeling once bee gone,
> Then may it well of us bee sayd, wee are a block or stone.
> This surely did the Poets meene when in such sundry wyse
> The pleasant tales of turned shapes they studied to devyse.
> (Preface, 89–93, 111–16)

For Golding, the most frightening and vile kind of metamorphosis dilated on is Circean, associated with witchcraft and the feminized hybridization of human and animal bodies. While the preface asserts the figurative nature of metamorphosis—this is "surely" what the poets meant—the attention devoted to this issue reveals a concern that the poem might be read literally and that it might therefore be associated with the heretical and feminized world of bodily transformations.

In other Protestant writings of the period, metamorphosis is also linked with the horrors of Catholicism and the paganism of witchcraft. Reginald Scot, for instance, in his 1584 *Discovery of Witchcraft*, which is the subject of Chapter 4, links metamorphosis to transubstantiation and refers to bodily change and the transformation of the Host by this same term.[4] Debunking the apparently widespread belief that witches had power to physically transform their victims, Scot writes,

> What a beastlie assertion is it, that a man, whom God hath made according to his own similitude and likenes, should be by a witch turned into a beast? What an impietie is it to affirme, that an asses bodie is the temple of the Holy-ghost? Or an asse to be the child of God and God to be his father; as it is said of man? Which Paule to the Corinthians so divinelie confuteth, who saith that Our bodies are the members of Christ. In the which we are to glorifie God: for the bodie is for the Lord and the Lord is for the bodie. Surelie he meaneth not for an asses bodie as, by this time I hope appeareth.[5]

Metamorphosis, as actual bodily change rather than as a metaphor for changes in the internal person, while central to the Ovidianism pervasive in this period, carried with it dangerous and feminized associations, associations that make it a seemingly unlikely discourse for representing Elizabeth, the female head of the state and church.

And yet, surprisingly, and I would argue, as a strategic response to this depiction of metamorphosis as a threatening fantasy of feminized power, the political discourse of Elizabeth's later reign deployed Ovidian metamorphosis to figure positively valued political flexibility, but also, more profoundly, to loosen and transform stable gender categories, especially in the person of the queen. The fact that such Ovidianism is present in Elizabethan courtly drama and entertainments reveals a concern to represent the queen's body as more than just the distant, inviolate, and virginal whole that is the depiction privileged especially in her later propaganda and the focus of scholars studying Elizabeth's representations. In her Ovidian representations, marked as they are with the dangers of monstrous gender and pagan emotion, there is a deeper commitment to bodily flexibility than to stasis. Ovidianism in Elizabeth's courtly productions operates in explicit contrast to representations of her body as uniquely stable, and it allows for negotiations of her gender that are central to her political fashioning. While one of Elizabeth's favorite mottos, *semper eadem*, might seem to be evidence to contradict this claim, it is precisely the Ovidian sense of the passionate body as both always in flux and always mysteriously stable that made Ovidianism an appropriate discourse for the queen's metamorphic political negotiations.

Not all associations of the queen with metamorphic change are explicitly or exclusively Ovidian—she is often linked, for instance, in her guise as Cynthia or Diana, with the changeable nature of the moon—but in these cases, she is removed from the natural realm, governing over change, rather than implicated in representations of desire and bodily transformation. Her transcendence of earthly change, marked as it is in associations of her with these moon goddesses, is probably a response to many of her detractors who, like Knox, based their objections to her rule on the belief that women were by nature weak, fickle, and emotionally inconstant. Ovidianism, however, repeatedly places the queen in the position of both goddess of change *and* metamorphosing mortal body, and in doing so, it riskily asserts her claims to a metamorphic gender identity. It also suggests, especially in her later political performances, control over the mutable nature of female desire, a control that Elizabethan propagandists might want especially to emphasize.

Bodily metamorphosis was especially important as a trope in Elizabeth's representations because the court discourses of her regime famously defined her gender through the refashioned medieval doctrine of the king's two bodies. This Elizabethan legal premise posited that a ruler by divine right has a "body politic," established by his position as king, that takes precedence over his "body natural," his mortal body, and also many of the attributes of what we might consider individual identity.[6] Elizabethan political writings, those written by both the queen and by others, often used this division to affirm that the weakness of the queen's female private person was outweighed by the strength of her public role as inheritor of Henry VIII's authority and God-chosen protector of the true faith. The most famous example of this self-fashioning is from the speech she reportedly made at Tilbury to the troops assembled to defeat the Spanish Armada in 1588, in which she asserted, "I may have the body of a weak and feeble woman, but I have the heart and stomach of a king, and a king of England too."[7]

Most of Elizabeth's articulations of her doubled gender are much more subtle, however, as she was generally very careful in her writings to seem to affirm traditional gender roles even as she subverted them. In her speech responding to the Parliament's request that Mary Queen of Scots be executed for treason in 1586, for instance, Elizabeth fashions herself as endowed with more than masculine bravery: "These former remembrances [of violations of trust and political betrayals], present feeling, and future expectation of evils, I say, have made me think an evil is much the better the less while it endureth, and so, them happiest that are soonest hence; and taught me to bear with a better mind these treasons than is common to my sex—yea, with a better heart, perhaps, than is in some men."[8] Drawing on the traditional association of courage with masculinity, Elizabeth skillfully undercuts this gendered stereotype as she seems to be asserting it. Although she begins to state that she can bear more than is common to her sex, she slyly ends up implying that she can bear more than is common to men as well, eroding the difference she seems to have just established. While such rhetoric has been read as reinforcing her uniqueness and thus representing her as anomalous to her gender, she says that she surpasses expectations of not only her own gender but both of them, deconstructing the dualism from her place beyond it.

Similarly, in her "Golden Speech" to parliament in 1601, which was reprinted many times and became her most famous parliamentary speech in the seventeenth century, she expresses her value as a ruler by asserting and then deconstructing her gender identity: "And though you have had and may have many princes more mighty and wise sitting in this seat, yet you never had or shall have any that will be more careful and loving. Shall I ascribe anything to myself and my sexly weakness? I were not worthy to live then, and of most unworthy of the mercies I have had from God, who hath ever yet given me a heart which never feared any foreign or home enemy."[9] Here again, Elizabeth seems to be emphasizing her "sexly weakness," affirming initially that she may not be as "mighty" as a male ruler, but investing her reign with the "womanly" emotional qualities of care and love. Immediately following these assertions, however, she reveals her mightiness, drawing attention to her fearless heart, the gift of the God who placed her in position as prince. Again, she asserts the femininity of her natural body only to subtly draw gender distinctions themselves into question.

Her use of this double-bodied theory of royal identity was, as these examples reveal, quite complex, and Stephen Cohen has posited that through her shifts of the genders of both parts of her self, she radically destabilized Renaissance notions of an interior, essential identity that took precedence over an exterior person.[10] For instance, her address at Tilbury asserts the femininity of her body as subordinate to the masculinity of her heart and stomach, implying that her "truer" self is manifested in the more interior organs, rather than the external body. In this equation, she is arguably more male than female, as her masculine, kingly identity is merely hidden, or disguised, by the weakness of her feminine body. In other circumstances, however, Elizabeth went out of her way to emphasize her inward femininity, and she often asserted the sway her interior feminine identity had over her exterior role as king. The entire cult surrounding her as Petrarchan mistress is only the most obvious evidence of this utilization of her perceived femininity. She also, as Cohen points out, routinely exploited her supposedly emotive and essential feminine self to excuse unpopular political decisions, such as when she attributed her delay in executing Mary Queen of Scots to her womanly predilection for mercy. These maneuvers must have left it difficult to say whether she was inwardly, and possibly "truly," more male or female. She did not, therefore, just assert a feminine "body natural" that was neatly suppressed by a masculine "body politic." Instead, as Cohen argues, she negotiated and renegotiated her gender to suit immediate political circumstances and in doing so challenged the emerging notion of a stable gendered modern self with a fixed interior and exterior identity.

While Elizabeth's own writings only rarely invoke literary discourses, are only occasionally allusive, and never, as far as we know from surviving documents, invoke Ovidian figures of any kind, Ovidianism offered her court artists a literary discourse that could reinforce Elizabeth's own potentially transgressive gender negotiations, especially in the last decade of her reign, reenvisioning the nightmare of Knox's picture of female rule into a politically viable reality. Ovidian representations in the period's writings outside the immediate context of the court, I would argue, while part of literary movements with many investments, were also often weighted with associations to the queen, and not only when she was present explicitly as Cynthia, Mutability, or Gloriana. The heightened interest in Ovidianism during the late 1580s and 1590s, the later part of Elizabeth's reign, partly reflects a cultural interest in the metamorphosis of gender identity introduced by the queen and her courtly publicists.

Before turning to an analysis of the Ovidianism of two later productions of Elizabeth's court (one an entertainment and one a court play), a comparison to an earlier courtly Ovidianism reveals a shift in the relations between the queen and her closest courtiers and artists over the course of her reign. Such political developments have been the focus of recent scholarship on Elizabeth's representations. Francis Yates and Roy Strong initiated the critical discussion of how court symbolism and pageantry were tied to constructions of the queen's royal authority, and Strong's articulation of Elizabeth's representations as forming a "cult" still governs the debate about this representational politics. A number of scholars have since complicated this description, however, citing the various and shifting ideological stances presented in most Elizabethan visual and verbal portraiture.[11] Philippa Berry, in *Of Chastity and Power*, describes the shifts that take place in the emphases and valences of courtly performances over the course of Elizabeth's reign. She outlines an early attempt by Elizabeth's courtiers to establish their masculine and military natures in order to govern the young queen. Later, she finds the queen influencing to greater degrees her own representation until in her final decade she becomes a mystical symbolic presence that preserves her feminine authority.[12] John King also provides a diachronic reading of her iconography. He similarly charts the changes in Elizabeth's representations from marriageable to mystical and perpetual virgin and attributes these changes to specific political exigencies.[13] Susan Frye in *Elizabeth I: The Competition for Representation*, argues that the distinct transformations in Elizabeth's self-presentation are the results of competition between the queen and those with vested political interests, such as her courtiers, ministers, and financiers.[14] Finally, Louis Montrose has produced many complex readings of the reciprocal power relationships formed between the Elizabethan court and artistic and other cultural representations in the period. He has argued that Elizabethan courtiers employed a "strategic ambiguity" in their representations of the queen. He remarks on the "coy and calculating performativity" of the Elizabethan court and outlines a cultural dynamic rather than a static "cult."[15] Ovidianism was only one of many discourses circulating in the political milieu of the court, but its representations were especially marked by this ambiguity, and in this respect they offer a unique perspective on the larger questions that still surround Elizabeth's representation.

By comparing two highly Ovidian entertainments from different political moments—those at Kenilworth Castle in 1575 and at

Sudeley Castle in 1592—we can trace the changing representations of the queen's body as she produces metamorphoses in other figures and governs over metamorphosis itself. At Kenilworth, metamorphosis is used to trope the courtier's transforming desire for his queen, and the queen's denial of that desire is marked and significant. In this early entertainment, the cruelty of the queen as mistress is associated with a dangerous and effeminizing metamorphic power, but she herself, physically present in the grove, does not perform an actual change, as she will in the Sudeley entertainment. Her metamorphic powers are repeatedly distanced, and they are depicted as threatening to her noble and loyal male subjects. They do represent, however, an early version of the link between her gendered body and metamorphosis. In the later Sudeley entertainment, this metamorphic power is both embodied by the queen and celebrated—it is co-opted and refigured—and it is associated with the feminine rescue of a Daphne figure and the power of political change and flexibility. More profoundly, metamorphosis in this later entertainment serves to loosen and transform stable gender categories, especially in the person of the queen.[16]

METAMORPHOSING THE COURTIER'S DESIRE: KENILWORTH IN 1575

In Elizabeth's most famous and republished entertainment at Kenilworth Castle, written in 1575 by George Gascoigne for her host, the Earl of Leicester metamorphosis is not specifically associated with the queen's body; instead, it is used to trope the courtier's transforming desire for his queen and the queen's denial of that desire. At the end of that entertainment, which is filled with Ovidian figures—nymphs, dryads, Diana searching for a lost nymph, Echo—Elizabeth's rejection of her suitors leads them to be "converted into most monstrous shapes and proportions; as some into fishes, some others into foules, and some into huge stony rocks and great mountains."[17] The nymph Zabeta, who is a very thinly veiled figure for the queen (the play on her name being only one among many obvious allegorical signs), in fact, has created many of the trees surrounding them at Leicester's castle, where this entertainment takes place. The wood god Sylvanus, who was probably played by Gascoigne himself, gives the queen a tour of the trees who were once Zabeta's suitors and elicits her pity for their transformed conditions:

> Behold, gracious Lady, this old Oke; the same was many years a faithfull follower and trustie servant of hyrs, named *Constance*, whome

when shee coulde by none other means overthrowe, considering that no chaunge coulde creepe into his thoughts, nor any trouble of passions and perplexities coulde turne his resolute minde, at length she caused him, as I say, to be converted into this Oke, a strange and cruel metamorphosis! But yet the heavens have thus far forth favoured and rewarded his long continued service, that as in life he was unmoveable, even so now all the vehement blasts of the most raging windes cannot once move his rocky body from his rooted place and abiding. (519)

Metamorphosis here is influenced by the queen, but the heavens have a share in this power, as they seem to be responsible for the way the transformation fits the nature of the desire (as in Dante's many metamorphic *contrapassi*). Zabeta "caused" Constance to be metamorphosed—ironically, since it is his inability to change that elicits her response—but it is by the heavens that he is "rewarded" in the nature of his transformed shape. Not all of Zabeta's suitors appear to deserve pity, though, as they are also Inconstancie, Vaineglory, Contention, and Ambition. Elizabeth's power to deny her male courtiers is figured here as metamorphic, and while it is critiqued when directed against Constance, some of her denials are just. The episode so far is only subtly critical, since she is responding to both good and bad suitors, but her metamorphic abilities seem to be of the Circean, dangerously feminized kind.

The entertainment concludes, however, with a stronger critique of the metamorphosis-producing Zabeta, along with an appeal for clemency. An unjustly transformed suitor, Deepedesire, who is surely a figure for Elizabeth's host, Leicester himself, and may in fact have been played by him, has become a Holly bush. Elizabeth negotiates the metamorphosed landscape animated verbally by Gascoigne, dressed as the wood-god Sylvanus, and physically by a man hiding in a holly bush:

Her Majestie came by a close arbor, made all of Hollie; and whiles Silvanus pointed to the same, the principal bush shaked. For therein were placed both strange musicke, and one who was there appointed to represent Deepedesire. Silvanus, perceiving the bush to shake, continued thus:

Behold, most gracious Queene, this Hollybush doeth tremble at your presence; and therefore I believe that Deepedesire hath gotten leave of the Gods to speake unto your excellent Majestie in their behalfe, for I myself was present at the Council-chamber of Heaven, when Desire was thought a meete messenger to be sent from that Convocation unto your Majestie as Ambassadour: and give eare, good Queene; methinks I heare his voice. (520–21)

The queen must have approached this shaking, musical bush in order to hear his speech, and this encounter served as the symbolic farewell between the queen and her host and controversial favorite, the Earl of Leicester. Most scholars agree that this particular entertainment tropes Leicester's bid for the queen's hand (in the present or after the fact) and his desire to pursue military intervention in the Netherlands, but critics vary in their evaluations of the results and overall political seriousness of this power struggle.[18] On the most basic level, this metamorphosed figure, and those before him in the same entertainment, represent conventional lovesick courtiers, and therefore participate in the Petrarchan discourse of unrequited desire that marks so many representations of the Elizabethan court. This bush, however, is more than just a pining lover; he is a metamorphic figure and therefore evokes the discourse of Ovidianism, in which bodies are prone to transformations and the self is both constantly affirmed beyond the mutable body, and—paradoxically and simultaneously—is always under threat of erosion. Ovidianism is a literary discourse unmistakably linked to court politics in this entertainment from the first half of Elizabeth's reign, and it functions to undercut stable representations of the body and the body's multiplicitous desires. It draws attention, in fact, to the instabilities and flexibilities of the queen's ambiguously gendered person.

What Gascoigne's trembling bush actually speaks is a narrative of his origins and then a long lament over the queen's departure. The bush introduces himself as

> that wretch *Desire*   whom neither death could daunt;
> Nor dole decay, nor dread delay,   nor fayned cheere inchant:
> Whom neither care could quench,   nor fancie force to change:
> And therefore turned into this tree,   which sight percase seems strange.
> (521)

Strange indeed, this encounter with the speaking bush is a highly overdetermined moment of intertextuality. While the queen's and the reader's interpretations of the bush are supposedly dictated by the self-consciously present poet in the guise of Sylvanus, metamorphosed bushes calling themselves desire would have had larger cultural resonances not accounted for by Sylvanus' moralized reading. A bush with music and words issuing from it might have evoked in Renaissance audiences an association with the burning bush of Exodus 3:1–10, an interpretation that makes sense since the bush says it has a message from heaven. While it is not burning, the widespread association of desire with the hotter humoral spirits and the Petrarchan convention of the lover existing in a perpetual state of icy fire would have made this association. The bush might also be a warning with a different type of uncanny message, since a speaking bush (though myrtle, not holly), warns Aeneas that he is the metamorphosed Polydorus and that they have landed on desecrated ground in Thrace in book 3 of *Aeneid*. Holly also had associations with various ancient fertility customs, and like other evergreens, was used to decorate homes around the winter solstice and then Christmas and was associated with Christ's crown of thorns in Christmas legends that linked the red berries to Christ's blood. The bush, therefore, might be harbinger of good or evil, a sign of God's or nature's promise, or a monument of violent, and possibly redeeming, death. It is, in other words, a metamorphic figure that needs to be read, and the entertainment offers a guide to the queen's interpretations.

While the speaking bush might evoke these many associations, Sylvanus/Gascoigne has prepared the queen for this encounter to be Ovidian, and he represents himself mainly as the Ovidian Orpheus. As Elizabeth approaches the desiring bush, Sylvanus invests all of the surrounding plants with Ovidian etiologies. He laments the fact that Diana's nymph Zabeta (the queen), has created a landscape of transformed lovers in this location:

> The tears stande in mine eyes, yea, and my tongue trembleth and faltereth in my mouth, when I begin to declare the distresses wherein some of them doe presently remayne. I could tell your Highnesse of sundry famous and worthy persons, whome shee hath turned and converted into most monstrous shapes and proportions . . . but because diverse of her most earnest and faithfull followers, as also some cicophants, have bin converted into sundry of these plants whereof I have charge, I will on shew unto your Majestie so many of them as are in sight in these places where you pass. (519)

Sylvanus proceeds to enumerate the different allegorical lovers, and the plants they have become: Constance becomes an Oak, Inconstancie a Poplar, Vaineglory an Ash, Contention a Bramble, Ambition an Ivy. This listing of metamorphosed trees is a direct allusion to Orpheus' tree-catalogue in *Metamorphoses* 10, in which the trees draw nearer to the tragic voice of Orpheus as he sings the songs of those transformed by various kinds of unlawful or unsanctioned love.[19] Orpheus is the narrator or singer of all the tales in book 10, and they are complex analyses of the relationship between transgressive desires and the losses and grieving to which these loves lead. Orpheus is associated with

Cyparrisus, who is overly fond of a stag, Ganymede and Hyacinthus, both youths loved by male gods, the Propoetides, the first prostitutes, Pygmalion, who desires a statue, and Myrrha, who desires her father. Orpheus' final tales are slightly different: Venus and Adonis invert and challenge the roles of pursuer and pursued in love, and, as if to conclude by associating these at least potentially transgressive desires with heteronormative structures, the book ends with the tragic story of Atalanta and Hippomenes, who are granted a brief romantic union and then are suddenly punished (by being transformed to lions) for failing to credit their normative happy ending to the goddess of love. Although there are many ways to read Ovid's notoriously shifting and ironic narrative, what is at stake in these stories seems to be love that lies outside expected social structures that govern desire. That the entertainment concludes with an allusion to this part of *Metamorphoses* may signal the poet's distancing of himself, as the Orphic singer, from the desires of his host and patron. Orpheus, who is associated also with the misogyny represented in many of these tales, and who is ultimately dismembered by women in an ironic Bacchic frenzy, becomes the intertextual persona of Leicester's fearful poet.

If the poet is defined as a grieving Orpheus in this episode, then Leicester's desire for the queen is also placed in the context of the transgressive loves lamented by Ovid's narrator. Politically, meaning is created intertextually with the Orphic tales in *Metamorphoses*, and the episode could be read as an intentional, or perhaps unconscious, acknowledgment of the transgressive nature of Leicester's own ambitions. If Leicester is one of Orpheus' trees, he is both trapped in grief and transformed by it, and it is tempting to read this as evidence of the queen's expressed annoyance at her treatment during her visit. This is the entertainment in which Elizabeth famously seems to have cancelled some of the events, miffed about a marriage masque on the first day that challenged her decision not to marry and specifically not to marry Leicester. This sense that Leicester may have transgressed his bounds is reinforced when the entertainment ends without the queen accomplishing the remetamorphosis of the bush back into a lover. Sylvanus pleads,

> because the case is very lamentable, in the conversion of Deepedesire, as also because they knowe that your Majestie is so highly favoured of the Gods, that they will not deny you any reasonable request; therefore I do humbly crave in his behalfe, that you would either be a suter for him unto the heavenly powers, or else but only to give your gracious consent that hee may be restored to his prystinate estate. Whereat

> your Highnesse many be assured, that heaven will smile, the earth will
> quake, men will clap their hands, and I will always continue an humble
> beseecher for the flourishing estate for your royal person; whom God
> now and ever preserve, to his good pleasure, and our great comfort.
> Amen. (523)

This final speech moves from a plea to the queen to a prayer, a request
to the only possible greater authority in the rhetoric of the court. The
fact that this release from metamorphosis is not accomplished or narrated in the entertainment as published, however, leaves the reaction
of the queen to this display in doubt and the figure of desire trapped.[20]
The ambiguity of the queen's power over metamorphosis, as she can
either be a heavenly mediator or just grant her consent (to heaven!?!),
distances her from control specifically over the courtier's body, even
as the Ovidianism of the scene suggests the lack of control over a
transforming passion. The queen's body, actually present at this performance, is symbolically removed from the threat embodied in the
speaking bush, but at the same time all bodies, and by implication I
would argue, all identities are called into question by the landscape of
Ovidian figures. In this entertainment, the link between the emotive
body and the identity of the courtier is made allegorically, and they
inhabit a landscape where individual identity seems to have been dif-
fused into a grove of desiring trees. The subjects here are subject to a
queen with threatening Ovidian powers of transformation, and in fact,
Deepedesire/Leicester is especially vulnerable, as Silvanus tells the
queen that Zabeta (she herself) "did never cease to use imprecation,
invocation, conjuration, and all means possible, until she had caused
him to be turned into this Hollybush" (520). The queen's metamorphic power over the bodies of her courtiers is witchlike, Circean, and
uncontrollable, and it is potentially potent enough to make Gascoigne
fear his own dismemberment.

Ovidianism, however, inflects the gender politics of the episode in
a number of ways. In this entertainment, the bush is specifically a
"he-holly," which has prickly leaves, as opposed to the "she-holly"
whose leaves are smooth, and the sexual connotations of this fact are
made explicit when Sylvanus tells the queen, "As he was in life and
worlde continually full of compunctions, so is he now furnished on
every side with sharpe pricking leaves, to prove the restlesse prickes
of his privie thoughts. Mary there are two kinds of Holly, that is to
say, He-Holly, and She-Holly. Now some will say, that She-Holly hath
no prickes; but thereof I intermeddle not" (520). This bawdy joke

emphasizes Deepedesire's masculinity, but it is a phallic power kept in check, as he suffers from the pricks of his metamorphosed state. This humor is ostensibly an affirmation of impotence, offering submission to the female ruler, but it implies a masculine potential for violence that the Ovidianism of the episode enforces. When a desiring figure is metamorphosed in Ovid's poem, especially in the most popular Renaissance tales, it is usually a god transforming himself in order to rape a mortal, a nymph or other less-powerful figure. Rape involving a god's transformation, is, in fact, the most exemplary tale in *Metamorphoses*, and while it is usually a male figure who pursues a female figure, in the section of the poem narrated by Orpheus and in a few other tales as well, a male god (or occasionally a female one, in the case of Venus and Adonis), pursues a less-powerful male. Because the rape narrative is the most pervasive and repeated in the poem, Ovidianism is often evoked to trope love as a hunt, and the actual hunting and previous rape narrative in this entertainment—in which Elizabeth rescues the Lady of the Lake from Sir Bruise sans Pitie—suggest the way this Ovidianism helps define the rigid gender politics of the whole entertainment. While rapists are usually metamorphosed into higher forms of life than bushes, the encounter between a queen and a deeply desiring metamorphosed male figure marks the potential for violence signified by Ovid's repeated rapes and therefore affirms in more subtle, covert ways, Leicester's power.

QUEEN OF METAMORPHOSIS AT SUDELEY, 1592

In contrast, during the entertainments at Sudeley Castle, performed before the queen in 1592, as her natural body entered its sixties, a different type of metamorphosed form begged for her attention. The queen made a progress that summer that included entertainments at Bisham, Sudeley Castle, and Ricoyte, and these were published together at the end of the summer. The fact that they were quickly published may suggest that they were written by John Lyly, whose renown as a court writer might have ensured quick publication.[21]

In September, the queen approached Sudeley Castle, the seat of Lord Chandos, a member of Parliament, and his wife, Lady Chandos, who may have served as the primary hostess on this occasion, as she was in 1574 and 1602. In this entertainment the queen watched as Apollo chased Daphne and then was met by a shepherd, who told her a directly reworked Ovidian tale. The shepherd begins by citing Ovid in the original Latin:

Nescis temeraria; nescis
Quem fugias; ideoque fugis.

[Thou knowest not, rash one, thou knowest not whom thou fleest, and
for that reason dost thou flee.][22]

This is a citation from Apollo's boastful attempt at persuasion in
the first book of *Metamorphoses*. In Ovid, the statement emphasizes
Apollo-the-seer's claims to an epistemological power—Daphne cannot know because she flees, and in the act of flight, according to
Apollo, she neglects her own self-interest. The Ovidian irony of this
moment inheres in the fact that Daphne actually does seem to know
who is pursuing her, or at least the power of the one pursuing her. The
original tale in Ovid, therefore, deflates Apollo's claims to superiority
by revealing that this nymph knows more than he thinks she does, and
this emphasis suggests her perspective as an important one for interpreting the affect of the story. Apollo's godly power is also deflated by
his silly love rhetoric. His facetious concern that Daphne not injure
herself while running ("me miserum! ne prona cadas indignave laedi
/ crura nontent sentes et sim tibi causa doloris!" [Ah me! I fear that
thou wilt fall, or brambles mar thy innocent limbs, and I be cause of
pain to thee; I. 508–9]) manages to be both comical and terrifying,
an example of the dark humor pervasive in *Metamorphoses* and often
imitated in Renaissance translations of it.

In the entertainment, the shepherd, in a triangulation of the Ovidian tale, loves Daphne, and is persecuted by Apollo:[23]

> Apollo, who calleth himselfe a God (a title among men, when they will
> commit injuries tearme themselves Gods), pursued my Daphne with
> bootlesse love, and myself with endlesse hate; her he woed, with faire
> wordes, the flatteries of men; with great gifts, the sorceries of Gods;
> with cruell threates, the terrefiing of weake damosels . . . Me he terri-
> fied with a monstrous word metamorphosing, saying he would turne
> me into a woolfe, and of a Shepheard make me a sheepe-biter; or into
> a cockatrice; and cause mine eies, which gazed on her, to blind hers,
> which made mine dazell; or to a molde, that I should heare his flatter-
> ing speech, but never behold her faire face. (137)

Rather than metamorphosis as an escape or at least a compromised
resolution, as it is in the Ovidian intertext, metamorphosis here is first
evoked as a threat, and a threat made to a male rival. The poor Shepherd is helpless against this god, who threatens him with a "monstrous

word." Either that monstrous word is itself "metamorphosing," or perhaps the incantation used by Apollo to effect this metamorphosis. At this initial point in the performance, the idea of metamorphosis is monstrous, as it was at Kenilworth, although in this case it is a powerful male figure threatening another man.

Immediately, however, the actually metamorphosed figure becomes Daphne herself:

> It was four of the clocke, when she, flying from his treason, was turned into a tree; which made me stand as though I had bene turned into a stone, and Apollo so enchanted as wounded with her losse, or his own cruelty: the fingers, which were wonte to play on the lute, found no other instrument then his owne face; the gulden haire, the pride of his heade, pulde off in lockes, and stampt at his feete; his sweete voice turned to howling; and there sitteth he (long may he sorrowe) wondring and weeping, and kissing the lawrell, his late love, and mine ever. Pleaseth your majestie to viewe the melancholy of Apollo, my distresse, and Daphne's mischance; it may be the sight of so rare perfection will make him die for grief, which I wish; or Daphne returne to her olde shape, which must be your wonder; if neither, it shal content me that I have revealed my griefes, and that you may beholde his. (137)

Unlike at Kenilworth, the queen is here urged to intervene in a male rivalry to rescue the female object of desire, rather than the desiring courtier, and to enforce her connections of gender with Daphne. In his description of the possibility that Elizabeth's presence can rescue the three of them from this dire situation, the shepherd seems to associate Daphne with the queen explicitly, suggesting that Apollo might die for grief if he saw Elizabeth's "rare perfection." Such perfection would only kill him if the grief were an intensification of the grief he feels at the loss of Daphne, who was an example of perfect chastity.

The queen does create this miraculous remetamorphosis, but first she is taken to another location, where she witnesses Apollo's grief being expressed in first a poem and then a song. He first recites these lines:

> Sing you, plaie you; but sing and play my truth;
> This tree my lute, these sighes my notes of ruth:
> The lawfull leafe for ever shall bee greene,
> And Chastety shall be Apolloes Queene.
> If Gods maye dye, here shall my tombe be plaste,
> And this engraven, "Fonde Phoebus, Daphne chaste."
> (138)

Apollo's declaration that Chastity will be his queen is a fairly unam-
biguous celebration of Elizabeth's chaste persona.[24] He admits to the
failure of his attempts to possess her. Such an apology may well refer
to some slight Lord Chandos may have made to the queen's person
at court, but it could just as easily be a more general celebration of
Elizabeth's transcendence of the narrative of masculine desire. Apollo's subsequent song emphasizes the truth of his love, acknowledges
again his defeat, and requests that a second motto be engraved on the
laurel: "That neither men nor gods, can force affection." This statement is a central part of the queen's propaganda in this entertainment
and is evidence of the cultural link being made between Ovidianism
and queenly "affection." In Ovid's retelling of the Daphne story, Lyly
finds a source for a representation of resistance to male desire that
defines Elizabeth's affections as transcendent of the limiting structures of power that dominate literary relationships between the sexes.

After his lament, the tree suddenly breaks open, Daphne emerges,
and Apollo immediately renews his chase, only to tell the audience
that he will abandon her to her shepherd, who will never be able to
truly appreciate her beauty. The nymph proceeds to run to present her
majesty with celebratory verses on tablets, saying, "I stay, for whither
should Chastety fly for succour, but to the Queene of Chastety. By
thee was I entered in a tree, that by crafte, way might be made to Lust:
by your Highnes restored, that by vertue there might be assurances
in honor" (139). That she describes her metamorphosis as making
way to lust may actually be a printing error, leaving out an essential
"not." It may also suggest, however, that the queen has devised her
metamorphosis to test the desires of Apollo and to affirm the honor
of the faithful shepherd. Whatever the case, she presents her gifts for
the queen with these words: "With this vouchsafe a poore Virgin's
wish, that often wish for good husbands; mine, only for the endlesse
prosperity of my soveraigne." In this case, Elizabeth is the agent of
metamorphosis, and this metamorphosis is a rescue from the gender
politics of love as a hunt.

The final moments of this episode are a validation of Daphne's
independence rather than her submission to the shepherd (although
the union is certainly implied). The overall effect is to privilege Chastity over marriage and thus to affirm the queen's choices not to marry
and to assume her position as Queen of Chastity. Metamorphosis is
affirmed as a power the queen holds, a means for allowing Daphne
a new life, rescued from her destiny in her Ovidian source. On the

surface, at least, this entertainment celebrates the queen's power and may possibly be using the Apollo and Daphne tale to seek forgiveness for either a specific or general attempt to force the queen's affections. Apollo is explicitly associated with the Petrarchan lover and Petrarch himself, however, so we may be witnessing an even more general acknowledgment and celebration of the queen's transcendence of the rhetoric of limiting Petrarchan sexual politics.

The episode points, however, to the queen's implication in the realm of such masculine desires, even as it represents her transcendence of them. If the queen must read herself in Daphne, she is, on the one hand, the Daphne of Ovid's tale, fixed in her nonhuman form, but still ambiguously released from the pursuit of Apollo. She is also the Daphne of this tale, engaged to the crude shepherd. In this case, the lowly shepherd is probably the host himself, suggesting the humility of his devotion to her in contrast to the prideful Apollo. In both cases, however, the threat to Daphne, and therefore to all chaste virgins, is not eliminated, only partially foiled. The power of male desire, embodied in the threat of rape, is, in fact, the heart of this tale, and even if the queen transcends that narrative, the ambiguities of both artistic creations implicate her in it. Treading the line between celebration and critique, the entertainment is an excellent example of how Ovidianism can accomplish a risky evaluation of the nature of and possibilities for female resistance to a masculine power.

This refigured metamorphosis, finally, is the site of a deeper celebration of the queen's political strategies. It is, after all, the only means of escape, however incomplete and qualified, for the female subject of both text and intertext. Although used as a "monstrous" threat by Apollo and represented that way in the Kenilworth entertainment, metamorphosis is ultimately a process in the queen's control in this retelling, and this may be a broader celebration of the queen's attempts to define a "metamorphic" royal person. While Daphne's metamorphosis into a tree suggests the dangers of an unstable bodily fluidity, her release implies her transcendence of these dangers. The queen can cleverly use metamorphosis as a tool to evade subjection, and this is precisely what she did by metamorphosing her gendered body throughout her reign. Drawing on the Ovidian emphasis on metamorphosis as a destabilization of the gendered body, this late entertainment acknowledges the dangers to the queen as a figure of female chastity, but still more profoundly celebrates her strategically metamorphic destabilizations of her gender.

JOHN LYLY'S COURTLY METAMORPHOSES

The most important instances and perhaps the sources of the Ovidianism that is associated with the Elizabethan court are the plays of John Lyly, who may also have been the author of the Sudeley entertainment. The particular Ovidianism of his court writings reveals a persistent attempt by at least this one author to engage with the queen's androgynous gender through Ovidian themes and images. Because of the complicated performance history of *Love's Metamorphosis*, it can actually be said to frame the Sudeley entertainment, to which we can with confidence assign a date of 1592. Although the play was not entered in the Stationer's Register until 1600, based on the evidence we have of when certain companies were producing plays, it was probably first produced by the Paul's Boys from 1586 through 1588 and then revived (and R. Warwick Bond argues, revised or partially rewritten) in 1599 or early 1600 by the Chapel Children.[25] It is frustrating to be without access to the possible revisions made to the play, given the turbulence of this period of Elizabeth's reign.

Lyly's plays, unfortunately, are usually approached by literary critics looking to him as an inferior predecessor of Shakespeare. Rarely do readings of the plays involve a sensitive analysis of the workings of Ovidian intertextuality; instead, they usually approach the explicit Ovidian borrowings as myths or mythic patterning.[26] Political approaches, unfortunately, tend to leave the Ovidianism of the plays out of the analysis altogether, focusing instead on topical historical allegory and Lyly's rhetorical maneuverings between celebration and critique.[27] Perhaps as a result of this critical history, there has not been a great deal of attention given to *Love's Metamorphosis*, the play by Lyly that most fully displays the Ovidian politics of Elizabeth's court.[28] Structured around two Ovidian tales and including not one but five metamorphosing figures, *Love's Metamorphosis* is the limit case for analyzing the political resonances of Ovidianism as a discourse of the court.

In the confrontation that begins the fifth act of *Love's Metamorphosis*, Cupid insists on his superior power over Ceres: "Thou, Ceres, doest but gouerne the guts of men; I the hearts" (V. i.8–9).[29] As even those who are unfamiliar with this particular play can guess, Ceres is a figure associated in important ways with Elizabeth, who was probably in the play's audience at some point in its performance history. Although traditionally a maternal goddess of fertility and natural abundance, in this play Ceres is a virgin goddess, and until the marriages that end the play, her followers are virgin nymphs. She maintains a distinctly regal presence throughout, her chastity is repeatedly emphasized, and she is only slightly less powerful than Cupid, who threatens to, but never actually does, infect her with unwanted desire. Since we cannot with confidence date the play, a reading of its topical allegory is impossible, but it seems clear that the play represents the queen and her ladies-in-waiting as engaged in energetic disputes over chastity. The opposing figure to Ceres in the play is Cupid, who is represented not as a willful naughty boy but as a mature god, and in fact the greatest god, to whom all, including Ceres, must pay respect. In the second act of the play, Ceres tells her nymphs, "But let vs to the Temple of *Cupid* and offer sacrifice; they that thinke it straunge for chastitie to humble it selfe to *Cupid*, knowe neither the power of loue, nor the nature of virginitie: th' one hauing absolute authoritie to commaund, the other difficultie to resist: and where such continuall warre is betweene loue and vertue, there must bee some parlies, and continuall perils; *Cupid* was neuer conquered, and therefore must be flattered; Virginitie hath, and therefore must be humble" (II. i. 38–45). Such a statement of defeat by the goddess of the play must operate as at least a mild critique of the Virgin Queen, placing her in a subordinate position to Cupid. This submission, however, is complicated by the insistent renegotiations of power associated with metamorphosis throughout the play.[30]

The play consists of two interwoven plots, which draw on two of the central kinds of stories within *Metamorphoses*, one exposing the violence to female figures inherent in the narrative of love as a hunt and the other questioning the stability of gender categories themselves. In both lines of the plot it is only female figures who metamorphose, making the play an extended commentary on metamorphosis in its relation to female subjectivity. The play opens focusing on three foresters, who complain of the unrequited loves of three of Ceres' nymphs. The three couples are a witty division of the most salient characteristics of Petrarchan and courtly love: Ramis loves Nisa, who has hardened her heart to all love. Montantus loves Celia, who is proud, haughty, and beautiful, and not interested in one she considers an inferior. Silvestris loves Niobe, who is unwilling to forgo her flirtations with many men to choose Silvestris from among the others. These masculine lovers write verses on the trees to their beloveds, and in the following scene, the three nymphs read them and reply, providing an opposing feminine view on their reasons for resistance:

> *Celia*. Alas poore soules, how ill love sounds in their lips, who telling a long tale of hunting, thinke they have bewray'd a sad passion of love!

> *Niobe.* Give them leaue to love, since we haue libertie to chuse, for as great sport doe I take in coursing their tame hearts, as they doe paines in hunting their wilde Harts.

This self-consciousness about the gender politics of love as a hunt is given another dimension when act 3 opens with Ramis speaking the famous lines of Apollo to Daphne in the opening book of *Metamorphoses*, the same lines that announce the Ovidian politics of the hunt in the Sudeley entertainment: "Stay, cruell Nisa, thou knowest not from whome thou fliest, and therefore fliest" (III.i.1–2). The echo of Ovid's lines is quite close:

> Nescis temeraria, nescis,
> quem fugias, ideoque fugis.

> [Thou knowest not, rash one, thou knowest not whom thou fleest, and for that reason dost thou flee.] (I.514–15)

This allusion sets off an act in which each forester attempts a verbal persuasion to love and is soundly rebuffed, and it situates the foresters as part of the long-standing tradition of hunters in love like Apollo, who are both terrifying and ridiculous.

In Ovid's account, Apollo's affirmation of Daphne's ignorance of her own good is ironized by the narrative insistence on his lascivious gaze and the comparison of his pursuit to that of a dog snatching at a hare:

> ut canis in vacuo leporem cum Gallicus arvo
> vidit, et hic pradeam pedibus petit, ille salutem;
> alter in haesuro similes iam iamque tenere
> sperat et extento stringit vestigial rostro,
> alter in ambiguo est, an sit conprensus, et ipsis
> morsibus eriptur tangentiaque ora relinquit:
> sic deus et virgo est hic spe celer, illa timore.

> [Just as when a Gallic hound has seen a hare in an open plain, and seeks his prey on flying feet, but the hare, safety: he, just about to fasten on her, now, even now thinks he has her, and grazes her very heels with his outstretched muzzle; but she knows not whether she be not already caught, and barely escapes from those sharp fangs and leaves behind the jaws just closing on her: so ran the god and maid, he sped by hope and she by fear.] (*Met.* I. 533–39)

The Ovidian Apollo vacillates between being a threat and a parody of a threat, and these lovers occupy a similar position in their own desirings. The tale of Apollo and Daphne, implicated so heavily in Petrarchan renegotiations, is the first rape narrative in Ovid's poem; it is Ovid's first investigation of the gender politics of desire, and it emphasizes sexual difference even as it begins to suggest the instabilities of such differences, as Daphne is transformed from a figure with a female body to the Laurel.[31] This Ovidian allusion in the play places the plot of the three love hunts in the context of Ovidianism, as do the metamorphoses of the nymphs that constitute the main action of the second half of the play. The play, therefore, sets up an intertextual dialogue between itself and *Metamorphoses* on questions of gender difference, parodying the stability of the subject–object binary of sexual desire implied in the metaphor of the hunt. While the foresters believe they are Apollos, the nymphs assert their ability to choose and disregard the threat of the narrative in which they seem to be implicated.

At the same time, the play negotiates gender in different ways through its other plot line. Scenes involving the three foresters and three nymphs are interspersed with scenes that are even more self-consciously Ovidian, as they rewrite the tale of Erysichthon from book 8 of *Metamorphoses*. In Lyly, Erysichthon, described (by Golding) as "a churlish Husbandman," comes upon Ceres' nymphs dancing and making offerings at her sacred tree. He blasphemes the goddess, abuses her nymphs and begins to chop down her tree. As he does so, the tree bleeds and then the nymph confined within begins to speak:

> Monster of men, hate of the heauens, and to the earth a burthen, what hath chast *Fidelia* committed? It is thy spite, *Cupid*, that having no power to wound my vnspotted mind, procurest meanes to mangle my tender body, and by violëce to gash those sides that enclose a heart dedicate to vertue: or is it that sauage Satire, that feeding his sensuall appetite vpon lust, seeketh now to quench it with bloud, that being without hope to attaine my loue, hee may with cruelty end my life? Or doth *Ceres*, whose nymph I have beene many years, in recompense of my inuiolable faith, reward me with vnspeakable torments? Diuine *Phoebus*, that pursued *Daphne* till shee was turned to a Bay tree, ceased then to trouble her; I, the gods are pittifull: and *Cinyras*, that with furie followed his daughter *Mirrha*, till shee was changed to a Mirre tree, left then to prosecute her; yea, parents are naturall: *Phoebus* lamented the losse of his friend, *Cinyras* of his child: but both gods and men either forgot or neglect the chaunge of *Fidelia*; nay, follow her after her chaunge, to make her more miserable: so that there is nothing more hatefull then to be chast, whose bodies are followed in the world with

lust, and prosecuted in the graues with tyrannie; whose minds the freer
they are from vice, their bodies are the more in daunger of mens loue;
nor being changed, because of their hates; nor being dead, because of
their defaming. (I.ii.90–112)

This speech continues for many more lines, and at the end of it, the
stage direction tells us, she dies. I have quoted it at some length because
it makes explicit the ideological link between chastity, Elizabeth's celebrated virtue, and metamorphosis that is central to a reading of the
play's politics. Rather than being set in contrast to metamorphosis as
an erosion of an inviolate body, chastity, and by extension Elizabeth
as a chaste figure, are here preserved by metamorphosis. Her metamorphosed form as a tree offers at least compromised protections for
Fidelia's body from "lust" and "tyrannie." While transformation is
also listed in the last sentence of this quotation as one of the evils
suffered by chaste women's bodies—sexual vulnerability, change, and
death are the three named—it is Fidelia's recourse to escape from
the dangerous world. Metamorphosis functions, according to Fidelia's complaint, as a bitter but effective evasion, and it is also set in
explicit contrast to "lust" and "tyranny," code words for the negative
gender politics and corrupted political systems of a patriarchal power.
Metamorphosis is associated, here as elsewhere in these Ovidian plays,
with a feminized escape from a masculinized social world, and more
specifically, a corrupted political system.

Fidelia's complaint is also a truly spectacular moment of overdetermined intertextuality. As Bond points out in his preface to this play, the
bleeding tree that speaks to tell the story of transformation is a trope found
in Spenser (Fradubio and Fraelissa transformed indirectly by Duessa; *FQ*
I. 2. 30–45) and Ariosto (Astolfo transformed to a tree by Alcina; *Orl.
Fur.* vi. 26–53). It is also found in Tasso's *Gerusalemme Liberata* and
derives ultimately from the episode at the beginning of the third book
of *Aeneid*, in which Aeneas find Polydorus transformed into a tree when
he lands in Thrace. A close relationship between the texts of Spenser and
Lyly is likely because both texts also combine Daphne and Myrrha in surprising ways as similar instances of flight and transformation. Because of
the difficulty dating the play, the imitation might work in either direction,
although Bond seems sure that Lyly is derivative of Spenser. Whatever
the case, Lyly's play turns most self-consciously to its source in Ovid,
where the being in the tree is female and therefore linked to the other
female figures who have been transformed in the poem.

While the episode in Lyly dilates on the nymph's lament, Ovid's narrative focuses instead on the violence of the deed. In *Metamorphoses*,

Erysichthon orders his men to fell a great oak in a grove sacred to Ceres, blasphemously vowing,

> non dilecta dae solum, sed et ipsa licebit
> sit dea, iam tanget frondente cacumine terram.

[Though this be not only the tree that the goddess loves, but even the goddess herself, now shall its leafy top touch the ground.] (VIII.755–56)

When one of his followers hesitates, Erysichthon chops off his head. In Ovid, not only does the tree bleed, but it also, rather mysteriously, grows pale:

> obliquos dum telum librat in ictus,
> contremuit gemitunque dedit Deoia quercus,
> et pariter frondes, pariter pallescere glandes
> coepere ac longi pallorem ducere rami.

[while he poised his axe for the slanting stroke, the oak of Deo trembled and gave forth a groan; at the same time its leaves and its acorns grew pale, its long branches took on a pallid hue.] (VIII.757–60)

When the tree speaks, we have nothing approaching Lyly's highly rhetorical lament. In Ovid's poem a plaintive voice within the tree frighteningly predicts Erysichthon's doom:

> nympha sub hoc ego sum Cereri gratissima ligno,
> quae tibi factorum poenas instare tuorum
> vaticinor moriens, nostri solacia leti.

[I, a nymph most dear to Ceres, dwell within this wood, and I prophesy with my dying breath, and find my death's solace in it, that punishment is at hand for what you do.] (VIII. 771–73)

The terror of punishment overshadows the death of the nymph.

While in Ovid the focus of this moment is the violent pride of Erysichthon, in Lyly's scene, the nymph's complaint takes center stage, and she quite explicitly comments on the larger role of metamorphosis in both Ovid's poem and her play. The nymph first wonders who could be committing this violence against her—Cupid, who is the avouched enemy of her virginity? The Satyr, whose attempted rape caused her metamorphosis? Ceres, who has abandoned her follower?—and this implies that her metamorphosed state was at least a qualified refuge, preserving her chaste identity. Strangely, she likens herself to both Daphne and Myrrha, presumably because both are turned through divine intervention into trees. The reference to Myrrha, however, destabilizes the alliance she seeks to represent between herself and other chaste figures in Ovid's poem, since Myrrha's love for her father can hardly be considered chaste. It implies that not chastity but gender is the defining characteristic of these tree figures. The main thrust of Fidelia's comparison, however, is that these other female figures were granted pity and peace through metamorphosis and her peace has been violently disturbed. It is this sense of metamorphosis as not necessarily a monstrous but primarily a merciful change that is Ovid's distinct contribution to the literary history of bleeding trees. Polydorus, Fradubio, and Astolfo are pained at their transformed state, miserable that they have left the social worlds of the texts they occupy. In Polydorus' case, he is a monstrous sign, transfixed to warn others of the unholy nature of the land, and both Fradubio and Astolfo are the victims of evil feminine enchantment. Only in Ovid is metamorphosis not a vile and monstrous state, operating as it often does as release from human suffering or impotence. While it is ambiguous in Ovid how comfortable the nymph is in her changed form, in Lyly the ambiguity dissipates, and we find a nymph living a preferable life in a transformed body. Her lament is not only for the dangers of living a chaste, explicitly feminine, life, but also for the loss of metamorphosis as a way to avoid violence from larger systems of tyrannous power.

This first defense of metamorphosis as the recourse for chaste women is followed by a similar validation in the other narrative line. But first the play dilates, as Ovid does, on the nature of Ceres' revenge. Ceres summons Hunger, who breathes herself into Erysichthon's body while he sleeps, making it impossible for him to be sated. Both Ovid's poem and Lyly's play emphasize the link between Ceres and natural abundance, making Erysichthon's punishment especially appropriate and especially horrifying. Meanwhile, in act 4, the Foresters, rejected by their Petrarchan mistresses, seek their own parallel revenge, calling upon Cupid to metamorphose the nymphs as punishment for their unavailability. Cupid turns Nisa to a stone, because of her hard heart; Celia to a rose, so that her beauty will be fleeting; and Niobe to a bird, so that she may never touch the ground, remaining forever inconstant. In this storyline, metamorphosis seems initially to be punishment, but then the play takes a sharp turn in the final scene.

In act 5, Ceres agrees to free Erysichthon from her curse in exchange for the remetamorphosis of her nymphs. Her concession to Cupid is that the nymphs will marry the foresters. Although she will lose her followers, she appears not to have ordered a vow of virginity, angrily calling the nymphs disobedient (V.iv.3–4), and chastising the foresters because they did not involve her instead of Cupid. She tells them, "You might have made me a counsel of your loues" (V.iv.12). This line, of course, begs a topical historical reading, especially because by this period Elizabeth had gained a reputation for being very protective (or envious) of her ladies-in-waiting. Her defeat at this point in the play is certainly at least gentle critique, as Cupid seems to have taken the day.

The final surprise, however, comes when the nymphs are commanded to marry the foresters once they have reassumed their human forms. Remetamorphosed, they hesitate to fulfill the expectations for the closure of this pastoral comedy and do not fly into their lovers' arms. Ceres asks, "Why speake you not, Nymphes? This must bee done, and you must yeeld" (V.iv.52–53). The nymphs reply, "Not I! Nor I! Nor I!" (V.iv.54–56). The comedy of this moment of generic play is intensified when the nymphs explain that they would prefer their metamorphosed states to marriage. They would, essentially, prefer to be Ovidian nymphs, for whom metamorphosis offers escape, than English nymphs, who must yield to marriage. Their main complaint is the dishonesty of men; all three declare that they would choose their metamorphosed states over living with the lies and dissembling of their partners. At this point, the comic threat that the play will not end in marriage is also a moment in which Lyly's text self-consciously engages the larger politics of its intertext, and Ovidian metamorphosis is upheld as the refuge of female figures who refuse to be subordinated to masculine desire. Such a witty moment of delay must have served to lighten the critique implicit in the final marriages of the play, allowing the playwright to acknowledge the ways in which Ovidianism might better serve the interests of chaste female figures than what seems to be an inevitable generic consummation in marriage.

Metamorphosis is refigured one more time, however, turning from refuge for Ceres' nymphs to the Circean kind of metamorphosis Knox conjures up in his diatribe against female rule. A frustrated Cupid threatens to turn the nymphs into things more monstrous than their previous metamorphic states: "*Ceres*, I vowe here by my sweete mother *Venus*, that if they yeeld not, I will turne them againe, not to flowers, or stones, or birds, but to monsters, no lesse filthie to bee seene then to bee named hatefull: they shall creepe that now stand,

and be to all men odious, and bee to themselves (for the mind they shall retaine) loathsome" (V.iv.104–9). Faced with this more disturbing threat, that they will loathe themselves, the nymphs relent, but on condition that they can use this instance of their lovers' cruelty and folly in the power struggle they anticipate in their marriages:

> *Nisa*: I am content, so as *Ramis*, when hee finds me cold in loue, or hard in beliefe, hee attribute it to his owne folly; in that I retaine some nature of the Rocke he changed me into.
> . . .
> *Celia*: I consent, so as *Montantus*, when in the midst of his sweete delight, he shall find some bitter ouerthwarts, impute it to his folly, in that he suffered me to be a Rose, that hath prickles with her pleasant-ness, as hee is like to haue with my loue shrewdness.
> . . .
> *Niobe*: I yielded first in mind though it bee my course last to speake: but if *Silvestris* find me not euer at home, let him curse himselfe that gaue me wings to flie abroad, whose feathers if his jealousie shall breake, my policie shall imp.
> (V.iv.133–35, 140–43, 149–52)

Remarkably, the nymphs determine to retain the qualities of their metamorphosed forms, and they use those qualities to assert dominance in their marriages. The play ultimately figures metamorphosis, in this part of its plot, as both a threat of monstrousness and an equalizer between the genders in the politics of marriage. Drawing on the many meanings of metamorphosis in Ovid's poem, Lyly's play reveals the tension between its conception as a positively valued refuge and a negatively valued degradation. The play also explicitly alludes to the monstrousness of metamorphosis as it is characterized in the Protestant writings that were analyzed at the beginning of this chapter. Cupid's attempts to punish the nymphs with Ovidian metamorphoses into familiar features of the landscape is not threatening enough, since the metamorphoses are bodily extensions of their defining identity characteristics. Instead, the play alludes to metamorphoses that are more beastly and more threatening, and while such metamorphoses exist in Ovid's poem, they are not the primary type of metamorphosis defined by Ovidianism throughout the play.

In fact, through these elaborate negotiations of various kinds of metamorphosis, the play critiques virginity while still preserving the dignity of its queenly central figure. While the marriages that end the play certainly do not celebrate virginity, Ceres as a figure does not seem ever to be committed to this for her nymphs, and she retains the dignity of being personally unaffected by Cupid's powers. As a figure for the queen, Ceres' body does not change, but she and Cupid negotiate the power of metamorphosis between them, and bodily metamorphosis is found surprisingly to offer female characters flexibility and freedom from the social constraints lamented by Fidelia as she dies at the beginning of the play: "Farwell Ladies, whose liues are subject to many mischieues; for if you be faire, it is hard to be chast; if chast, impossible to be safe; if you be young, you will quickly bend; if bend, you are suddenly broken" (I.iv.124–27).

In Lyly's revision to the Erysichthon tale, finally, metamorphosis is also celebrated in the surprising figure of Protea, Erysichthon's daughter, who saves him from starvation through her ability to take many different bodily forms, most significantly the bodies of men. Protea as a character figures metamorphosis of her gender as a moral personal power. Unnamed in Ovid, Erysichthon's daughter is sold into slavery in exchange for food by her desperate father. Calling upon Neptune who raped her, she receives from him the ability to change her form at will to escape her master, and she uses this ability to be continuously resold to feed her father. She is transformed first by Neptune to a fisherman, and Ovid's narrator emphasizes her happiness at the doubling of her identity as a method of preservation. When her master asks this fisherman if he has seen a girl, she denies having seen one and inwardly rejoices:

> illa dei munus bene cedere sensit et a se
> se quaeri gaudens his est resecuta rogantem.

> [She perceived by this that the god's gift was working well, and, delighted that one asked her of herself, answered his question in these words.] (VIII. 862–63)

In this passage, it is the doubleness of her bodily gender identity that delights her, and in fact this description of her happy awareness of her metamorphosed self is echoed very closely in Lyly, who emphasizes even further the strength of her position as arbiter of her own metamorphosis.

Lyly elevates Protea's character and links her to a metamorphic sense of the body as a flexible attribute of identity. Giving her a name that more explicitly links her to Proteus (a link made in Ovid through an extended digression on his powers at the start of the tale), and thus to all metamorphic characters in Ovid's poem, Lyly also makes her more the heroine of her tale by making the master—now a merchant—who buys her more the villain. As the merchant expresses his desire for her, she asserts the independence of her will:

> *Mar.* You are now mine, *Protea.*
> *Pro*: And mine owne.
> *Mar*: In will, not power.
> *Pro*: In power, if I will.
> (III.ii.60–63)

Her metamorphic abilities are here used to counter both the threat of rape and the threat of male mastery and ownership over her body and mind. This specifically feminized form of metamorphic power rescues her father, herself, and finally her lover in the play, affirming that this gift can counter forces arrayed against both male and female persons.

Her power to change is further linked to the moral strength of her character when she impersonates the ghost of Ulysses to rescue her lover, Petulius, from the clutches of a siren. Petulius has been searching the shore for the transformed Protea and instead comes upon a siren who traps him with her song. Protea watches their encounter and explicitly distinguishes between her own metamorphic abilities and the monstrous powers of the siren and her desire for revenge on men for their emotional betrayals. Coming upon the Siren she hears her railing against men:

> *Syren*: Accursed men! Whose loues haue no other meane then extremities, nor hates end but mischiefe.
> *Pro*: Vnnatural monster! No maide, that accuseth men, whose loues are built on truth, and whose hearts are remoued by curtesie: I will heare the depth of her malice.
> *Syren*: Of all creatures most unkind, most cunning, by whose subtilties I am halfe fish, halfe flesh, themselves being neither fish nor flesh; in loue luke warme, in crueltie red hot; if they praise, they flatter; if flatter, deceiue; if deceiue, destroy.
> *Pro*: Shee rayles at men, but seekes to intangle them . . .
> (IV.ii.24–33)

By setting Protea in contrast to the siren, the play elevates Protea's kind of metamorphosis above the monstrousness associated with "unnatural" and "monstrous" female characters who experience or inflict bodily change. Like Circe, the siren figures the dangers of monstrous desire through metamorphosis. She, however, is a metamorphosed figure herself, unlike Circe, so she is directly set in contrast to Protea. As two metamorphic characters, the siren and Protea represent two cultural extremes in the evaluation of the female body: Protea is the moral defender of both the desire of male characters and herself, while the Siren is the more familiar figure for the dangers of excessive feminized desire. That Protea defeats this figure, so similar to herself, by assuming the masculine form of Ulysses registers the play's ambivalent but pervasive attempts to assert a positive evaluation of female metamorphosis, even as it acknowledges the threat of feminized bodily change in its more monstrous forms. This scene comments on and supports the negotiations of metamorphic power and gender occurring throughout the play, holding up Protea, a metamorphic female character, as one of the play's heroic figures.

The resolution of Erysichthon's tale in Ovid is particularly gruesome. Having exhausted all of his resources for food, he eats himself. As in most of the other tales in which mortals proudly challenge the power of the gods, the punishment is severe and fitting; disrespectful of the principle of fertility and natural abundance embodied in Ceres, he is perversely forced to consume himself. In Lyly, instead, he is rather easily excused. Having been saved from starvation by Protea, Erysichthon is warned to pay respectful homage to Ceres. In fact, Erysichthon ironically offers to host the multiple marriage feast at the end of the play. While Lyly's resolution does hierarchize the powers of these gods—making Cupid controller of "hearts," and therefore minds and souls, and Ceres sustainer of "guts," or bodies—the Ovidianism of the play actually destabilizes this split. While the subjectivities of the play's metamorphosing female figures clearly survive bodily changes, and are in this sense essentialized, the emotive attributes of their desiring identities are not only reflected in, but strengthened by, their changes of bodily form. The three nymphs determine that they will continue to be some of the things they were as transformed beings, so rather than having been punished by their experience of change, the supposed flaws that made them disobedient are reified in their reintegrated human selves. Similarly, Protea not only suffers bodily change but also welcomes it—it defines who she is (and is inherent in her name), rather than being secondary to an interior, not bodily, sense of identity. In fact, in the spectacle of Fidelia's death that opens the play, the link between her body as tree and her voice emphasizes the mortality of the body as the true end of the self. While implying that the queen only rules the "guts" of her subjects may subordinate her in some ways to the masculine power of Cupid, dictator of a disembodied kind of Petrarchan and courtly desire, the play also insists on the essential power of the body as a constituent of identity.

The play also more obviously allows that having power over bodily change gives female figures a greater freedom in the face of straightened political circumstances. In the figure of Protea, especially, the play offers a picture of female agency achieved through power over the metamorphic body (and as a gender-switching character, she is linked in interesting ways to figures like Spenser's Britomart, a more explicit shadow of the queen). While the play subordinates female rule in the figure of Ceres to male rule in the figure of Cupid, it also validates the queen's political strategies in more fundamental ways by revealing metamorphosis as a feminine kind of power. In doing so, it justifies Elizabeth's continual renegotiations of the gender of her doubled person. When we recall, finally, that boys performed this play, the celebrated destabilization of gendered bodies becomes even more marked. As boys turned to girls, and then turned to stones, roses, birds, and various types of men, much of the play's humor and erotic interest must have arisen from these changes. Playing with gender-inversion and metamorphosis in a comedy that celebrates a truce between Ceres and Cupid counters the vituperative rhetoric of monstrous gender change found in writings like those of Knox cited to begin this chapter. The many metamorphosing female characters in the play control their own transformed bodies with varying degrees of social success—from Fidelia, who can only evade rape and then lament her loss after that evasion, to the courtly nymphs, whose metamorphoses solidify the continuation of their positions of limited power as desired rather than possessed mistresses, and finally to Protea, whose self-willed metamorphoses make her the most heroic human character in the play. In each case, agency for female figures is enabled by metamorphosis, and an acknowledgment of their desires is shown to be not just permissible but essential for smooth social functioning, government stability, and generic closure. With a queen who manipulated her bodily gender identity in the audience, such a celebration of metamorphosis as a source of a feminized agency supports this metamorphic political strategy. Not necessarily dangerous to individual or state, the queen's metamorphic negotiations of her body and her desires are subtly revealed as essential to her agency by Lyly, her most Ovidian propagandist.

CHAPTER 2

OVIDIAN EMOTION AND ALLEGORY
IN *THE FAERIE QUEENE*

Like Lyly, Spenser writes his most important work, *The Faerie Queene*, with the explicit understanding that the queen (as well as her propagandists and her detractors and all those invested in the politics of representing her person) will be paying attention.[1] It is not surprising, therefore, that Spenser's great epic romance draws on Ovidianism to represent the self and its emotions, and that it stands out as in many ways the most Ovidian literary project of the late Elizabethan period.[2] In important ways, however, Spenser's Ovidianism is not focused on the metamorphic body and instead negotiates pagan emotional states that lie outside the prescribed limits of Elizabethan and Protestant experience. When Spenser alludes to Ovid's text directly or employs an explicitly Ovidian aesthetic, however—and these intertextual moments take many forms and are the results of various strategies of signification—the poem both highlights and then often struggles to contain the disorder that results. It is these moments—the moments in which Spenser's poem, to use Harry Berger's term, "kidnaps" Ovidianism—that reveal a deep and conflicted cultural engagement not just with Ovidian stories but with the politics of Ovidian emotion.[3]

The intertextual dialogue between Spenser's Protestant romance-epic and Ovid's pagan antiepic results in a number of different kinds of ideological negotiations, but from very small allusions to larger rewritings of Ovidian tales, *The Faerie Queene* is repeatedly interested in the ways Ovid's poem associates potentials for agency with the interior experience of grief. This Ovidian construction of an often-feminized emotion operates as an intertextual theme in all books of the poem, and it is made explicit when the narrative self-consciously envisions a feminine response to the conventions of male heroism in epic or romance that depend upon the often violent objectifications or demonizations of female figures. Ovidianism opens, through intertextual means, a narrative space for emotional response or commentary and often a space for various types of social or symbolic agency. In Spenser's text, written for a larger public but also explicitly for the queen and negotiating the period's other challenges to the constructions of gender, this one strain of Ovidianism serves to explore the interior emotional space of grief and politicize that grief as a response to cultural and literary systems of power.

In addition, as an allegory uniquely tied to the queen and indeed her body, *The Faerie Queene* posits through Ovidianism the etiology of allegory in emotion, as it is figured to depend on the metamorphosis of characters into allegorical daemons.[4] The process of allegorical abstraction is revealed to be analogous to the process of metamorphosis, and if all allegorical figures carry the history of their creations as characters into the text, masculine and feminine figures are defined by very different histories determined by the gender politics of the poem's action. Furthermore, the world of Ovidian metamorphosis that is posited through analogy as the source for all allegorical figures, both male and female, is a highly feminized and female-oriented world, and this effeminizes that sense of allegorical abstraction that removes figures from the action of the romance epic to another symbolic realm. Acknowledging the possibilities that a feminized meaning can be constructed at this abstract allegorical level, the poem suggests the potential for an alternate form of representational power, one that lies outside the conventions and ideologies of heroic epic.

Reading Ovidianism in *The Faerie Queene* calls for a number of different reading practices, as the Ovidian intertext adds a layer of complexity to already diverse and demanding processes of allegorical signification. In order to accomplish a broader investigation into how this most essential intertext functions in dialogue with the poem, I have organized each section of the following chapter around an allusion or set of allusions to a single Ovidian tale or a central thematic crux in *Metamorphoses*, ranging from a stanza-long digression on Cyparissus in book 1 to the poem's most definitive Ovidian encounter in the House of Busirane. In addition, except in my analyses of the central Ovidian episodes in book 3, I have deliberately chosen to analyze moments of Ovidianism that have not been the focus of extensive critical commentary. I hope through this technique to expand the current critical understandings of both Ovidianism and the representations of emotion in the poem. While the significances of these intertextual encounters are usually read in terms of their local resonances, my readings attempt broader analyses. As a whole, the accumulated readings argue for a crucial but largely unexplored role for Ovidianism as a discourse in the poem engaged in the cultural work of defining and gendering subjects through their passions.

REVIVING SYLVANUS' "ANCIENT LOVE"

In canto 6 of Spenser's legend of Holiness, by "eternall providence exceeding thought" (I, vi, 7) Una is rescued by a troop of satyrs from Sansloy who was attempting to rape her.[5] They lead her to their god, Sylvanus, who meets her inflamed with a similarly threatening desire:

> So towards old *Sylvanus* they her bring;
> Who with the noyse awaked, commeth out,
> To weet the cause, his weake steps gouerning,
> And aged limbs on Cypresse stadle stout,
> And with an yuie twyne his wast is girt about.
>
> Far off he wonders, what them makes so glad,
> Or *Bacchus* merry fruit they did inuent,
> Or *Cybeles* franticke rites haue made them mad;
> They drawing nigh, vnto their God present
> That flower of faith and beautie excellent.
> The God himselfe vewing that mirrhour rare,
> Stood long amazd, and burnt in his intent;
> His owne faire *Dryope* now he thinkes not faire,
> And *Pholoe* fowle, when her to this he doth compare.
> (I.vi.14–15)

The lascivious desires of this wood god threaten a repetition of the attempted rape that was the matter of the beginning of this canto, as Sylvanus compares Una to his other mistresses. But then strangely and rather abruptly, Sylvanus' desire is rewritten as Ovidian and associated with nostalgic grief:

> And old *Sylvanus* selfe bethinks not, what
> To thinke of wight so faire, but gazing stood,
> In doubt to deeme her borne of earthly brood;
> Sometimes Dame *Venus* selfe he seemes to see,
> But *Venus* neuer had so sober mood;
> Sometimes *Diana* he her takes to bee,
> But misseth bow, and shaftes, and buskins to her knee.

By vew of her he ginneth to reuiue
His ancient loue, and dearest *Cyparisse*,
And calles to mind his portraiture aliue,
How faire he was, and yet not faire to this,
And how he slew with glauncing dart amisse
A gentle Hynd, the which the louely boy
Did loue as life, aboue all worldly blisse;
For griefe whereof the lad n'ould after joy,
But pynd away in anguish and selfe-wild annoy.
(I.vi.16–17)

While represented as a potential threat, Sylvanus turns out not to be a rapist in the poem, and in fact the canto ends with Satyrane, another male figure associated with the satyr-like propensity to rape (and the child of a rape himself), helping Una leave the satyrs to pursue her rightful love, Redcrosse. At first, Sylvanus cannot decide whether the goddess before him is Venus or Diana, the suggestion being that Una's Christian perfections transcend the dualism of these pagan deities. Sylvanus' moment of confusion is also a subtle rewriting of the moment in book 3 of *Aeneid* in which Aeneas meets his mother, Venus, disguised as a Diana-like huntress. In this intertextual moment, Sylvanus is placed in the position of hero, rather than rapist, and then he is further distracted from his desire for Una by his memory of Cyparissus, the first youth whose metamorphosis is described as an inserted tale in book 10 of *Metamorphoses*, where most of the narrative is both about and sung by Orpheus.

This allusion, which is particularly self-conscious because it actually inserts an Ovidian figure, Cyparissus, into the personal history of a Spenserian figure (and one who has wide cultural associations in Elizabethan literature), serves to characterize Sylvanus as experiencing a fairly complex set of emotions, including sexual desire, regret, and most interestingly, nostalgia. As Sylvanus "revive[s] / His ancient love, and dearest Cyparisse" (I.vi.17), however, the narrative of the poem itself enacts a revival, as the characters who come to worship Una all belong to a pagan literary past that Spenser's Christian epic constantly negotiates. This moment in the poem, therefore, which in one allegorical sense asserts the supremacy of Christian truth, simultaneously enacts nostalgia for pagan emotion and specifically for "ancient," or same-sex desire. While readers might expect a condemnation of such pagan desires in figures like the satyrs (who are notoriously lusty in classical myth, being half goat, and therefore beastly, and half man), the episode represents the satyrs as Una's rescuers and grants the grief of their leader Sylvanus a notable dignity. Rather than insisting on the primacy of Christian truth as allegorized in Una, in fact, the episode instead subtly points to the difficulty and at least potential inadequacy of her emotional characterization. The episode evinces nostalgia for the "emotional culture" of the pagan past constructed in Ovid's poem.

An analysis of Sylvanus' stanza-long memory of his previous love links Una's vulnerability to rape to the loss and grief for the boy that are the import of this Ovidian narrative. Sometimes such allusions, which on the surface seem digressive or irrelevant, can alert us to larger intertextual relationships developed throughout the allegory. In book 1, for instance, the most overtly Protestant book of *The Faerie Queene*, many of the allusions, including this one, are to the tenth book of *Metamorphoses*. Syrithe Pugh, in fact, has outlined the way book 1 engages insistently and repeatedly with Orpheus' song of pagan love. Book 10 of *Metamorphoses* is unique in that it is framed by the tale of Orpheus and is comprised of the tales he tells through his songs: Cyparissus, Ganymede, Hyacinthus, the Propoetides, Pygmalion, Myrrha, Adonis, and Atalanta. Orpheus has just lost Eurydice, and the narrator tells us that after grieving for three years, he recovered some joy in his love for young men:

> ille etiam Thracum populis fuit auctor amorem
> in teneros transferre mares citraque iuventam
> aetatis breve ver et primos carpere flores.

> [He set the example for the people of Thrace of giving his love to tender boys, and enjoying the springtime and first flower of their youth.]
> (X.83–85)

Rather than a celebration of the giving and taking of love, in Arthur Golding's 1567 translation of this tale, Orpheus' same-sex desire is more roundly condemned:

> He also taught the Thracian folke a stewes of Males to make
> And of the flowring pryme of boayes the pleasure for to take.
> (Golding, 10, 91–92)

Golding's translation, however, is an intensification of the theme of sexual transgression that runs throughout the Orphic tales.

Although Orpheus has found some consolation for his loss of Eurydice, the implication is that Orpheus' own grief indirectly determines the kinds of tales he tells, and the tales are thematically linked in their explorations of the grief caused by what the poem seems at first to consider perverse transgressions of normative heterosexual desire. Orpheus calls on his mother, the Muse Calliope:

> nunc opus est leviore lyra, puerosque canamus
> dilectos superis inconcessisque puellas
> ignibus attonitas meruisse libidine poenam.

> [But now I need the gentler touch, for I would sing of boys beloved by gods, and maidens inflamed by unnatural love and paying the penalty of their lust.] (X.152–54)

Although he implies that his tone will be light—"leviore lyra"—his tales are marked by grief that is weighty, and they reveal the consequences of socially transgressive desire.[6] The tales of Cyparissus, Ganymede, and Hyacinthus are all tales of same-sex desire like Orpheus', and they all involve the metamorphosis (or apotheosis in the case of Ganymede) of the youths desired by male gods as consolations for the gods' loss: the Propeotides, who deny Venus, are punished as the first prostitutes; Pygmalion's tale, though it has a happy ending, is about the fetishization of an object, the maker's artistic production; Myrrha's is about incestuous desire of daughter for father; Venus and Adonis reverse the traditional gender roles of pursuer and pursued. In typical Ovidian fashion, the possibly moralistic reading that this Orphic grouping might imply is undercut both by the narrator's sympathies for all of these transgressive figures and by the insertion of the tale of Atalanta, which is in many respects an assertion of the dangers of traditional heterosexual desire in the poem. Atalanta, a great runner who is prophetically advised to avoid marriage, vows to marry only the winner of a race with her. When she sees a new suitor, Hippomenes, she regrets this and hopes he can win. Hippomenes cheats, with the help of Venus, who gives him golden apples to toss to distract Atalanta from her running. He wins the girl. The two are later transformed to lions who draw Cybele's chariot because they do not show proper gratitude to Venus, who inspires Hippomenes with lust so that he defiles Cybele's temple. Their punishment fulfills Atalanta's prophecy. As the broad outlines of this tale make clear, the race is essentially an intensification of the typical pursuit of male for female and is justified by Atalanta's expressed desire to be caught. It is not, therefore, mainly the transgressive nature of these tales that unite them, but the expressions of the grief that the figures suffer in the throes of desire that is not socially sanctioned, or in the case of Atalanta, that comments on the similarities between transgressive and mainstream desires.

Within the context of this book about desire and grief, the tale of Cyparissus is brief, and it is the etiology of the Cypress as a tree symbolic of mourning. The tale is told by the narrator as a digression from the catalogue of trees that approach Orpheus to shade him while he sings his grieving songs. The iconography of Sylvanus leaning on the Cypress staff at the start of this episode suggests a similarly etiological function for the retelling of the tale in *The Faerie Queene*. Sylvanus as a character leans on a symbol of his mourning for Cyparissus and Cyparissus' mourning for the object of his desire. Sylvanus is associated with the specifically funereal tree, and with the series of losses that are the content of this tale, suggesting his dependence as a figure on the emotions constructed by Ovid's poem.

Ovid's Cyparissus is a youth excessively attached to a tame stag with golden horns and bejeweled collar who is beloved by the local population:

> sed tamen ante alios, Ceae pulcherrime gentis,
> gratus erat, Cyparisse, tibi: tu pabula cervum
> ad nova, tu liquidi ducebas fontis ad undam,
> tu modo texebas varios per cornua flores,
> nunc eques in tergo residens huc laetus et illuc
> mollia purpureis frenabas ora capistris.

[But more than to all the rest, O Cyparrissus, loveliest of the Cean race, was he dear to you. 'Twas you who led the stag to fresh pasturage and to the waters of the clear spring. Now would you weave bright garlands for his horns; now, sitting like a horseman on his back, now here, now there, would gleefully guide his soft mouth with purple reins.] (X. 120–25).

The poem stops just short of overtly stating the sexual nature of this relationship between man and stag, although the sensuality of the union is implied by the final lines of this description (and it is generally read as a tale about bestiality in Renaissance commentaries). The tragedy of the tale occurs when Cyparrisus accidentally kills his stag with a javelin as it is resting in the shade at noon, a moment with phallic and sexual overtones. Although he is counseled not to excessively grieve by Apollo who loves him, Cyparissus is inconsolable and begs for metamorphosis as relief:

> quae non soalcia Phoebus
> dixit et, ut leviter pro materiaque doleret,
> admonuit! gemit ille tamen munusque supremum
> hoc petit a superis, ut tempore lugeat omni.
> iamque per inmensos egesto sanguine fletus

in viridem verti coeperunt membra colorem,
et, modo qui nivea pendebant fronte capilli,
horrida caesaries fieri sumptoque rigore
sidereum gracili spectare cacumine caelum.
ingemuit tristique deus "lugebere nobis
lugebisque alios aderisque dolentibus" inquit.

[What did not Phoebus say to comfort him! How he warned him to grieve in moderation and consistently with the occasion! The lad only groaned and begged this as the boon he most desired from heaven, that he might mourn forever. And now, as his life forces were exhausted by endless weeping, his limbs began to change to a green colour, and his locks, which but now overhung his snowy brow, were turned to a bristling crest, and he became a stiff tree with slender top looking to the starry heavens. The god groaned and, full of sadness, said: "You shall be mourned by me, shall mourn for others, and your place shall always be where others grieve."] (X. 132–42)

The apparent dignity afforded Cyparissus' grief is difficult to read, especially given Orpheus' previous call for a light tone, but the descriptions of his weeping and metamorphosis are sympathetic, and the fact that he becomes associated with the funereal Cypress further suggests a level of seriousness to the tale. Furthermore, in Spenser's engagement with this tale, when Sylvanus, in the position of Apollo, recalls this youth, it is his grief he recalls. In Spenser's retelling of the tale, Sylvanus remembers a "he" who killed the stag, and Hamilton in his note assumes that, like Boccaccio and Comes before him, Spenser has rewritten the tale so that Sylvanus, rather than Cyparissus, accidentally killed the stag.[7] Spenser's text, however, is fairly ambiguous about who is responsible for the death of the stag, and this ambiguity serves to increase the sense that the stag represents an alternate love object, whose death might have furthered the desires of Apollo. Instead, the loss of this love leads to the kind of permanent grief symbolized by the Cypress that Cyparissus becomes.

What makes this digression in Spenser's poem especially interesting is that it is Una who inspires Sylvanus to remember this love turned to grief. At this moment of her own danger and grief over the loss of Redcrosse, Una's encounter with another potential rapist becomes instead, through the narrated memory of a transgressive Ovidian love story, a moment of identificatory grief. The Ovidianism of this episode produces a strange encounter between the Christian poem and its pagan intertext. It is traditionally read as allegorizing Sylvanus' inability to worship the divinity of the true church, distracted as he is by his pagan love, and the satyrs have been convincingly read as early Christians, Jews, the Irish, Egyptians, the unlearned masses, men in a state of nature—any group unable to conceive or hold on to the religious truth Una represents. What the episode also reveals, however, is a subtle analysis of the function of grief in relation to sexual desire. In describing Sylvanus' grief over Cyparissus' grief, the narrator of Spenser's poem becomes another Orpheus, the "Poet born of Goddes" (X, 95), as Golding calls him. In addition to linking the narrator with the transgressive pagan poet, though, even more surprisingly, the episode highlights Una's lack of this highlighted emotional response to the loss of Redcrosse. As many critics have pointed out, Una is an underdeveloped character, even as allegories go. In contrast, we might say Sylvanus is an overdeveloped character, as we know more about his sense of loss through intertextuality than we should, considering his minor role in the allegory. While the Ovidian intertext does not disrupt the operations of the Christian allegory, and in fact makes it possible, the transgressiveness of Sylvanus' love and the seriousness of his nostalgic grief highlight the suppressions of pagan (and possibly bestial) love occurring in the episode with the satyrs. At the same time, the encounter unifies the Christian figure of Truth and this potentially transgressive pagan figure in a shared moment of grief and loss. This initially incongruous digression negotiates the significance of grief, which is an absolutely central issue in a book about a solemn and sad knight who is plagued and almost defeated by despair. While Protestantism and the book of holiness must distinguish between worldly grief that leads to destruction (as in the cave of Despair) and Christian repentance that leads to salvation (as in the House of Holiness), this earlier episode sympathetically emphasizes the similarities between Una's loss of Redcrosse and Sylvanus' loss of Cyparissus (and by extension, his loss of the stag). Through intertextuality, therefore, book 1 engages in an extended nostalgic negotiation with Orpheus' book in *Metamorphoses* on the significance of pagan grief, and it constructs a potentially subversive link between this Ovidian mourning and the dangerous but requisite Protestant grief that leads to repentance.

OVIDIAN LOVE AND SELF-CONSCIOUSNESS IN THE HOUSE OF BUSIRANE

While many of the moments of overt Ovidianism in the poem are allegorically central but occur on the margins of the poem's action, as similes or digressions, the House of Busirane is partly defined as a house of Ovidianism, and it is the culminating challenge in Britomart's quest in book 3. Here Spenser overtly engages the gender politics of his own inherited literary discourses and comments on the effects such discourses have on the meanings of the poem. The narrator also explores, through the episode's Ovidian intertext, the gendering of desire itself. The tapestries hanging in the outer room of the House depict the transformations the gods engage in to deceive and rape mortals, and they are imitations of Arachne's tapestry from *Metamorphoses*.[8] Arachne—because she proudly defies Minerva by depicting in her weaving the capricious violence of the gods toward the mortals they desire and are transformed to attain—has traditionally been read as a figure for the artist of *Metamorphoses*, since the tales she weaves are those Ovid himself has woven into his own poetic narrative. Given the importance of Arachne as a figure in Ovid's text, Spenser's room filled with imitations of her tapestry must be read as an engagement with the whole of *Metamorphoses*, a poem exploring the gendered nature of power and desire in ways important to Spenser's own concerns. Although the tales told on Busirane's tapestries are not all found in Ovid's text, Spenser's primary aesthetic engagement is with Ovid, and this episode is a staged encounter between the gender politics of *The Faerie Queene* and those of its most pervasive and challenging pagan intertext.

The Ovidianism of Spenser's house of demonic love is related to the Ovidianism of his poem as a whole, and in the following analysis, I will unravel the complex intertextual encounter that occurs when Arachne's tapestry, the literalization of a self-conscious ekphrasis in Ovid, finds its way into Spenser's own self-conscious examination of the ways poetry about love may "pen" its female figures. Focusing on the way Spenser's and Ovid's texts negotiate gender politics in their moments of artistic reflexivity, I offer a new reading of this episode, which has been identified rightly as central to the gender politics and aesthetics of Spenser's poem, and by extension, the culture that produced it.

Having passed easily through the first peril of the House, the wall of fire, Britomart enters the "utmost" room and passes through the "foremost" door (III.xi.27). Whether we read the house as an externalized allegory of a mind, imagination, or the artistic process itself, or link it to more political or material spaces, the narrator throughout the episode establishes the interpretive importance of Britomart's progress through the house, implying that the significance of the episode is to be gained for both Britomart and the reader through a careful interpretation of the spaces she passes through.[9] In this first room she sees that

the wals clothed were
With goodly arras of great maiesty,

and the first characteristic of these tapestries she notices is that they are

woven with gold and silke so close and nere,
That the rich metall lurked privily
As faining to be hid from envious eye;
Yet here, and there, and every where unwares
It shewd it selfe, and shone unwillingly;
Like a discoloured Snake, whose hidden snares
Through the greene gras his long bright burnisht backe declares.
(III.xi.28)

The "majesty" of this arras is in its making, and that idea is figured through the incongruous simile of the gold threads hiding like a snake in its woven surface. The narrator's (and Britomart's to whom the narrator is closely aligned at this moment in the poem) initial wonder at the "majesty" of the arras is ironic, especially once we know the tapestries are Arachne's, because while Arachne's tapestries must certainly have been majestically beautiful, Arachne is punished precisely for mocking the "majesty" of the gods in the scenes she depicts.

According to Ovid, Arachne's metamorphosis results from two specific affronts to Minerva. First, the girl refuses to acknowledge the goddess' influence on her own skill, and this is what draws Minerva's attention to her in the first place. Having just approved how the Muses punished Pierus' mortal daughters who challenged their skills, Minerva says to herself,

laudare parum est, laudemur et ipsae
numina nec sperni sine poena nostra sinamus.

[To praise is not enough; let me be praised myself and not allow my divinity to be scouted without punishment.] (VI.3–4)

She goes off to confront Arachne. Arachne's second transgression is to weave the "heavenly crimes" (caelestia crimina; VI.131) of the gods into her tapestry, rather than showing respect for their divinity. The threat posed by Arachne is a threat to Minerva's *numina*, that is, her divine will or command and hence her abstract ability to command, her power. When this attribute is translated into English in the Renaissance by Arthur Golding, it is translated as "majesty," rather than "divinity." According to the *O.E.D.*, *majesty* could mean primarily either the "dignity or greatness of a sovereign" (1.a.), "the greatness and glory of God" (1.b.), "the external magnificence befitting a sovereign" (3.) or "kingly or queenly demeanor or bearing" (4.).[10] Majesty, therefore, is both an abstract and an external quality of authoritative power, and this double sense of the word has the effect of suggesting that Minerva may be more analogous to a queen than a goddess, transforming pagan narrative to political commentary. In Ovid, this power is already not purely divine, as the power of the gods has been shown to be associated throughout his works with the godlike but mortal power of Augustus. In Golding's Renaissance translation of this narrative and in Spenser's allusion to it, this power belongs to the earthly political, rather than heavenly realm. When Spenser alludes to the confrontation between Minerva and Arachne and emphasizes that it is a critique of majestic power, he reveals an anxiety about the majestic power of his own time, which, like Minerva's, attempts to exercise control over its own images. Arachne's tapestries in Busirane's house refer immediately to insecurities surrounding Elizabethan political power, a majestic power very much concerned with the dignity of its images.

In addition to allegorizing the relationship between divinity or majesty and art, the theme of Arachne's story in Ovid, the snake simile does something else that helps us read the significance of these tapestries for interpreting the allegory of Busirane's house. In his final alexandrine, Spenser draws attention to his own self-conscious artifice, making his line, in Hamilton's words, "measure the snake's length" (note to stanza 28). In doing so, the narrator allies his sinister simile with his own self-consciousness about his artistry. The image of the snake behind his tapestries might be a clever figure for Spenser's Ovidianism itself, which hides here but contributes to meaning by acting as the subtle background for Spenser's own verbal tapestry.

Spenser's narrator does not identify these tapestries directly as Arachne's. He does not, for instance, reveal that they are narrative images of the gods' "heavenly crimes" but rather informs us that they are pictures of "Cupid's warres" (III.xi.29). Because this is the house governed by Cupid, he is made responsible for those crimes so offensive to Minerva and so central to Arachne's critique of the patriarchal and capricious Olympian system. On the one hand, attributing the cause of corruption to Cupid has the effect of distancing that cause from the powerful Olympians (or rulers) themselves, since they are subject to the whims of Cupid. However, the deleterious effects of these crimes are portrayed as much more far-reaching in Spenser's text, creating a breakdown in the social system that exists as a threat in Ovid's poem, but is represented as an actuality in Spenser's. Cupid, an allegorical figure for the external impingement of desire on the behavior of those with power, creates such chaos in the universe depicted on these tapestries that it affects all mortals—not just those whose narratives have been told, but "Kings Queens, Lords Ladies, Knights and Damzels" and the "raskall rablement." Spenser's affront, if he like Arachne is depicting the crimes of those with godlike power, is to a much more pervasive power, one which has the ability to affect everyday life for citizens of every social stratum.

Aside from attributing these crimes to the forces of a different and perhaps more threatening power, however, the descriptions of the tapestries themselves are structurally quite remarkably like those of Arachne in Ovid's poem. As Hamilton notes, "In Ovid, the order of the gods and the number of stories is: Jove (9), Neptune (6), Phoebus (4), Bacchus (1) and Saturn (1). S. varies and extends this order, but keeps much the same emphasis: Jove (12), Phoebus (8), Neptune (5), Saturn (1), Bacchus (1), Mars (1), and unnamed nymphs" (note to stanzas 29–46). Spenser's additions and changes to his own ekphrasis, rather than being evidence of his rejection of Ovidianism, mark his assumption of the Ovidian mode. That the narrator becomes an Ovidian narrator, able to describe an Ovidian scene with the leisure and obvious descriptive pleasure of Spenser's narrator, enforces the sense that Spenser is linking his own poetic reflexivity to Ovid's at this moment in the poem.

Given the similarities, however, the most striking difference between the ekphrases of Ovid and Spenser is that while Arachne's tapestry serves as a sympathetic rendering of the narrative method of her author, Spenser's parodies that author's method by reproducing the tapestry in the context of Busirane's house of evil representation and in a manner that suggests his superiority to his intertext. In *Metamorphoses*, Arachne's tapestry is produced at the end of the section of the poem in which Ovid has been telling tales about the often-violent relations between gods and mortals. Arachne ends up depicting in metamorphic fashion a series of rapes that are equivalent to the crimes Ovid has just left off narrating in his own poem. Because of this, it is common to read Arachne's tapestry as a representation of Ovid's art, and to point to his sympathies with her as a figure for the metamorphic artist that he is himself.[11] The tale, therefore, becomes a commentary on the dangers of Ovid's own art that represents the gods (or those with a more immediate political authority) as abusers of their power. When this self-consciousness about the artist's vulnerability to

external power structures is imported into Spenser's text, the suggestion seems to be that not only is Busirane a dark double for Spenser,
but his tools of representation make Spenser vulnerable to Minerva-
like figures in his own political sphere. The fact that it is Britomart,
however, who confronts these representations of the dangers of an
authoritative power like Elizabeth's, creates profound and meaning-
ful ambiguity in the allegory, since Britomart is both identified with
Amoret, Busirane's victim, and is also associated with Elizabeth herself (within the fictional geneaology of the poem she is her ancestor).
Britomart's encounter with these tapestries leads readers to question
whether Britomart will be Minerva or Arachne when she reads Spenser's intertextual complexity, and this confusion draws attention to the
central problem of writing as a male artist for a female ruler and trying to represent with some sympathy a female subject and her desires.
Spenser's Ovidian allusion highlights the difficulty of producing art
that attempts to celebrate female authority from within a tradition
often characterized by its female victims.

It is not surprising, as we have seen, that Arachne is a female artist and that Ovid aligns himself with her specifically, rather than a
male figure or perhaps Minerva, a goddess of course, but one heavily
invested in the patriarchal Olympian system. Arachne's tale, with its
depiction of the bestial extremes to which the gods will go to rape
mortal women, is another commentary on the gendered systems of
power in Ovid's own text. Ovid fashions a female artist who represents a sympathetic rendering of the vulnerability of his own art to
the whims of a godlike Augustan/imperial power but also offers a
feminized critique of the tales he has been telling. Minerva's ire at
the representation of the male divinities as they rape mortal women
effectively highlights this critique as essentially dependent on gender differences, since she expresses shame at her peers' exploits and
ultimately takes pity (Pallas miserata) on Arachne, transforming her
into a spider to continue her weaving rather than allowing her to
hang herself or offering her a more gruesome metamorphic end.
Even Minerva, it seems, recognizes the faults of the gender system
in which she is implicated.

Spenser's tapestries, which extend Ovid's twenty-six lines of poetry
into eighteen stanzas, represent both male and female victims of the
gods' crimes, adding the tales of Ganymede and Hyacinthus to those
of Europa, Leda, and the rest. While the overwhelming number of
mortal figures are still women, the widening of the victims of these
assaults to include both genders is another way of emphasizing the
injustice of this system and the feminized position within it rather

than an essentialized sexual difference. In his redescription of Ovid's tale of Leda, however, Spenser actually makes Leda a knowing participant in her rape, perhaps directly mocking the critique of male violence implicit in Arachne's weaving:

> Whiles the proud Bird ruffing his fethers wyde,
> And bruching his faire brest, did her inuade;
> She slept, yet twixt her eyelids closely spyde,
> How towards her he rusht, and smiled at his pryde.
> (III.xi.32)

This is a common representation of the tale in Renaissance art, but the attempted comedy of this revision undermines the force of Ovid's self-consciousness about the repetitive violence of the rape structure underlying his own text. By neutralizing this critique in the Ovidian intertext at this moment, Spenser's narrator becomes surprisingly like Busirane. Rewriting the tale of an explicit rape, Spenser's narrator gets lost in his Ovidian descriptions and seems more and more distant from the feminized perspective of Britomart, who is witnessing them. By the end of this episode, in fact, it will be clear that he is, at least in some respects, Busirane himself.

Spenser's tapestries, therefore, as direct importations from Ovid's poem, engage, I would argue, with both central concerns of Ovid's Arachne story—its focus on the dangers for the poet who produces metamorphic and antiauthoritarian poetry and its exploration of the gendered nature of power in the narratives of male desire Ovid has focused on in the first part of his poem. As specimens of verbal artistry, the tapestries in Busirane's outer room are a parody of *Metamorphoses* itself, imitating in their concision the way in which the episodic narrative of Ovid's poem creates meaning by repetition and accretion. In that sense, they might be read as Spenser's attempt to outdo his poetic predecessor. They are, however, an artistically self-conscious rendering of an artistically self-conscious rendering, and as such they betray not anxiety of influence, but more sympathy toward Ovid's text and its author's admittedly complex but essentially antiauthoritarian ideological vision. The parody here is subtle and unites Spenser's poem with his self-critical pagan intertext rather than distancing from it as an example of the violence of male desire.

Spenser's postive engagement with these Ovidian themes makes sense when one considers the Ovidianism of Spenser's poem as a whole. *The Faerie Queene*, as Leonard Barkan points out, "may well be the fullest poetic exploration of metamorphoses since Ovid's time," and to read these tapestries as dismissive or simply critical of Ovidian discourse is to miss the fact that Spenser here aligns himself quite strongly with Ovidianism as a self-reflexive discursive resource.[12] While it is certainly true that Spenser alludes to the violence of Ovidian love in order to associate it with the evil kind of art Busirane produces, he also chooses a moment of Ovidianism in which Ovid himself critiques his own text on similar grounds. In doing so, he presents us with an exploration of artistic power that is vulnerable to external pressures, from the gods or a queen, who is free to criticize art on the grounds that it does not do justice to her feminine kind of "majesty."

Spenser is not just imitating Ovid's text; he is imitating Ovidian self-consciousness. Just as Ovid uses Arachne, a female figure, to critique the violent structure of male desire underlying his own narrative, Spenser has Britomart critique his own poetic practices and resources. Britomart, however, occupies the position of consumer, rather than producer, of art, and she can't read these tapestries. The narrator tells us that as she leaves, marveling at the other piece of self-conscious artistry in the room, the statue of Cupid, she

> was amazed,
> Ne could her wonder satisfye,
> But evermore and more upon it gazed,
> The whiles the passing brightnes her fraile sences dazed.
> (III.xi.49)

Her experience of the room is wonder, and her amazement and confusion are understandable. As a figure for Elizabeth, Britomart can represent both the mortal woman embedded in violent narratives of desire and the Minerva-like arbiter of authority who can punish artists for their representations. Her inability to do more than wonder at this room may actually be a sign of Spenser's own ambivalence about which role the queen will take when she reads his poetry. As Britomart proceeds through the house and slowly conceives that she, through her links of gender with Amoret, is subject to the dangers of these Ovidian representations (especially when she is wounded in this very house), her anger is both Arachne's and Minerva's. In Ovid, Minerva breaks Arachne's loom and beats her with it until the girl hangs herself in despair. The goddess then takes pity on her and transforms her to a spider to memorialize both her hanging and her weaving. Britomart, on the other hand, with the help of Amoret, who tells her that only forcing Busirane to reverse the figures of his discourse can end her torment, manages to make Busirane's allegory of Ovidian rapes reverse itself and just disappear. In doing so, Britomart enacts Spenser's fantasies for both his powerful female reader and himself as a poet, erasing the signs of female subjection to discourses of male desire and the demonic magician, while preserving the intertextual engagement with the self-consciousness of Ovidianism as a discourse. The House of Busirane, ultimately, allegorizes both aspects of *The Faerie Queene's* encounter with Ovidianism. It represents the dangers of masculine desire and authoritarian power that are the central terrors of Ovid's poem. It also, however, acknowledges Ovidianism's self-consciousness about its own highly gendered violence, and similarly suggests a feminized response to that violence that defines an emotional, wondering female self.

BRITOMART'S OVIDIAN GENDER

Britomart's encounter with Ovidianism in Busirane's tapestries is actually the second time she has read Ovidian tapestries in the poem, and it is the second time she is wounded after reading them. Her first consumption of this particular kind of art occurs in canto 1, just at the beginning of her quest, when she enters Malecasta's Castle Joyeous with Redcrosse. As the figure of unchastity—or as her name implies, bad or evil chastity—Malecasta is the chaste Britomart's antithesis as well as her potential double, and their comic encounter when Malecasta slips into her bed represents the dangers of Britomart's aggressive cross-dressed identity to her own figuration as chastity. Because Britomart is disguised as a knight, Malecasta makes her almost fatal mistake, and Britomart receives her first narrated wound in the poem. This wound is traditionally read as allegorizing Britomart's initiation into love after seeing Artegall, as it is inflicted by Gardante, the allegorical figure for the first stage of courtly love—seeing. The Ovidianism of this episode, however, suggests another allegorical meaning, as Britomart only seems to receive such wounds when she is in episodes of Ovidianism that define her as a character in the poem.

Britomart has already experienced, although we don't know it yet, a more dangerous internal wound of love. Right after Britomart's encounter with Malecasta, in canto 2, she tells Redcrosse the story that has generated her quest. Looking into Merlin's magic mirror in her father's bedroom, Britomart sees the image of Artegall and describes her love as an experience of being baited or poisoned. When her Nurse asks if a man has caused her insomnia, nightmares, and constant sighing, Britomart explains,

Nor man it is, nor other liuing wight;
For then some hope I might vnto me draw,
But th'only shade and semblant of a knight,
Whose shape or person yet I neuer saw,
Hath me subiected to loues cruell law:
The same one day, as me misfortune led,
I in my fathers wondrous mirrhour saw,
And pleased with that seeming goodly-hed,
Vnwares the hidden hooke with baite I swallowed.

Sithens it hath infixed faster hold
Within my bleeding bowels, and so sore
Now ranckleth in this same fraile fleshly mould,
That all mine entrails flow with poysnous gore,
And th'vlcer groweth daily more and more.
(III.ii.38–39)

Britomart's festering ulcer is an intensification of the traditional imagery of lovesickness, but it also figures something else, because it is a mirror that has presented this "shade and semblant" that inflicts the wound. This episode in the poem has been read from various psychoanalytic perspectives, and these readings all acknowledge that this moment is unique in the poem in that it creates a deeper characterization of Britomart than of any other figure.[13] What the mirror reflects to Britomart is, of course, partly herself, as she notices when she compares her desire for the object in the mirror to the desire of Ovid's Narcissus:

I fonder, then *Cephisus* foolish child,
Who having vewed in a fountain shere
His face, was with the loue therefore beguiled;
I fonder loue a shade, the bodie farre exild.
(III.ii.44)

Britomart figures her desire for the representation of Artegall in the mirror as more perverse than Narcissus' because while Narcissus loved his own present face, hers is a love entirely disembodied. Her love is "fonder" because she loves a "shade," or a figure. But she is, of course, a shade herself, and explicitly a shadow of the queen. This moment, therefore, operates as a metacommentary on Spenser's own representational strategies with regards to Britomart's character—it figures Britomart's desire, something represented as intensely bodily, as generated from "shadows," which are figures generally, but in this case specifically intertextual ones. Through accumulated allusions to Ovidian tales, this episode reveals Britomart's emotions to be the product of Ovidian intertextuality. When Britomart laments that she is fonder than Narcissus, therefore, in one sense, she is worried about the way her desire has been engendered. In another allegorical sense, however, her vision of Artegall in her father's mirror is the vision of herself, and specifically the shadowy nature of that self in the poem. When she pursues Artegall, she is also pursuing her own characterization.

Britomart's Nurse, Glauce, who previously expressed her relief that Britomart was not like Myrrha, Byblis, or Pasiphae—

> Such shamefull lusts who loaths not, which depart
> From course of nature and of modestie?
> (III.ii.41)

—tells Britomart that her love is not Narcissus-like because the object in the mirror is embodied elsewhere, and they can find him through her magic or their cross-gendered pursuit. The fact, however, that the Nurse recalls these Ovidian tales, and especially the tale of Myrrha, suggests that she may also be a dangerous influence on Britomart's self-definition and her experience of desire. In Myrrha's tale, it is her nurse who arranges access for Myrrha to her father's bed under cover of darkness, and in fact, the way Britomart hesitates and must be convinced to reveal her suffering to her nurse is explicitly modeled on this Ovidian story. Britomart's desire, therefore, for her love object and for her own subjectivity, is made dangerous by its numerous Ovidian associations. While Ovidianism is the discourse that constructs Britomart's character, it is a dangerous discourse, filled with the possibilities for perversion and violence that will be more explicitly allegorized at the end of Britomart's quest in the House of Busirane. It is both generative, because it creates her as a character with agency, and dangerous, because the desire that sets off her narrative may also be destructive or violent. Ovidianism is allegorized as playing a crucial but frightening role in Britomart's self-definition.

Part of what defines Britomart's character is also her transgressive assumption of a masculine role, and as we have previously noted in the analysis of the Ovidian representations surrounding Queen Elizabeth, erosions to stable categories of gender are characteristic of the politics of Elizabethan Ovidianism. When Britomart creates gender confusion in Castle Joyeous, therefore, she is acting out her Ovidian nature, and this is further emphasized when her cross-dressing is examined through an encounter with the Ovidian tale of Venus and Adonis. The tapestries in Castle Joyeous depict this tale, which is the culminating tale sung by

Orpheus in book 10 of *The Metamorphoses*. While the narrative is not very long or descriptive in Ovid, and it contains an extended digression as Venus tells the tale of Atalanta, it is one of the most commonly retold in the Renaissance, most likely because it explores so explicitly but ambiguously two of the cultural issues that I argue are central to the period's interest in Ovidianism: the reversal or erosion of stable gender categories and the inevitability of grief. Ovid's narration of Venus' desire for Adonis emphasizes the major change resulting from her brush with Cupid's arrow, as she abandons her traditional feminine role and pursues, like Diana, her anomalous virgin counterpart:

> caelo praefertur Adonis.
> hunc tenet, huic comes est adsuetaque semper in umbra
> indulgere sibi formamque augere colendo
> per iuga, per silvas dumosaque saxa vagatur
> fine genus vestem ritu succincta Dianae.

> [Adonis is preferred to heaven. She holds him fast, is his companion, and, though her wont has always been to take her ease in the shade and to enhance her beauty by fostering it, now, over mountain ridges, through the woods, over rocky places set with thorns, she ranges with her garments girt up to her knees after the manner of Diana.] (X.532–36)

Venus has become a hunter, literally and in love, and the incongruity of her assuming this role is the source of the humor of the tale. The gender-inverted behavior of pursuit for Venus is emphasized because she joins Adonis, the male figure, in his hunting, and because it links her with the virgin goddess Diana, who shuns traditional female behavior. As a story confronted by Spenser's Britomart, a shadow of the Virgin Queen who is repeatedly associated in her choice of virginity with Diana, the Venus and Adonis tale, like Malecasta's mock-tragic decision to enter Britomart's bed, operates to remind readers of the dangers of Britomart's cross-dressed behavior. While she may not be hunting, she is engaged in the analogous masculine activities of knightly chivalry, and this opens her to the wound she receives in her confrontation with Malecasta's knights, just as Venus' cross-gendered behavior opens her to the grief and loss of Adonis. While Britomart seems on many levels to transcend the limiting condemnation of gender inversion that might be the allegorical import of the Ovidian tale, her wound more ambiguously marks the way her character is still vulnerable to the critique implied in these tapestries.

Ovid makes the connection between Venus' challenges to her feminine role and Adonis' death by linking Venus' warning to Adonis with his description of the kind of weaker hunting she pursues. Venus does not hunt the boar, and this reminds her to warn Adonis not to as well:

> te quoque, ut hos timeas, siquid prodesse monendo
> possit, Adoni, monet, 'fortis'que 'fugacibus esto'
> inquit; 'in audaces non est audacia tuta.
> parce meo, juvenis, temerarius esse periclo,
> neve feras, quibus arma dedit natura, lacesse,
> stet mihi ne magno tua gloria.

> [She warns you, too, Adonis, to fear these beasts, if only it were of any avail to warn. "Be brave against timorous creatures," she says; "but against bold creatures boldness is not safe. Do not be rash, dear boy, at my risk; and do not provoke those beasts which nature has well armed, lest your glory be at great cost to me."] (X.542–47)

Golding, in his Renaissance translation, makes the value judgment placed on Venus' advice clear when he translates Venus' admonition as "Bee bold on cowards" (Golding, X.628). The weighted word "coward" implies that if Adonis follows this advice, he will join Venus in her reversal of gender roles, going from masculine hunter to effeminized weakling and abandoning his "glory." Adonis' resistance to this gender inversion has tragic consequences. The narrator (Orpheus) tells us that his *virtus*, that is, his manly power or spirit, or as Golding has it, his "manhood," could not be influenced by Venus, and it is this resistance to Venus' advice that results in his death. That he is gored in the groin by the phallic boar's tusks enforces the tale's emphasis on the tragic nature of Adonis' commitment to his manhood. Venus' grief, however, which she immortalizes in the short-lived anemone into which she metamorphoses Adonis' blood, aestheticizes Adonis' destruction, marking it as natural and inevitable. While Venus' advice is subtly critiqued and mocked, the tale seems also to critique the character traits associated with manhood, since they result in the masculine hunter's death. Venus' grief over Adonis' death is granted dignity through metamorphosis as she asserts,

> luctus monimenta manebunt
> semper, Adoni, mei, repititaque mortis imago
> annua plangoris peraget simulamina nostri.

[My grief, Adonis, shall have an enduring monument, and each passing year in memory of your death shall give an imitation of my grief.]
(X.725–27)

Both solidifying, and in many respects celebrating, essential notions
of what constitutes masculine and feminine behavior and at the same
time suggesting the need for the loosening of gender boundaries to
save beautiful youths like Adonis from death, this tale partly resolves
its ambiguity through its final focus on the finality of death and the
survival of grief, which is imitated in each rebirth and quick demise
of the anemone. The tale is about gender politics and the possibilities for transgressions of gender, but it ambiguously resists either
affirmation or critique of gender-inverted behavior, essentially transcending these questions through the final emphasis on the inevitability of Venus' grief.

When the disguised Britomart encounters this tale, she does so
as a character engaged in gender role reversals of her own, so her
wonder at the depiction of Venus and Adonis is a result of her own
implication in just such a negotiation of gendered behaviors. While we
might expect the tale depicted in this house of dangerous, but conventional, love to critique Britomart's gender transgression, the narrator instead is moved by his description to grieve with Venus. When the
poem turns to describe the tapestries, the narrator himself becomes
so inspired by Ovidian beauty that he describes tapestries that cannot
exist, relating instead the pathos of the Ovidian tale. In one allegorical
sense, the position of these Ovidian tapestries as the main decora-
tion in Castle Joyeous implicates Ovidianism in the dangerous kind
of erotic love figured by the house and its inhabitants. What is most
notable about the description of these tapestries, however, is that they
are impossible on the literal level of the poem's action and instead
reveal the sympathies of the poem's narrator. Like the Ovidian intertext, Castle Joyeous reveals the dangers of gender-inverted behavior
but offers us a Venus-like narrator, who avoids moralization in favor
of affirming the emotional relevance of the tale.

After first emphasizing his inability to describe the "goodly frame"
and "stately port" of the castle (III.i.31), the narrator attempts to
avoid describing this place, ostensibly because words are inadequate:

But for to tell the sumptuous aray
Of that great chamber, should be labour lost:
For liuing wit, I weene, cannot display

The royal riches and exceeding cost,
Of euery pillour and of euery post;
Which all of purest bullion framed were,
And with great pearles and pretious stones embost,
That the bright glister of their beames cleare
Did sparkle forth great light, and glorious did appeare.
(III.i.32)

While the narrator insists that "living wit" cannot describe these decorations, he actually manages to describe them quite well in the lines that follow. In fact, the narrative creates a vivid visual image, employing words like "glister" and "sparkle" to create a verbal picture. The next stanza might account for the narrator's hesitance to describe this beauty, as we are told that Britomart and Redcrosse are in a state of wonder at the "superfluous riotize" of the room. These characters, as well as their narrator, seem at least initially aware of the moral dangers of such beauty, but the narrator, once he begins the description of the Ovidian tapestries, gets carried away.

The ekphrasis devoted to the tapestries describes events from Ovid's narrative of Venus and Adonis that seem to defy visual representation, and thus that cannot really exist in the literal action of the poem. The narrator asserts that

First did it shew the bitter balefull stowre,
Which her assayd with many a feruent fit,
When first her tender hart was with his beautie smit.
(III.i.34)

The description is of Venus' interior emotional condition—the turmoil she suffered in her first pangs of love for Adonis—and this is the narrator's first visual impossibility. The tapestries cannot literally show this emotional state, but they can signify it, just as Ovidian intertextuality can define Venus' emotional experience. The verbal narrative description privileges Ovidian art, which defines emotion, over this form of visual art, as well as the art of Spenser's own poem. After this first description of what cannot possibly be fully visually represented, the narrative continues to describe events, persuasions, and feelings—things very difficult to represent through visual means. Venus, in her tapestry, woos him with "sleights and sweet allurements" (III.i.35). She leads him from his peers to shady places and bathes him in fountains. She also lasciviously watches him:

> And whilest he bath'd, with her two crafty spyes,
> She secretly would search each daintie lim,
> And throw into the well sweet Rosemaryes,
> And fragrant violets, and Pances trim,
> And euer with sweet nectar she did sprinkle him.
> (II.i.36)

After these increasingly verbal descriptions of this supposedly visual artistry, the narrator imitates Ovid's narration of events quite closely, leaving behind the mode of ekphrasis entirely:

> So did she steale his heedlesse hart away,
> And ioyed his loue in secret vnespyde.
> But for she saw him bent to cruell play,
> To hunt the saluage beast in forrest wyde,
> Dreadfull of daunger, that mote him betyde,
> She oft and oft adviz'd him to refraine
> From chase of greater beasts, whose brutish pryde
> Mote breede him scath vnwares: but all in vaine;
> For who can shun the chaunce, that dest'ny doth ordaine?
> (III.i.37)

At this point in the middle of the description of the tapestries, the narrator has strayed very far from the ekphrastic mode into an obvious emotional engagement with the tragedy of the story that figures love's subjection to death and grief. Although he is brought back to description by the apparently literal depiction of Adonis dying on the tapestry, the narrator never fully regains the composure to continue the description:

> Lo, where beyond he lyeth languishing,
> Deadly engored of a great wild Bore,
> And by his side the Goddesse groueling
> Makes for him endlesse mone, and euermore
> With her soft garment wipes away the gore,
> Which staines his snowy skin with hatefull hew:
> But when she saw no helpe might him restore,
> Him to a dainty flower she did transmew,
> Which in theat cloth was wrought, as if it liuely grew.
> (III.i.38)

Rather than a static description, the tale is presented as existing paradoxically both in and outside narrative time: Venus makes an "endlesse mone" and wipes away his blood for "euermore," but she also makes the decision to turn him into the flower. The entire description pulls between a static description of visual artistry, existing outside of human and narrative time, and its effect on the narrator's own present emotional response. While the tapestries will be associated with moral decay by a description of the hall in which they are placed as "swimming deepe in sensual desires" (III.i.39), suggesting a more distanced moral evaluation of the allegorical place, the narrator has been emotionally moved himself. While his heroes seem to see the dangers of this lascivious kind of beauty, he forgets the purpose of his own description and relates the tragic power and beautiful grief of the Ovidian tale, not the tapestries themselves. The episode, therefore, privileges emotional experiences, of aesthetic pleasure and grief, over rational attempts to judge this tale of gender-inverted desire. Drawing on the ambiguity of its Ovidian intertext, Castle Joyeous similarly figures both the dangers and beauty of art that memorializes both gender inversion and the grief it cannot prevent.

For Britomart, however, these tapestries also mean something else. While the narrator is moved by his descriptions of this tale's picture, we have no indication that Britomart is moved, and the fact that she does not remove her armor in the house and is described as constantly on her guard suggests that she transcends the weakness of her narrator. Her strength and superiority, in fact, are emphasized in this house as precisely a result of the fact that she occupies both genders simultaneously. When she removes her visor, her beauty is compared to that of Cynthia, the moon, and Britomart is represented as far surpassing the six knights who are already Malecasta's followers:

> For she was full of amiable grace,
> And manly terrour mixed therewithal,
> That as the one stird vp affections bace,
> So th'other did mens rashe desires appall,
> And hold them backe, that would in errour fall;
> As he, that hath espied a vermeil Rose,
> To which sharpe thornes and breres the way forstall,
> Dare not for dread his hardy hand expose,
> But wishing it far off, his idle wish doth lose.
> (III.i.46)

Unlike Venus, whose gender-inverted behavior as pursuer of Adonis creates beauty but cannot forestall death, Britomart's dual-gendered self in pursuit of her love object is celebrated here as inspiring only the chastest, most reasonable kind of love. Britomart's connection with Elizabeth is made particularly firm here, as she is linked to Elizabeth's guise as Cynthia and then, in this passage, the Tudor rose that retains its thorns, unlike the symbolic rose of courtly love that doesn't have the thorns to protect lovers from error. Britomart in this episode, therefore, is defined by these Ovidian tapestries as more perfect in her erosions of stable gender categories than Venus. As a figure for the queen, she functions for Spenser to celebrate the queen's similarly transformed gender identity and Ovidian representation. She cannot, however, transcend death, the dangers of desire that will be directed to her by such figures as Malecasta, or her masculine knight and equivalent, Gardante.

Britomart's wound in this Ovidian castle, finally, also operates to comment on her participation in the powerful and yet dangerous feminine position in the discourse of Ovidianism. *The Faerie Queene* will itself attempt a representation of the transcendence of these dangers in the allegory of Adonis' boar, imprisoned in the Garden of Adonis. The only thing that seems to rescue Britomart from death or the violent masculine desire of the boar or the artist himself in both Castle Joyeous and the House of Busirane, however, is her apparent obliviousness to her own figuration through this discourse. It is important to recall that when Britomart identifies herself with an Ovidian character, it is Narcissus, a male figure, while the Nurse worries that she might be constructed through allusion to more troubling female figures. As I have argued above, Britomart wonders about but ultimately cannot read the meanings for herself of the Ovidian tapestries in Busirane's house because she is both Arachne and Minerva, both female victim and feminized authority. In this case, Britomart, prefiguring her culminating encounter with the artist constructing her character, similarly does not fully see her own danger: that because she is acting as a knight, she has inspired in Malecasta a desire too much like her own. Britomart does sympathize with Malecasta's feminine suffering:

> Full easie was for her to haue beliefe
> Who by self-feeling of her feeble sexe,
> And by long triall of the inward griefe,
> Wherewith imperious loue her hart did vexe,
> Could iudge what paines do liuing harts perplexe.
> (III.i.54)

She cannot, however, prevent the danger of her implication in the gender politics of Ovidianism. Her wound highlights the fact that while Britomart may be more perfect in her dual-gendered nature than any previous intertextual double and may transcend the gender politics of this specific Ovidian tale, she is still identified with her female body, its pains and emotions, and therefore she is still in danger of being wounded by the masculine power to gaze at that body, figured by Gardante. As in the House of Busirane, Spenser creates through Ovidian intertextuality a powerful figure of female authority, a representative of the queen's transformative and transcendent gender, but also figures the vulnerability of that figure to the violence so self-consciously explored in Ovid's poem. Again, through self-consciousness about its own gender politics and its own articulations of desire, Ovidianism can both celebrate and represent the dangers for a majestic female authority.

SPENSER'S GRIEVING ADICIA AND THE GENDERING OF OVIDIAN ALLEGORY

No other book in *The Faerie Queene* is as pervasively Ovidian as book 3, but Spenser does not leave this intertextual discourse behind in the second (1596) part of the poem. In fact, leading up to the Mutability Cantos, where metamorphosis is revealed to be at least potentially the central trope behind the poem, Spenser includes a number of self-conscious Ovidian allusions, the most stunning of which is Adicia's transformation in book 5. In the figure of Adicia, who metamorphoses in V.viii into a tiger in a dramatic imitation of Hecuba's transformation in *Metamorphoses*, the questions of gender politics that are central to Ovid's critique of Augustan imperialism take on new resonances in Spenser's Elizabethan present. Operating in relation to Elizabeth's court, Spenser's choice to imitate the metamorphosis and exile of an Ovidian female ruler at this moment in the poem should be read as an attempt to counter and complicate other codified forms of Elizabethan female subjectivity and to comment on that notably gendered and regendered representative of her sex, Elizabeth herself. In book 5 alone, Spenser has just shadowed Elizabeth in the beheaded Radigund as well as the triumphant Britomart, and he will explicitly allegorize her role in the execution of Mary Stuart in the figure of Mercilla in the next canto.[14] In this context, Adicia is another, differently realized but equally important, picture of female sovereignty, because as an Ovidian figure she participates in a long history of counterheroic, often grieving heroines.

In addition to complicating Spenserian gender politics, Adicia's Ovidian metamorphosis enacts her transition in *The Faerie Queene* from character to allegorical daemon, so this episode points to some of the ways Renaissance Ovidianism intersects with the mode of allegory. Adicia goes from being the villainized consort of the Souldan to inhabiting the woods of Faeryland as a ferocious tiger, a more abstract figure for the Injustice her figure was also supposed to represent.[15] Rather than interpreting her transition from active figure to abstraction of Injustice as a complete loss of Adicia's authority and agency, this analysis explores how Adicia as a figure gains representational power through her exit from the action in the poem. When Adicia becomes a tiger and flees out of her castle's postern door to haunt the woods of Faeryland, as a figure she escapes from the limits placed on her by the constructed social world of the poem. Her metamorphosis memorializes her once active figure and haunts the text as an allegory for the grieving female figure who must be demonized and then sacrificed to ensure the stability of heroism and the progress of heroic narrative. The structure of Spenser's allegory of allegorical abstraction, in fact, mimes Ovid's repetitive narrative structure, and this suggests a deeper connection between Renaissance Ovidianism and the same period's allegorical constructions, especially those created through representations of excessive emotional states.

In V. viii, Adicia metamorphoses into a tiger in her rage and grief at the murder of her husband, the Souldan, by the heroic knights of Justice, Artegall and Arthur. The knights have just rescued the good queen Mercilla's messenger, Samient, from the clutches of two pagan knights sent to despoil her by Adicia and have learned that the Souldan and his wife, affirming themselves enemies of Justice, vex Mercilla, going so far as to threaten her very life. Using a bit of deception, Artegall disguises himself to enter the Souldan's court, and with his help Arthur manages to take the castle and kill the Souldan, leaving Adicia alone with her conquerors. After attempting first revenge and then suicide, Adicia metamorphoses and simultaneously escapes out of her castle's postern door to haunt the woods of Faeryland. As such a plot summary suggests, on the level of heroic action Adicia's defeat is the triumph of the poem's heroes, and as simple allegory the episode can be read as divinely sanctioned Justice, embodied in Arthur and Artegall, triumphing over Injustice in the figure of Adicia. Adicia is also the explicit enemy of Mercilla, an allegorical figure representing Elizabeth in the next canto, so on one level she must function as a negative double of the merciful queen. Reading one sense of the allegory, then, Adicia is a powerful villain, but she is also a female ruler, and her Ovidian characterization enforces her status as a figure of female authority and grief for whom the poem generates noticeable sympathy. As is the case in many episodes of Spenserian allegory, this representation of Mercilla/Elizabeth's dark double as Injustice is too complex, and in this case sympathetic, to allow a straightforward reading of her as an antitype to Mercilla or Elizabeth.[16]

Reading Adicia's representation involves negotiating the intertextual effects of Spenser's Ovidian allusion, and Spenser self-consciously draws attention to the troubled nature of reading itself at the start of Adicia's tale. Adicia's husband, the Souldan, has been dragged to death under his own chariot wheels, and according to the narrator his body is so disfigured and dismembered "that of his shape appear'd no litle moniment" (V.viii.43). Shortly following this description, the narrator wittily remarks that as a symbol of his victory over this monument-less body, Arthur hangs the Souldan's arms on a tree "to be a moniment forevermore" (V.viii.45). When Adicia reacts with rage to this display, the narrative emphasizes that her anger is not just over the physical death of her husband but over the reading or interpretation of that death, the "moniment" that ought to remain to memorialize their encounter in the absence of the Souldan's violated body. Arthur's interpretation, which is closely allied with the narrator's at this point in the poem, is that his arms will

> remain for an eternal token
> To all, mongst whom this storie should be spoken,
> How worthily, by heavens high decree,
> Justice that day of wrong her selfe had wroken,
> That all men which that spectacle did see,
> By like ensample mote for ever warned bee.
> (V.viii.44)

Justice, according to Arthur and the narrator, has "wroken" herself on Wrong; that is, she has vented or given expression to her emotional motivations for revenge. The reflexive use of "wroken" here suggests that Justice in this battle takes a just revenge on Wrong, since according to the *O.E.D.* such a construction "frequently implies that revenge is taken by the injured party."[17] Arthur's interpretation of the Souldan's defeat as the revenge of Justice on Wrong is the one which most critics take to be the authoritative one for the whole episode—for them Arthur's monument succeeds. Such a monologic reading is undercut immediately, however, by Adicia, an Ovidian female figure whose reading of the spectacle of her husband's defeat leads to a narrative digression on her extreme grief and rage and her subsequent metamorphosis.

The description of Adicia's metamorphosis itself is one of the most overt moments of Ovidian intertextuality in *The Faerie Queene* and the only extended representation of Adicia as a figure. The narrator works here through indirection and allusion, never actually describing the metamorphosis and thereby insistently drawing attention to its derivative status. Adicia,

> breaking forth out at a posterne dore,
> Unto the wyld wood ranne, her dolours to deplore.
>
> As a mad bytch, when as the franticke fit
> Her burning tongue with rage inflamed hath,
> Doth runne at randon, and with furious bit
> Snatching at every thing, doth wreake her wrath
> On man and beast, that commeth in her path.
> There they do say, that she transformed was
> Into a Tygre, and that Tygres scath
> In crueltie and outrage she did pas.
> (V.viii.48–49)

The narrator tells us that "they do say" Adicia's metamorphosis took place, which distances him from the darkly Ovidian "wyld wood" she retreats to, but which also signals the intertextuality of this episode, reminding the reader that in another context the story has been told before.

The Ovidian tale most directly alluded to is Hecuba's from *Metamorphoses*; in her metamorphosis Adicia is like a "mad bytch," the animal Hecuba becomes in her own rage and grief.[18] Hecuba and Adicia share many parts of their stories—both are female rulers facing the defeat and death of their kinsmen and both attempt to be revenged on a figure incidental to the main causes of their suffering. Most importantly, though, it is the parallel structure and outcome of their transformations that link these two figures, as both metamorphose into raging animals at the limits of their human endurance of suffering and become magical beasts haunting and therefore memorializing the natural places of their transformations. The invocation of Hecuba's story defines Adicia primarily in relation to Hecuba's status in the Renaissance as a symbol of misfortune and mourning. Boccaccio, for example, in *De Mulieribus Claris*, tells us, "Hecuba Trojanorum preclarissima regina fuit, eque perituri splendoris fulgor eximus et miseriarum certissimum documentum" (Hecuba, the most famous queen of the Trojans, provides a notable illustration of fleeting glory as well as a sure example of human misery).[19] Adicia, if she is like Hecuba, is figured mainly through her suffering.

The simile that links Adicia to Hecuba, therefore, serves in some sense to explain the Ovidian logic of Adicia's metamorphosis, implying that extreme emotion is the ultimate cause of her transformation. As occurs in many of the tales of *Metamorphoses*, Hecuba's metamorphosis in Ovid's poem is explicitly described not as a bodily change but more as an extension of the human responses to extremes of emotion:

> clade sui Thracum gens inritata tyranni
> Troada telorum lapidumque incessere iactu
> coepit, at haec missum rauco cum murmure saxum
> morsibus insequitur rictuque in verba parato
> latravit, conata loqui.

> [The Thracians, incensed by their king's disaster, began to set upon the Trojan with shafts and stones. But she, with hoarse growls, bit at the stones they threw, and, though her jaws were set for words, barked when she tried to speak.] (*Met.* XIII.565–69)

Her growls could arguably be human, until we are told she can no longer speak, which signals her movement from the discursive realm of human identity to the world of beasts. This movement from one state of being to another is not represented as a punishment or, as it is in some cases in *Metamorphoses*, a literalization of a flaw, but instead as in some sense a release from the limits of her human suffering. Intimately tied to emotion in this tale, metamorphosis becomes a marker of the line between endurable human grief and animalistic passion that pushes Hecuba outside the realm of recognizable human identity.

While the internal cause of Hecuba's metamorphosis may be grief, however, that grief is linked to a loss of control over external political forces. Hecuba's transformation comes in response both to extreme suffering and to the actual physical attack by the Thracians; Adicia's rage and metamorphosis, on the other hand, result from her extreme impotence in the face of Arthur and Artegall. While the narrator asserts that Adicia is *like* Hecuba, her metamorphic trajectory suggests that she is a more extreme version of such a figure. Hecuba is driven to a mad grief, so she becomes a rabid dog. Adicia, on the other hand, is driven to rage in addition to grief, and the tiger is a more terrifying and violent figure in the landscape of *The Faerie Queene*. Spenser takes this story of excessive emotion a step further than Ovid and increases the violence associated with the transformed female figure. The allusion to Hecuba's story exposes *The Faerie Queene's* own concerns over the extreme suffering it has produced in this figure of a female ruler, one who will haunt the poem, even if she does not appear again.

It is the intertextual mingling of Ovid's representation of extreme female emotion in Hecuba and Spenser's in Adicia that produces the complex negotiations of female identity that occur in this episode. Adicia's metamorphosis is the result of two extreme emotional states: despair over the death of her husband and frustration over her powerlessness to take revenge on her offenders. Both of these emotions are at issue in Hecuba's tale in *Metamorphoses*. In Ovid's narrative, Hecuba is given significant narrative space to grieve her losses and reveal her nobility as a Trojan queen. In dialogue most explicitly with Euripides and Virgil, Ovid retells the Troy story from Hecuba's point of view, casting the Greeks as her violent enslavers. Her grief, the narrative suggests, exceeds endurable bounds, as she watches her last daughter, Polyxena, sacrificed to appease the ghost of Achilles and then finds her last son, Polydorus, murdered by the Thracian king entrusted with preserving him from the dangers of the war. Ovid tells us that her suffering is much lamented by both sides of the war and even by the furious Juno herself:

> illius Troasque suos hostesque Pelasgos,
> illius fortuna deos quoque moverat omnes,
> sic omnes, ut et ipsa Iovis coniunxque sororque
> eventus Hecaben meruisse negaverit illos.

> [Her sad fortune touched the Trojans and her Grecian foes and all the gods as well; yes, all, for even Juno, sister and wife of Jove, declared that Hecuba had not deserved such an end.] (*Met.* XIII.572–75)

Such universal lament is significant here, since Adicia, Spenser's metamorphic imitation of Hecuba, is supposed to be the criminal, not the generally approved victim. Hecuba's narrative in Ovid's text associates her extreme grief both with her nobility and therefore her agency, but also with her powerlessness after the Trojan war. In her case, as in many in *Metamorphoses*, Hecuba's emotion emphasizes her human self at the moment it is lost, so Spenser's allusion to her story links Adicia's grief both to her agency as a subject and the loss of that agency.

In fact, Adicia's metamorphosis, while it imitates Hecuba's, alludes more broadly to the pagan poem's obsession with extreme emotion and female agency. Ovid's retelling of Hecuba's tale is the paradigmatic example of the poem's implicit project to represent the moments in which female grief leads to metamorphosis. Ovid devotes forty-three lines to Hecuba's lament, which ends with the tragic "all is lost" (Golding, *Met.* 634), and most of the narrative space of Hecuba's tale is devoted to descriptions of her grief and suffering. In addition, Hecuba's grief serves public as well as private purposes, as she fulfills the symbolic mourning assigned to women, who are central to rituals surrounding the end of life. Hecuba is found grieving over the graves of her sons, fulfilling the ritualistic role of, as Golding calls her, "Queene of moothers all" (Golding, *Met.* XIII.578):

> Last of all tooke shippe ageinst her will
> Queene Hecub: who (a piteous cace to see) was found amid
> The tumbes in which her sonnes were layd. And there as Hecub did
> Embrace theyr chists and kisse theyr bones, Ulysses voyd of care
> Did pull her thence. Yit raught shee up, and in her boosom bare
> Away a crum of Hectors dust, and left on Hectors grave
> Her hory heares and teares, which for poore offrings she gave.
> (Golding, *Met.* XIII.507–13)

That Ulysses is "voyd of care" is Arthur Golding's interpretative translation of the Latin, which suggests such cruelty.[20] This and other of his interventions reveal Golding's understanding that the tale presents the Trojan queen as a foil to the guileful and cruel Greek heroes. The Greeks are guilty in this instance of not respecting Hecuba's social role, and this calls Adicia's social and political function similarly into question. Her grief, if she is like Hecuba, is culturally and politically significant, which makes Arthur's thwarting of that social role in Spenser's episode more marked. Hecuba's extensive laments make it clear that the power of female grief is one of the main things at stake in Hecuba's representation, and this makes her story an especially appropriate subtext to that of Adicia, who has cause for excessive grief but is not allowed the narrative space to lament, as the narrative focuses on her attempt at revenge and metamorphosis instead.

As I have noted, it is Arthur's monument—the Souldan's arms hanging on tree, read by Adicia as a symbol of the dismemberment of her husband's body—that leads to her transformation, and a dismembered body also serves to precipitate Hecuba's excessive grief and then transformation in *Metamorphoses*. In a moment of typically Ovidian melodramatic irony, readers know that at first Hecuba still believes that she has one child still living, Polydorus, the son Priam sent to Polymestor to be saved from the dangers of the war. In Ovid's version of this story, Hecuba recalls her son in the midst of her enumeration of her sorrows only to find his body on the shore when she goes to wash the body of her sacrificed daughter:

> adspicit eiectum Polydori in litore corpus
> factaque Threicis ingentia vulnera telis;
> Troades exclamant, obmutuit illa dolore,
> et pariter vocem lacrimasque introrsus obortas
> devorat ipse dolor, duroque simillima saxo
> torpet et adversa figit modo lumina terra,
> interdum torvos sustollit ad aethera vultus,
> nunc positi spectat vultum, nunc vulnera nati,
> vulnera praecipue, seque armat et instruit ira.
> qua simul exarsit, tamquam regina maneret,
> ulcisci statuit poenaeque in imagine tota est . . .

[And there she saw the body of Polydorus, cast up upon the shore, cov-ered with gaping wounds made by Thracian spears. The Trojan women shrieked at the sight; but she was dumb with grief; her very grief engulfed her powers of speech, her rising tears. Like a hard rock, immovable she stood, now held her gaze fixed upon the ground, and at times lifted her awful face to the heavens; now she gazed upon the features of her son as he lay there in death, now on his wounds, but mostly on his wounds, arming herself with ever-mounting rage. When now her rage blazed out, as if she still were queen, she fixed on vengeance and was wholly absorbed in the punishment her imagination pictured.] (*Met.* XIII.536–46)

Hecuba's first response is stony immobility, recalling the metamor-phosis of Niobe, another mother witnessing the deaths of all her chil-dren, but then the repetitive naming of Polydorus' wounds focuses on the dismembered body as the unbearable sight and cause of her revenge, as she arms herself with the excessive rage that enables her violence. Her revenge is therefore in some sense an escape from stasis, and the violence is essential to Hecuba's sense of herself as the power-ful figure she has been, as the narrator tells us her

> rage blazed out,
> as if she still were queen.

This representation of her motivations for revenge serves to solidify the reader's recognition of her former agency, while at the same time drawing attention to the loss of that power.

Similarly, Adicia's first attempt at action on seeing the sign of her husband's dismembered body is revenge, and the narrator reveals at once a sympathy for her strong response as well as a misogynistic con-tempt for women as the unreasonable and weaker sex. When Adicia has seen her husband's "moniment,"

it much appald her troubled spright:
Yet not, as women wont in doleful fit,
She was dismayed, or faynted through affright,
But gathered unto her her trobled wit,
And gan eftsoones deuise to be aueng'd for it.
(V.viii.45)

Spenser's narrator characterizes Adicia's desire as unnatural and unwom-anly, linking her to the Amazon Radigund, who has just been beheaded in the poem, and indirectly to Britomart, that other cross-dressed figure of female authority negotiating her identity in book 5. The tone of the narrator here is hard to read, but although we would expect a condem-nation of such cross-gendered behavior, the misogyny of the narrator's commentary ends up valorizing her actions, since Adicia is contrasted with the weak women whom the narrator scorns. Such confusion of gendered sympathy may be an excellent example of what Dorothy Ste-phens calls Spenser's "flirtatious" narrative strategy, as Adicia's revenge is coded by the ostensibly masculine narrator at first as aberrant to her femininity and then immediately validated.[21] In fact, since she has been and will be further characterized as unreasonable in contrast to the rea-soned discourse of civil justice, the emphasis here upon her restraint and active plotting of her actions betrays not just an underlying sympathy, transported from the Ovidian intertext, for her feminized grief, but an interest in her ability to take a more masculine revenge, an ability she seems to gain through association with Ovid's heroic female revenger. Just as Hecuba's violence is celebrated as a just revenge, Adicia's agency for revenge is strangely validated, in this case riskily transcending expec-tations for a gendered response. In both cases, though, such agency is memorialized right before it is effaced through metamorphosis.

Adicia, unlike Hecuba, cannot take revenge, and although the nar-rator may betray some sympathy toward her point of view, Adicia's violence is not as clearly justified as Hecuba's in the action of the poem, since it is directed at Samient, Mercilla's messenger and an improper object, rather than Arthur or Artegall, the true perpetrators of her wrong. Rather than sharing a sympathetic bond of gender with Samient, Adicia is represented as a force of destruction to maiden innocence. Adicia's desire to be revenged, though, is coded immedi-ately as a maternal rage, as she is compared to

an enraged cow,
That is berobbed of her youngling dere.
(V.viii.46)

Although she does not appear to be a mother in Spenser's version of this tale, Adicia's figure is so elided with Hecuba's in this episode of Ovidianism that her anger is represented as maternal, the primary kind of rage in the Ovidian intertext. In addition to subtly contributing social sanction to her emotions, this simile also serves to naturalize her rage, justifying her actions as motivated by an instinctive maternal response. The comparison further highlights Adicia's troublesome resemblance to other, less explicitly villainized, female figures.

Adicia is also compared to a series of classical figures—Ino, Agave, Medea—who are linked in that their excessive violence is against their kin and therefore partially against themselves:

> Like raging Ino, when with knife in hand
> She threw her husbands murdred infant out,
> Or fell Medea, when on Colchicke strand
> Her brothers bones she scattered all about;
> Or as that madding mother, mongst the rout
> Of Bacchus Priests her owne deare flesh did teare.
> Yet neither Ino, nor Medea stout,
> Nor all the maenades so furious were,
> As this bold woman, when she saw that Damzell there.
> (V.xiii.46)

In addition to being Ovidian female figures who have murdered their children, all of these women are associated with madness or, in the case of Medea, irrational and destructive passion—Ino is driven mad by Hera for raising her sister's son, Dionysus; Agave is in a Bacchic frenzy when she dismembers her son; and Medea is a sorceress, using her magic to revenge herself on Jason, who has abandoned her. The narrator stresses that Adicia's rage exceeds all these others, outdoing the classical precedents of her situation. Because all of these figures murder their children, the comparisons suggest that Adicia's attempt to take revenge on Samient is caused by their kinship or similarity rather than Adicia's perception that Samient is the author of her misfortune. Ino and Agave also seek to end their own lives (and Ino succeeds), as Adicia does immediately after her comparison to these figures. The critique may be of female passion that destroys the innocent, but in each of these cases the passion is evoked by a family tragedy. Considering the larger comparison being made in this episode to Hecuba's revenge against the greedy and fraudulent Polymestor, these readings begin to suggest that what is at stake here is the female position in a larger system over which Adicia has little control. Her desire to kill

Samient is figured as a displacement of her rage against the heroic knights, and this fact becomes even clearer when she attempts suicide when she cannot take revenge on Samient.

Hecuba, in the Ovidian tale, does not explicitly attempt to take her own life. In fact, she shows herself at first to be resigned to life as a captive. Her metamorphosis, however, preserves her from the horrified vision of slavery she describes in her laments, so that she will never be (in Golding's translation),

> presented too Penelope a gift, whoo shewing mee
> In spinning my appoynted taske, shall say: this same is shee
> that was sumtyme king Priams wyfe, this was the famous moother
> Of Hector.
> (Golding, *Met.* XIII.614–17)

Although the focus of Hecuba's revenge in the Ovidian narrative is Polymestor, the point of the narrative is that the sources of her grief are so manifold that they exceed human limits of endurance. The narrator tells us it is her "ira" that causes her violence, which has been building until this point of excess. Although her revenge may be partly motivated by a desire to destroy herself to escape from slavery, her final transformation into a dog offers her freedom from human emotive limits and is a resolution that rescues her nobility, since she will never be a slave.

In addition to rescuing her from slavery, Hecuba's metamorphosis memorializes her grief in the landscape:

> locus exstat et ex re
> noment habet, veterumque diu memor illa malorum,
> tum quoque Sithonios ululavit maesta per agros.

> [The place still remains and takes its name from this incident, where she, long remembering her ancient ills, still howled mournfully across the Sithonian plains.] (*Met.* XIII.569–71)

Hecuba's suffering is granted an eternal symbolic presence, and in this sense Ovid's narrator implies that she is not completely powerless in this tragedy. Haunting the landscape, she ensures that the story will be memorialized from her perspective, and this suggests another way in which this intertext is in dialogue with Adicia's story.

Adicia too becomes in some respects a memorial to her own suffering, but her exile from the central discourse of the poem is both more urgent and more complete. As we have seen, Adicia's metamorphosis, which has been foreshadowed in such dramatic ways, is not actually described, and the suggestion of it occupies only half a stanza:

> There they doe say, that she transformed was
> Into a Tygre, and that Tygres scath
> In crueltie and outrage she did pas,
> To prove her surname true, that she imposed has.
> (V.viii. 49)

Already a place linked with moral errancy and danger, the woods in this case are also the site of a different kind of memorialization from Arthur's "moniment." The memorial to this once-active character in the poem is an allegorical tiger, and she has proven the "surname" imposed upon her to be true. She has, in other words, become the daemonic allegory of Injustice that was her name's destiny. Denied agency on the level of the fiction, Adicia ultimately gains representational power as a threateningly embodied allegorical figure existing in the woods, removed both from the social world of Faeryland and the level of figure and action.

Like Hecuba, Adicia is driven by her excessive grief and rage to become a wild animal preying on the surrounding countryside. Also like that of Hecuba, her presence as a wild animal in this place becomes legendary, marking the location of her transformation as a sort of natural monument to her disintegrated human identity. While Hecuba is turned to a dog, however, whose howling memorializes more her grief than her rage, Adicia becomes a tiger, fulfilling, the narrator tells us, her destined role as the name of injustice. It is clear, once this comparison has been drawn, that the primary difference between Ovid's telling of this tale and Spenser's is that Adicia cannot take revenge on any of her oppressors, not even Samient, who the text has suggested might be a desperate substitute for the masculinized forces in play around her. Adicia's revenge is thwarted, and impotence is the main cause of her rage. In addition, although both grief and rage lead to Adicia's and Hecuba's metamorphoses, Hecuba's satisfied anger is validated in her transformation as her human self escapes from slavery. Adicia, on the other hand, is driven to excesses of both anger and grief, and her metamorphosed figure is represented as much more threatening to the inhabitants of her world, but in a new, symbolic way.

The apparent misogyny of the resolution of Adicia's tale is reflected in the narrator, who, after all, began canto 8 with a stereotypical diatribe about the dangers of women:

Nought under heaven so strongly doth allure
The sence of man, and all his minde possesse,
As beauties lovely baite, that doth procure
Great warriours oft their rigour to represse,
And mighty hands forget their manlinesse;
Drawne with the powre of an heart-robbing eye,
And wrapt in fetters of a golden tresse,
That can with melting pleasaunce mollifye
Their hardned hearts, enur'd to bloud and cruelty.
　. . .
Such wondrous powre hath wemens faire aspect,
To captive men, and make them all the world reject.
(V.viii.1–2)

Such a narrative intervention must be at least partly ironic, since Britomart has just succeeded in rescuing Artegall from his subjection and
has been left behind so that Artegall can continue his heroic adventures. In fact, the narrative suggests that Britomart herself has some
control over Artegall's decision to leave her:

Full sad and sorrowfull was Britomart
For his departure, her new cause of griefe;
Yet wisely moderated her owne smart,
Seeing his honor; which she tendred chiefe,
Consisted much in that adventures priefe.
(V.vii.44)

Britomart chooses not to hinder Artegall in his adventures, and this
emphasis both reinforces the possibility that she could emasculate him
and characterizes her as a positive female figure, one who supports
his heroic endeavors rather than trapping him in the stasis that she is
capable of producing. The reliability of canto 8's narrator on matters
of women and their agency has therefore already been suitably called
into question when he relates Adicia's metamorphosis.

It is not surprising, then, that Adicia's excessive emotion (her rage
and despair) and metamorphosis disrupt the heroic ideology of the
text to such a degree that the narrator must intervene at the beginning of the next canto to remind readers of Adicia's allegorical significance and assure them that she has been safely exiled to the woods:

What Tygre, or what other salvage wight
Is so exceeding furious and fell,
As wrong, when it hath arm'd it selfe with might?

Not fit mongst men, that doe with reason mell,
But mongst wyld beasts and salvage woods to dwell;
Where they that most in boldness doe excell,
Are dreadded most, and feared for their powre:
Fit for Adicia, there to build her wicked bowre.

There let her wonne farre from resort of men,
Where righteous Artegall her late exyled;
There let her every keepe her damned den,
Where none may be with her lewd parts defyled,
Nor none but beasts may be of her despoyled.
(V.ix.1–2)

Ostensibly, the narrator is concerned to reassure his readers that Adicia's villainous person is no longer a threat to the people of Faeryland,
but his tirade against her degenerates into reviling her "lewd parts."
Because Adicia's only directly narrated crime is sending her knights
to assault the innocent messenger, Samient, readers might need to be
assured that she cannot "despoyle" additional maidens. We have had
no indication, however, that her motivations are primarily sexual; in
fact, it is her political power—her dangerous counsel to her husband,
the Souldan—that is emphasized as her primary crime. The anxious
narrator, therefore, reveals here a new kind of threat, both to the inhabitants of Faeryland and to the narrative he is telling. It is her female sex,
and, more importantly, her discursive power in the unreasonable realm
of emotion that are perceived by the narrator as the true sources of
threat to the heroic action of the poem. The extremity of that feminized
emotion and its ability to signal a subject about to undergo metamorphosis, as we have seen, are Adicia's most Ovidian characteristics.

This moment of Ovidian intertextuality and the specific comparison
of Adicia's situation to Hecuba's destabilizes the allegorical meaning
of the episode and to some degree the entire book by drawing sympathy to the conquered antiheroine. Spenser allies Adicia, his supposed
personification of Injustice, with a great Roman and British cultural
heroine, Hecuba, while insisting that she is the source of Mercilla's
danger, the "author" of Samient's wrong, and the epitome of the
forces that resist justice and the just knights of book 5. Throughout
Metamorphoses we find examples of female figures such as Hecuba
who comment on the masculinized violence that underlies classical
(often Virgilian) heroic discourse. The metamorphoses of such figures
are often answers to their prayers for release from the suffering of
their positions as victims of human or divine forces associated with
male heroism. On the one hand, the allusion here is specifically to

Hecuba, and her story is the one that troubles the episode to the greatest degree, but the metamorphic aesthetic employed at this point in the poem alludes to Ovid's entire work and calls into question the gender ideologies of both the ancient and Renaissance authors. When approached broadly as a moment of Ovidianism, Adicia's representation takes shape as a commentary on questions of female authority and power and betrays an anxiety over female emotion that has far-reaching consequences for reading the constructions of gendered figures in book 5 and throughout *The Faerie Queene*.[22] If Adicia is like Hecuba, Ovid's victim of extreme injustice, the justice of the poem's heroes, her enemies, is called into question. The narrative self-consciously creates a confusion of sympathy that highlights (or perhaps grieves over) the injustice of socially constructed gender roles in a heroic narrative.

In addition to relocating *The Faerie Queene's* concerns over Injustice to the heroes of the episode, Adicia's Ovidian representation profoundly influences Spenser's thematic exploration of female authority in this section of book 5. When Artegall meets Adicia, he has just been rescued from the dungeon of the Amazon Radigund, who kept him as her thrall in "womans weedes" (V.v.20). This section of the poem is one of the most explicitly misogynistic—Britomart rescues Artegall from his emasculated state, beheads Radigund and reestablishes patriarchy. Britomart,

> changing all that forme of common weale,
> The liberty of women did repeal,
> Which they had long usurpt; and them restoring
> To mens subjection, did true Justice deale.
> (V.vii.42)

Britomart and Radigund are, as many have noted, doubles of each other or one and the same, since both are female warriors who desire Artegall. The description of their battle suggests further the similarity between the two female figures when they are likened interchangeably to a tiger and a lioness:

> As when a Tygre and a Lionesse
> Are met at spoyling of some hungry pray,
> Both challenge it with equall greediness.
> (V.vii.30)

"Britomart's task," then, as Katherine Eggert puts it, "is to subdue herself."[23] Coming on the heels of such a repression of female authority and of Britomart's more active nature, Adicia's transformation into a tiger suggests that she, as well, is linked to both Britomart and Radigund, and hence to Elizabeth, the female ruler to whom all such figures refer.[24]

The threat embodied in Adicia—coming as it does after the apparent resolution of the threat of martial women such as Radigund and Britomart—is not, then, the danger of stasis, but rather what we should call "agency," the power of an active figure to promote her own interests. Katherine Eggert has analyzed what she terms the attempted "repeal of queenship" that takes place beginning in canto 8, a repeal that also involves the aesthetic realm, as the poem turns from the "effeminate" poetics of books 3 and 4 to the "most straightforward mode that the Faerie Queene will ever assume, historical allegory."[25] She argues that the language of these final five cantos of book 5 is deliberately unsuggestive and that the poem attempts to escape from feminine authority as well as feminine poetics in these cantos but ultimately cannot do so. She concludes, "In the end Book 5's historical episodes make the case that even when barren and driven poetry replaces seductive lyric, masculine heroism is still subject to an undirected feminine authority."[26] While the poem certainly displays such an ideological struggle, Adicia's representation operates to comment on the attempted shift Eggert identifies, actually drawing attention to the female agency and feminized poetry that has been lost. Adicia's Ovidian metamorphosis is such a dramatic shift in the aesthetic of the canto and the sympathetic treatment of her grief is so marked that it is difficult to characterize this portion of the poem as barren or as an abandonment of the complex and dialectical style of his earlier cantos and books. Indeed, the canto highlights and questions such abandonment. While Eggert rightly suggests that this section of the poem seems to be examining a more "masculine" (in Eggert's terms) mode of poetry and politics, the project may be called into question from the outset in this canto, when Adicia, a figure for all that transgresses and runs counter to the centralized discursive systems of the poem, escapes out a postern door to haunt the poem's woods. Because Adicia's narrative of metamorphosis is an imitation of Hecuba's, female authority is doubly at stake in her representation, and her grief in some ways marks the grief of the narrative over sacrificed female rulers and the poetics with which they are associated. Although the poem does turn eventually toward a more restrictive "masculine" style, as Eggert suggests, this turn is memorialized in Adicia's metamorphosis before it occurs. Adicia haunts the rest of the action of the poem, not as a figure of female authority but as a representation of the loss of that authority, the emotional costs of Spenser's heroic narrative.

When the text draws such attention to the despair its heroes produce, readers are asked to pay special attention to this particular moment of allegorical signification, and yet this episode has been largely ignored in studies of this book. Political history has been the privileged allegorical referent for all of book 5, and the small critical debate about this canto has centered not on the vividly Ovidian descriptions at play but on proving that the canto allegorizes the defeat of the Spanish Armada under Phillip II in 1588, about eight years before Spenser published the second installment of his poem.[27] The critics who have dealt with this canto have focused especially on the description of the Souldan's battle with Arthur, finding evidence to support a comparison between the tall, weapon-wielding chariots of the Souldan and the Spanish ships.[28] Richard Mallett provides strong support for such a historical reading, finding evidence in popular representations of the Armada's defeat that Spenser relied on contemporary commentary on that event.[29] In this reading, Arthur is a figure of divine intervention corresponding to the popular belief that the bad weather that forced the Armada to retreat was God's will, and the Souldan/Phillip is aligned with Antichrist.[30]

Although there is certainly evidence to suggest that at least in one sense the Souldan is indeed a figure representing Phillip II of Spain, there has been a surprising lack of attention to Adicia as a figure in this supposedly straightforward historical episode, and this has left the puzzle of Spenser's allegory partly unsolved. Phillip was unmarried at the time Spenser was writing his poem, so there is no obvious referent for Adicia as a historical figure. It is possible that she refers obliquely to Mary Tudor, who married Phillip and made him regent of England before Elizabeth's reign, but Phillip married after Mary's death, so the Souldan's consort could just as easily be another of his wives. Phillip also offered himself as a possible suitor to Elizabeth in the early decades of her reign, so Adicia could possibly be a demonic shadow of what Elizabeth might have been, but such a reading is strained by the fact that Elizabeth had spent about twenty years dallying with many other suitors before the writing of this poem. Adicia does indeed hold significance as a figure for a female ruler, but Spenser does not give strong suggestions that she is a contemporary historical woman, and this makes her figure more, not less, important for a reading of this part of the poem.

In addition to providing no satisfactory historical figure who might be Adicia's model, criticism of this canto has also rarely explored her significance in other terms. Those who do offer a reading of Adicia usually remark in passing that she must be an abstract idea, "the principle of injustice and lawlessness behind the Suldan,"[31] or as Gough puts it in the variorum edition of the poem, "the injustice to which the king of Spain was 'wedded,' and probably, in particular, the iniquitous government that he maintained."[32] Mallett's illuminating reading of the second half of book 5 nuances our understanding of the Souldan/ Phillip as a figure associated with Antichrist in postarmada apocalyptic rhetoric. Even he, however, does not question Adicia's representation and notes about this canto that "like other apocalyptic and patriotic polemic, the Souldan episode has little moral nuance, for the struggle is simply between right and wrong."[33] Other critics have been similarly dismissive. Sheila Cavanaugh, for instance, remarks that it is hard to take Adicia seriously when she is compared to an enraged cow.[34]

If Adicia's representation as Injustice conformed to widespread and culturally accepted iconography of Injustice, such a hasty reading of her significance might make sense, but in fact a quick survey of representations of Injustice reveals specific characteristics wholly missing from Adicia's description. In Cesare Ripa's *Iconologia*, for instance, which was published without illustrations in Rome in 1593, Ripa provides two different descriptions of this icon, both of which offer great possibilities for allegorical representation but have not found their way into Spenser's representation. Injustice is represented in both descriptions as a woman and in one as a "donna difforme" (a deformed woman). She is dressed in white, which is in the first case stained and in the other "sparta di sangue" (spattered with blood), signifying the stained moral figure of the unjust. In both cases she is blind in her right eye, seeing all things in an unbalanced way through her sinister left eye. She is also holding a sword in both, and the glosses tell us that this links her with civil violence. In her other hand she holds either a toad or a golden cup, both symbols of avarice, and she stands on a broken balance and "le tavole della legge rotte in pezzi" (legal tables broken in pieces), representing her destruction of the rules of law and perhaps reason.[35] As is clear from these descriptions, Spenser had some iconographical markers to choose from to represent Adicia, but they do not seem to have informed her characterization in any way. She is not, then, a simple or culturally stable allegorical figure; instead, she is an abstract allegory created before our eyes from a character through the process of Ovidian metamorphosis. The fact that Adicia is not clearly linked to a historical person does not make her a less historically relevant allegorical figure. Similarly, the fact that she is not an obvious icon of Injustice does not make her abstract allegorical status less culturally remarkable. In fact, as I hope this analysis has shown, she operates as a nexus for reading the various struggles of late Elizabethan culture over the authority and emotion of female rulers.

In addition, her metamorphosis, a performed transition from an allegorical figure into a daemon, comments in significant ways on the power of various kinds of allegorical signification and the way in which gender inflects that power. In only two instances in the poem does Spenser employ an Ovidian aesthetic to tell the tale of the metamorphosis of an expressly allegorical figure: once in book 3, when Malbecco is transformed in a fit of jealousy into an emblem of Jealousy itself, and once here in book 5, when Adicia is driven mad with anger and grief and becomes a tiger, a figure of Injustice. Malbecco's trajectory, from displaying his human emotion (excessive jealousy) to metamorphic resolution (allegorical jealousy), is particularly Ovidian; witness Narcissus, or a number of metamorphoses in Metamorphoses. Adicia's transformation, however, takes this Ovidian logic in a new direction, since her lack of agency is social rather than individual. Malbecco's story has been read as an allegory of the allegorical process itself, offering the reader an etiology of the allegorical figure of Jealousy.[36] It is significant, however, that when the figure involved is female, as Adicia is, the excessive emotion that brings about metamorphosis is an enraged grief, but her allegorical role is Injustice. Adicia is glossed by the narrator as "wrong, when it hath arm'd it selfe with might," but in fact it is Adicia's inability to take revenge, her inability to assume the might that is the provenance of only the masculine figures in this story that leads to her excessive rage and grief and then her metamorphosis.

By linking Adicia to Malbecco as two figures who become allegories as a result of excessive emotion, the poem signals that gender politics play a role in such allegorical abstraction. Whereas Malbecco's transformation occurs as the result of the impotence of his jealousy, Adicia's occurs as a response to her lack of agency in the action of the poem, and this locates the etiology of feminine allegory in political rather than personal failings. Just as Hecuba's suffering and grief are signs of the larger cultural loss of Troy, Adicia's forced exile from the poem acts as a sign of the consequences of the text's justice and heroic narrative. Adicia excessively responds to her husband's death because she cannot take revenge, but Spenser allows the rage of her figure discursive significance, and the image of her metamorphosis marks her as a subject no longer able to assert herself in the text. Her status as an allegorical abstraction calls attention to the fact that her figure must be excised from the poem's action, and this forces us to consider if this is the history of many or all feminized allegorical figures in the poem.

Through allusion to Hecuba's particular Ovidian narrative, Spenser draws into question the political role of powerful female figures and the allegorical process that reifies their emotional states. Canto 8 offers a commentary on the ways in which allegorical abstraction may sometimes be the consequence of excessive female emotion, a figurative response to the cultural threat such female emotion might engender. Although she moves from being a character who has agency in the fiction to being an abstraction roaming the woods of Faeryland, the loss of Adicia is explicitly noted by the poem. She becomes a specifically female figure for what must be sacrificed both in the political and cultural realms of heroic wars and in the literary world of heroic narrative. She also calls into question the nature of allegory itself, furnishing an example of the ways abstract allegorization of a female figure can diminish social agency while imbuing her with a symbolic power. Spenser's Ovidianism at this moment in the poem allows for a different kind of female agency, then: as a character, Adicia is shown to be powerless, constrained by her role in this constructed political world; as an allegorical abstraction, though, she gains significance and power outside the fiction, validating another kind of allegorical signification over narrative action.

Adicia's metamorphosis is the figurative equivalent of her escape out the back door in the fiction, and both are textual strategies that leave the reader aware of what has been excluded by the central systems of the poem. Adicia escapes out the postern door into the shady woods of Faeryland and haunts the action of the poem. There she join Cyparissus, Narcissus, Venus, and others in the world of Ovidian emotion that is a central but dangerous resource for representing power in the poem. Her Ovidian nature has erupted into action, but she returns to her intertextual location in Ovidianism, reminding readers of the possibilities for Ovidian moral and political critique and strategic ambiguity that the heroic Christian epic must memorialize and then exile.

CHAPTER 3

GRIEF AND THE OVIDIAN POLITICS
OF REVENGE IN *TITUS ANDRONICUS*

What's Hecuba to him, or he to Hecuba,
That he should weep for her?

—*Hamlet* II.ii.559–60[1]

As Spenser's use of Hecuba's story exemplifies, she is an important cultural figure for excessive female Ovidian emotion, and Hamlet asks the famous rhetorical question about her that stands as the epigraph to this chapter in an important moment of reflexivity on playwriting and the power of self-consciously imitated fictions to move audiences. Having just heard the player's dramatic adaptation of Aeneas' narration of the fall of Troy, Hamlet wonders out loud about how the player can produce such convincing affect, engendering a corollary emotional response in his audience. He asks himself,

Is it not monstrous that this player here,
But in a fiction, in a dream of passion,
Could force his soul so to his own conceit
That from her working all his visage wann'd,
Tears in his eyes, distraction in his aspect,
A broken voice, and his whole function suiting
With forms to his conceit? And all for nothing!
For Hecuba!
(II.ii.545–52)

As many critical readings of *Hamlet* have pointed out, Hamlet in this scene articulates a set of questions that are central to the mystery of theater, and especially Renaissance theater: what is the source of emotion as it is produced on the stage and transmitted to the audience? And more specifically, if the source is a classical tale or figure, why do the cultural productions of a previous (pagan) age create dramatically effective scenes, and why does this emotion matter to a Renaissance playgoer?

It is notable that Shakespeare indicates some ambiguity about the source of the player's emotional power (his soul is forced along with his "forms," more external qualities, to suit his conceit). Hamlet here expresses wonder as well as anxiety about the ability of actors from one period to represent emotional states from another. It is, in other words, the distance between the player in Hamlet's fictional-ized Danish court and Hecuba as a figure from the Troy story that troubles Hamlet's notions about how the emotion results in action. He seems especially concerned about the fact that those emotional expressions are the markers of the actor's assumption of a fictional character and are therefore the results of a "false" emotion, one not produced from the actor's lived experience. Hamlet chides himself for not being able to muster the necessary emotional intensity and attributes his inability to carry out his revenge to his own inadequate reserves of affect:

> What would he do
> Had he the motive and [the cue] for passion
> that I have? He would drown the stage with tears.
> (II.ii.540–42)

The answer to Hamlet's question about the connection between the player and Hecuba is not that they share some kind of transcendent human emotional state but that they are linked in a chain of imitation in which the player, Hamlet, and the audiences watching him are at only further imitative removes. This metatheatrical moment in *Hamlet* reveals an underlying interest in how a fiction, and specifically a self-consciously imitative fiction, can be powerful as the basis for emotional representation—a representation, Hamlet is quick to remind us, that may have serious and violent consequences. Hecuba's grief, inspiring grief in Aeneas and then an imitation of that grief in the player, seems for Hamlet to be the mysterious source of the agency for revenge.

Such interest in the power of Hecuba's grief to generate agency is played out in broader intertextual ways in Shakespeare's earliest revenge play, *Titus Andronicus*, where Ovid's, rather than Virgil's, version of Hecuba is one of the main classical figures alluded to in order to define the play's revenging characters. While Hamlet's play-ers are rehearsing a representation of Hecuba informed primarily by the Virgilian version of the fall of Troy, her figure in the period seems to be most associated with Ovid's retelling of her tale in *Metamorphoses*, where her grief and revenge are the central matter of the tale.[2] As I have outlined in the previous chapter, using Hecuba as the focal point of the actor's feigned sorrow is a culturally predictable choice; authors often refer to her in the period as the quintessential figure of grief and unjust suffering.[3] Hecuba serves as both a cultural symbol of mourning and grief and as a sign of Roman intertextuality, however, drawing attention to the representational power she gains as an imitation. She is also specifically cited, I would argue, because of her associations with Ovidian emotion. In *Titus*, her status as an Ovidian figure of extreme grief helps to define revenge in the play, and that grief is politicized, invested with all of the power and terror of revenge.

Titus Andronicus shares many similarities with *Hamlet*. They are both revenge plays—*Titus* a double one, involving Tamora and then Titus—and historically, critics have read *Titus* as Shakespeare's experiment with this popular genre before *Hamlet*.[4] In addition to being plays about individual responses to abuses of power, revenge plays are unique contexts for speculations about the self and agency, issues that are emphasized throughout *Metamorphoses*, partly because many revenge conventions use psychological suspense for dramatic effect. One of the defining elements of the revenge play is the period of delay during which the revenger must disguise, often through cunning language or by feigning madness, his motivations for revenge and therefore his emotional state. We see this behavior in *Titus* first in Tamora, who disguises her ambitions for revenge against the Andronici beginning in the first scene of the play. When Tamora uses her new position as Saturninus' wife to manipulate the people's favor by asking him to pardon Titus and his family, she speaks in the language of the dissembling revenger:

> On mine honor dare I undertake
> For good Lord Titus' innocence in all,
> Whose fury not dissembled speaks his griefs.
> Then at my suit look graciously on him;
> Lose not so noble a friend on vain suppose,
> Nor with sour looks afflict his gentle heart.
> [*Aside to Saturnine.*] My lord, be rul'd by me, be won at last,
> Dissemble all your griefs and discontents.
>   . . .
> Yield at entreats; and then let me alone,
> I'll find a day to massacre them all,
> And rase their faction and their family
> (I.i.432–43, 449–51)

In this passage, the villainous Tamora contrasts Titus' inability to conceal his grief with her own ability to do so, placing herself in the
position of agent of revenge. Titus spends most of the play in this situation, expressing the extremity of his suffering and thereby disallow-
ing his own agency. It is not until act 5 that we see Titus accomplish
his revenge by taking on the revenger's role when he feigns madness
in order to trap his enemies. The danger of Tamora's aside is, therefore, the danger that is obsessively central to the genre itself, which
highlights the fact that emotional states can be hidden while still pre-
cipitating acts of violence.

Titus generally has deep scholarly and humanistic investments.
Representing and examining the morality of classicism itself, it is a
play about Renaissance syncretism and intertextuality. Critics have
explored the many ways the play is an examination of the myths of
Rome and, some argue, their disintegration.[5] Although the play sets
up *Metamorphoses* as its most explicit and self-conscious source, its
"pattern" as Jonathan Bate rightly points out, it also draws from a
handful of other Roman texts, including most notably Virgil, Seneca,
Plutarch, and Livy, and may possibly have been based on an Italian
source now lost to us.[6] The play, in fact, interrogates the Renaissance
turn toward classical culture as the model for that most fundamental element of both character and the social self—emotion—and it
deploys a self-conscious Ovidianism to examine the relationship
between extreme emotional states and powerful action.[7]

In fact, because of its deep investments in Ovidianism, the play
notably feminizes agency, and especially female figures exist in relation to their models in the Ovidian tales structuring the play's action.
Lavinia, most explicitly, and Tamora as well, are defined in the play as
imitations of Ovid's Philomela and Hecuba, and perhaps most interestingly, Titus himself is also associated through allusion with these
tales. When Titus announces in the final bloody feast of the play that
"worse than Progne" (V.ii.195) he will take his revenge, he regenders
himself through allusion to Ovid's avenging sister in Philomela's tale.
In doing so, he aligns himself with the specifically Ovidian figures
who, from their feminized positions, comment on, lament over, and
eventually exceed their characterizations as impotent victims, often
committing acts of extreme political violence. While the story of
Philomela's rape in book 6 of *Metamorphoses* is familiar through its
many imitations in English literary history, in Ovid the focus of the
story is not actually the rape itself but the complex negotiations of
emotion the characters must experience to carry out violent acts:
rape, in the case of Tereus, and revenge, in the cases of Procne and

Philomela. The basic outline is familiar: Tereus, Philomela's brother-in-law, rapes her and cuts out her tongue to prevent her from revealing his crime to her sister. She circumvents his attempt to silence her by weaving the story into a tapestry, and the two sisters unite to take revenge on Tereus by serving him his son, Itys, at a bloody banquet. When the enraged Tereus chases the women, they are all three metamorphosed into birds. While the gruesome details of Philomela's rape are the most obvious borrowings from this tale in *Titus*, most of the narrative in *Metamorphoses* is devoted to how actions are accomplished under the duress of extreme emotion, and this concern underlies the representations in *Titus* in pervasive ways. It is not just Lavinia, in fact, who famously finds herself in Ovid's book when it is brought onto the stage in act 3, but Titus himself. The play wrestles with emotion through its connections with the excessive passions of Ovidian powerlessness and suffering, but it also explores the relationship between such a feminized position of impotence and the agency that seems to arise from this specific position to violently assert itself in the political act of revenge.[8]

Titus' most Ovidian representations cluster around Lavinia. Titus' only daughter, Lavinia is raped and mutilated by the sons of Tamora, the Goth queen whose extended revenge on the Andronici is the main matter of the play. In act 2, Marcus is the first of his family to discover his niece, "her hands cut off, and her tongue cut out, and ravish'd" (II.iv. stage direction) and conjecture that she is now a type of Philomela. At this moment of horror, Marcus produces a long rhetorical lament on her condition in which he sees and sarcastically admires the imitative work of the rapists Chiron and Demetrius. The hyperbolic rhetoric of this speech has made it a favorite of critics who accuse the play of insincerity in its representations of suffering. The allusions in the speech, however, are to Ovidian figures who are victims of violence, and the excess of its rhetoric figures the extremity of Marcus' shared grief and his attempt to understand it through the language of Ovidian intertextuality.

Marcus repeatedly in this speech encourages the audience to recognize and compare the play's Ovidian intertext to the action and thematic negotiations occurring on the stage. He exclaims, "But sure some Tereus hath deflowered thee / And, lest thou shouldst detect him, cut thy tongue" (II.iii.26), and

> Fair Philomela, why she but lost her tongue,
> And in a tedious sampler sewed her mind;
> But, lovely niece, that mean is cut from thee.

> A craftier Tereus, cousin, hast thou met,
> And he hath cut those pretty fingers off,
> That could have better sewed than Philomel.
> (II.iii.38–43)

In addition to insisting at this crucial moment that Lavinia is a type of Philomela, Marcus also alludes to other metamorphic figures, specifically Daphne, when he ironically urges Lavinia,

> Speak, gentle niece, what stern ungentle hands
> Hath lopped and hewed and made thy body bare
> Of her two branches, those sweet ornaments
> Whose circling shadows kings have longed to sleep in.
> (II.iii.16–19)

By comparing Lavinia's hands to branches, Marcus evokes the image of Daphne as she is metamorphosed to a tree to evade rape by Apollo.[9] This association of Lavinia, not just with Philomela but also with Daphne, makes her a figure for the many victims of rape in *Metamorphoses* and suggests the association of violence with metamorphosis that colors both of these narratives. Her grief, as read by her uncle at least, is paradigmatic of the female response to rape in Ovidianism.

In addition, Marcus alludes to two other Ovidian tales in this lament. First, he compares Lavinia's loss of blood to "a conduit with three issuing spouts" (II.iii.30), an image often mocked by detractors of the play. As Bate notes in his edition, this description echoes Golding's translation of Ovid's description of Pyramus' blood in the tale of Pyramus and Thisbe ("bloud did spin on hie / As when a Conduit pipe is crackt") in *Metamorphoses* 4. While this does seem a ludicrous way to describe the scene, and would be especially troubling with an actual, embodied Lavinia present on the stage, the excess of the description has the effect of heightening the horror rather than distancing the spectator through humor. It also links Lavinia to Pyramus, another unfortunate figure from *Metamorphoses*, in this case an ironic tragic victim. Finally, Marcus also compares Lavinia to Orpheus:

> O, had the monster seen those lily hands
> Tremble like aspen leaves upon a lute
> And make the silken strings delight to kiss them,
> He would not then have touched them for his life.
> Or had he heard the heavenly harmony
> Which that sweet tongue hath made,

> He would have dropped his knife and fell asleep,
> As Cerberus at the Thracian poet's feet.
> (II.iii.44–51).

Both in the image of her hands as aspen leaves and through the direct reference to Orpheus' charming of Cerberus in his descent to the underworld to retrieve Eurydice, Marcus associates Lavinia with Orpheus. Although Orpheus is a ubiquitous character in Greek and Roman mythology and literature, as I have outlined in previous chapters, he is an especially important figure in *Metamorphoses* because his grief is the impetus for the tale-telling of book 10. In the context of the Ovidianism of the play, he operates as an additional figure of Ovidian grief who helps explain Lavinia's and her uncle's experiences of suffering. That he is male suggests the ways the feminized grief over rape, associated with Philomela, is broadened by Marcus to include other kinds of tragedy and loss, as his own grief develops in response to the image of horror he is witnessing.

Marcus asserts that Lavinia is a type of Ovidian grief, and this speech expresses the play's central desire to represent the extreme suffering it has produced in its own characters. When Marcus finds Lavinia as Philomela, his first concern is that he cannot gain from her the name of her rapist to enable his revenge:

> Shall I speak for thee? Shall I say 'tis so?
> O, that I knew thy heart, and knew the beast,
> That I might rail at him to ease my mind.
> (II.iv.33–35)

His next concern, however, is notably Lavinia herself:

> Sorrow conceal'd, like an oven stopp'd,
> Doth burn the heart to cinders where it is . . .
>
> Do not draw back, for we will mourn with thee:
> O, could our mourning ease thy misery!
> (ll.36–37, 56–57)

Here Marcus worries about Lavinia's inability to express her sorrow, which operates as recognition of her interiorized emotions at the exact moment in which access to them has apparently been lost. The fact that Lavinia operates as such a visually shocking emblem of pain, however, makes Marcus' worry ironic, as her grief is being communicated most profoundly to the audience in this scene. The scene, in fact, highlights the link between bodily mutilation and assaults on the self. Marcus' catalogue of Ovidian figures attempts to read Lavinia in Ovidian terms, terms that highlight her interiorized state of distress, and therefore her potential for agency, even at this moment in which it seems most to be threatened by the violence of the play. What Marcus does in this long, rhetorical lament, therefore, is create through language a link between his own grief and Lavinia's, solidifying that empathetic bond through intertextual reference. It is not just violence, therefore, that these characters learn from their Ovidian educations and intertextuality, but where to find expressions of emotion and a possible response to violence and their own impotence.

Marcus' aphoristic statement about the dangers of unexpressed emotion serves another purpose, though, as it points to an understanding of grief as an interior state that can consume the self if not expressed. This commonplace notion of the threat of concealed grief is reinforced by the play's constant attention to the suffering of the Andronici, as they spend most of the time on the stage expressing their extreme grief and rage. Marcus' concern that Lavinia's sorrow, like Philomela's, will be concealed, turns out to be unfounded, as she manages to communicate with her father through less-conventional means: she kisses him and weeps with him when his sorrows mount, and she utilizes literature, the volume of Ovid's *Metamorphoses* on the stage, and a stick as a stylus between her stumps, to be more specific about the perpetrators of the crime against her person. The fact is, therefore, that Lavinia's sorrows are not concealed, just as Titus' are not until the final act of the play. She does operate in one sense, as many critics have argued, as an emblem of the injustice done to the family and perhaps the literalized metaphor of the rape of Roman civic virtue, but she also becomes an accessory to the Andronici revenge, just as her Ovidian type, Philomela, helps her sister Procne to punish Tereus.[10] She is more than a silenced victim.[11] Instead, she becomes an Ovidian agent of revenge who will fulfill her narrative trajectory as Philomela. As a figure, her interior suffering has been made external, her bleeding representing the suffering of the whole Andronici clan, and it is this horror that eventually inspires in Titus the specific breed of agency that is needed for revenge.[12]

While Marcus begins to define Lavinia in Ovidian terms when he finds her wandering after her rape, Lavinia herself is the greatest claimant for her participation in the play as an Ovidian revenger. In the famous moment I described to begin the introduction to this book, Lavinia searches for her own story in a volume of Ovid's *Metamorphoses* actually opened on the stage. Lavinia enters, mute and mutilated, chasing her nephew until he drops his schoolbooks and she frantically searches them:

Titus: How now, Lavinia? Marcus, what means this?
Some book there is that she desires to see.
Which is it, girl, of these? Open them, boy.
[*to Lavinia*]
But thou art deeper read and better skilled:
Come and take choice of all my library,
And so beguile thy sorrow till the heavens
Reveal the damned contriver of this deed.
Why lifts she up her arms in sequence thus?

Marcus: I think she means that there were more than one
Confederate in the fact. Ay, more there was—
Or else to heaven she heaves them for revenge.
(IV.i.30–40)

This scene opens as a moment of miscommunication, and of a very specific kind. Lavinia's father and her uncle at first cannot understand her actions, which place importance on the written text lying on the stage before her. Titus tries to instruct Lavinia about literature's place in social life—that it can entertain her, or distract her from the "real" sorrows occurring around her—but literature in this play, and especially Ovid's poetry, does not function in the way Titus describes. On the contrary, characters, plot, and imagery are self-consciously defined by classical fictions, and the characters seem strangely and horrifyingly aware of this.[13] Marcus has already guessed when he finds her in the woods that she is another Philomela, and it is not just her family who recognize Lavinia's implication in an imitated narrative; Aaron, the plotter of the rape, tells Tamora before the fact that Bassianus' "Philomel must lose her tongue today" (II.i.43), darkly foreshadowing the actual activities of the rape itself. Chiron and Demetrius also allude to the tale when they depart after her rape, as Demetrius mocks her with,

So, now go tell, and if thy tongue can speak,
Who 'twas that cut thy tongue and ravished thee.
(II.iii.1–2)

Although audience response to this scene must be dictated by how the physical prop of the book is constructed and used—whether it is labeled, how clearly it is *Metamorphoses*—when Lavinia pages through this book, dramatic irony produces the effect that places Lavinia in the powerful position as demonstrator of the play's dependence on the transmission of texts, and Titus appears to be spouting a useless and escapist aesthetic theory.

Titus' desire, however, that Lavinia retire from her sorrows to the solace of his larger library betrays another fantasy on the part of the play—that Lavinia may sooth her sorrows passively until the heavens dispense justice to the Andronici clan. This is the fundamental wish behind both Titus' and Marcus' response to Lavinia in her frenzy, and this desire becomes more clearly gendered when their second guess at Lavinia's behavior is that it is an expression of some kind of female sympathy:

> *Titus*: Lucius, what book is that she tosseth so?
>
> *Boy*: Grandsire, 'tis Ovid's *Metamorphosis*;
> My mother gave it me.
>
> *Marcus*:   For love of her that's gone,
> Perhaps she culled it from among the rest.
> (IV.i.41–44)

Again, the male Andronici are victims of the play's penetrating irony, misreading her behavior but raising the question of Lucius' absent mother and Lavinia's gendered allegiances.[14] Rather than reading Lavinia as engaged in an active behavior facilitating revenge for the Andronici, Marcus assumes she is expressing love, and presumably grief over the lack of a female community to grieve with her. Marcus firmly genders her activities, implying that expressing womanly affection must be her understood role in the family.

After such inarticulate delay, however, the revelation that Lavinia has found her own story in Ovid's *Metamorphoses* on the stage is accompanied by a recognition that they are all being written into Ovid's tale. Marcus, perhaps because he has already associated her grief with Philomela's in act 2, seems to be the first to notice the similarity between her story and Ovid's:

> *Titus*: Soft, so busily she turns the leaves!   *Helps her.*
> What would she find? Lavinia, shall I read?
> This is the tragic tale of Philomel,
> And treats of Tereus' treason and his rape—
> And rape, I fear, was root of thy annoy.
>
> *Marcus*: See, brother, see: note how she quotes the leaves.

> *Titus*: Lavinia, wert thou thus surprised, sweet girl,
> Ravished and wronged as Philomela was,
> Forced in the ruthless, vast and gloomy woods?
> (IV.i.45–53)

"Quotes," as Bates points out in his notes to his edition, can be more generally "observes," but preserves the specific sense of citing a particular passage of literature. The use of the word here suggests that this recognition has broader significance as a revelation about the nature of characterization in general in the play. Lavinia can "quote" her own identity in the play, but the recognition is not only hers, but the male characters'. What they see is their own implication in the literary narratives constructing the entire action of the play. In fact, Titus deplores the fictional setting in which this event took place:

> Ay, such a place there is where we did hunt—
> O, had we never, never hunted there!—
> Patterned by that the poet here describes,
> By nature made for murders and for rapes.
> (IV.i.55–58)

The setting for their destruction is "patterned" after Ovid. While it is possible to read Titus' concern as about his own inability to have learned from his reading to avoid shady woods, because Lavinia has just revealed her intertextual double, these lines are more clearly a moment in which Shakespeare stages his characters' own awareness that they are characters and that they are being constructed through intertextual means. This moment, therefore, is not just one of recognition for Lavinia, but instead extends this growing awareness to the other characters, including the male characters, who may not be the victims of rape but are the impotent victims of Tamora's and Aaron's own imitative and violent machinations.

In *Metamorphoses*, Philomela's tale actually begins with an examination of a different kind of extreme emotion, that of a highly masculinized passion or desire. Tereus must go to great lengths in order to conceal his desire for Philomela to accomplish his evil intentions:

> non secus exarsit conspecta virgine Tereus,
> quam si quis canis ignem supponat aristis
> aut frondem positasque cremet faenilibus herbas.

. . .

et nihil est, quod non effreno captus amore
ausit, nec capiunt inclusas pectora flammas.
iamque moras male fert cupidoque revertitur ore
ad mandata Procnes et agit sue vota sub illa.
facundum faciebat amor, quotiensque rogabat
ulterius iusto, Procnen ita velle ferebat.
addidit et lacrimas, tamquam mandasset et illas.
pro superi, quantum mortalia pectora caecae
noctis habent!

[The moment he saw the maiden Tereus was inflamed with love, quick
as if one should set fire to ripe grain, or dry leaves, or hay stored away
in the mow . . . There was nothing which he would not do or dare,
smitten by this mad passion. His heart could scarce contain the fires
that burnt in it. Now, impatient of delay, he eagerly repeated Procne's
request, pleading his own cause under her name. Love made him elo-
quent, and as often as he asked more urgently than he should, he would
say that Procne wished it so. He even added tears to his entreaties, as
though she had bidden him to do this too. Ye gods, what blind night
rules in the hearts of men!] (VI.455–57, 465–73)

The evil of Tereus' actions is related to the fact that he can so well
conceal his lust, and this aspect of the story is even more pointedly
represented in Golding's version of the same passage. In his translation he stresses,

There was not under heaven the thing but that he durst it prove,
So far unable was he now to stay his lawlesse love.
Delay was deadly: backe again with greedie minde he came,
Of *Prognes* errands for to talke: and underneath the same
He works his owne ungraciousnesse . . .
O God, what blindnesse doth the heartes of mortal men disguise?
(Golding, Met. VI.595–600, 603)

Although both of these translations, the modern one by Frank Justus
Miller and Golding's, emphasize Tereus' lack of control once he has
been inflamed with lust, Golding's translation betrays more anxiety
about the fact that Tereus can conceal this internal state even though
his passion is so extreme. He stresses that "underneath" Tereus' talk,
he "works his owne ungraciousnesse." He also makes the last line
more specifically about the way the heart, a strange concealing agent,
can disguise the blindness of men. We are left not knowing whether

the heart disguises its blindness from itself, somehow allowing Tereus to misrecognize his evil nature, or whether the heart disguises Tereus' moral blindness from others. Golding's narrator, therefore, takes what might be translated as a generalized comment on the darkness within human hearts and makes it a specific darkness in men like Tereus, who, in whatever way they can, disguise their blindness. The Renaissance translation betrays through this ambiguity a greater anxiety about internal emotional states that can be concealed to accomplish violence.

Tereus' violence, however, is matched by the violent revenge the two sisters enact at the end of Ovid's narrative, and the revenge itself cannot take place unless Procne conceals her rage to trap her husband into eating his own child at their hands. When she receives her sister's tapestry and reads of her husband's horrific betrayal, Procne becomes mute, like her sister:

> evolvit vestes saevi matrona tyranni
> germanaeque suae fatum miserabile legit
> et (mirum potuisse) silet: dolor ora repressit,
> verbaque quaerenti satis indignantia linguae
> defuerunt, nec flere vacat, sed fasque nefasque
> confusura ruit poenaeque in imagine tota est.

> [The savage tyrant's wife unrolls the cloth, reads the pitiable fate of her sister, and (a miracle that she could!) says not a word. Grief chokes the words that rise to her lips, and her questing tongue can find no words strong enough to express her outraged feelings. Here is no room for tears, but she hurries on to confound right and wrong, her whole soul bent on the thought of vengeance.] (VI.581–86)

Tereus is here referred to as a tyrant, associating him not just with private, but with political misdeeds, which reinforces the sense that he represents a larger social or political order in which his victims are seemingly powerless. Revenge, however, the narrator implies, is why there is "no room for tears" in Procne's experience of grief, and the action she takes confuses the morality of the story, making right and wrong less obvious when she commits horrific violence herself. Her concealment of her grief and rage enables Procne's revenge, just as concealing lust enabled Tereus' rape, and although the narrator generates considerable sympathy for Procne's suffering, her deeds are judged by the rhetoric of the poem to be wrong from the moment she conceives them in mute grief.

Ovid's description of the way grief initially turns Procne to silence is remarkably similar to the way Hecuba is described much later in *Metamorphoses*. When Hecuba finds that her last surviving son has been murdered by Polymnestor, the Thracian king entrusted with preserving him from the dangers of the Trojan war, she too experiences a grief that is too intense to be expressed and that leads her to a particularly gruesome revenge, as she gouges out the traitor's eyes:

> adspicit eiectum Polydori in litore corpus
> factaque Threiciis ingentia vulnera telis;
> Troades exclamant, obmutuit illa dolore,
> et pariter vocem lacrimasque introrsus obortas
> devorat ipse dolor, duroque simillima saxo
> torpet et adversa figit modo lumina terra,
> interdum torvos sustollit ad aethera vultus,
> nunc positi spectat vultum, nunc vulnera nati,
> vulner praecipue, seque armat at instruit ira.
> qua simul exarsit, tamquam regina maneret,
> ulcisci statuit poenaeque in imagine tota est . . .

[There she saw the body of Polydorus, cast up upon the shore, covered with gaping wounds made by Thracian spears. The Trojan women shrieked at the sight; but she was dumb with grief; her very grief engulfed her powers of speech, her rising tears. Like a hard rock immovable she stood, now held her gaze fixed upon the ground, and at times lifted her awful face to the heavens; now she gazed upon the features of her son as he lay there in death, now on his wounds, but mostly on his wounds, arming herself with ever-mounting rage. When now her rage blazed out, as if she still were queen, she fixed on vengeance and was wholly absorbed in the punishment her imagination pictured.] (XIII.536–46)

Although it is not clear from the translations, the last phrase of both of these descriptions is the same: "poenaeque in imagine tota est," which might be more literally translated, "she is completely in the image of the punishment."[15] The repetition of this expression in both narratives indicates its formulaic status and suggests that it is an attempt to represent the ambiguous interior state that enables violence. In both cases, the revenger's silence is constructed as a necessary state for the accomplishment of her revenge, both literally, because she must hide her grief and rage until she has trapped her victim, and figuratively, because the conception of that revenge takes over her entire interior life, making communication impossible. Golding's translations of the two narratives, in fact, stress the impossibility of expressing grief and rage as great as those suffered by the revengers. He tells us that Procne

> held hir peace (a wonderous thing it is she should doe)
> But sorrow tide her tongue, and wordes agreeable unto
> Hir great displeasure were not at commaundment at that stound,
> and weep she could not.
> (Golding, VI. ll.742–45)

Hecuba, similarly,

> was dumb for sorrow.
> The anguish of her hart forclosde as well her speech as eeke
> Her teares devowring them within.
> (Golding, XIII. ll.644–46)

In both narratives, Golding highlights most clearly the inability of his female characters to speak or weep once their interior states are wholly devoted to picturing revenge. Paradoxically, therefore, reaching this point of extreme passion, the female figures are granted the ability to conceal it, and through their silence they can revenge.

These Ovidian tales, therefore, outline a specific theory of the relationship between an excessive feminized emotion and possibilities for individual agency. Before their final metamorphoses, these figures from Ovid's poem express the extremity of their suffering through highly rhetoricized lament, and at the moment in which their imaginations can picture nothing but revenge they accomplish these acts of excessive violence. Titus, as the revenger of Shakespeare's play, follows an analogous trajectory. The play's Ovidianism, therefore, goes much deeper than previous criticism has recognized, because Ovid's text models how subjects can seize agency in moments of extreme grief. When Titus is pushed to the limits of human suffering, he joins Hecuba and Philomela in the feminized role of the impotent victim who is transformed through a mysteriously internal process into a revenger.

Both Tamora and Lavinia are also defined as descendents of Hecuba. Tamora, however, while initially associated through allusion with Hecuba, becomes the antitype to the sympathetic female grief Hecuba symbolizes. In the opening scene of the play, when Titus orders Alarbus' sacrificial death against the pleas of his mother, Tamora's son, Demetrius, suggests that she, like Ovid's Hecuba, may find opportunity for her own revenge:

> The self-same gods that arm'd the Queen of Troy
> With opportunity of sharp revenge
> Upon the Thracian tyrant in his tent
> May favor Tamora, the Queen of Goths
> (When Goths were Goths and Tamora was queen),
> To quit the bloody wrongs upon her foes.
> (I.i.130–41)

From this first scene, therefore, Tamora is associated with Hecuba, a famous Ovidian revenge figure and a queen, and this initial comparison generates sympathy for her plight, a sympathy that will be mocked by her progressively gruesome behavior in the play.[16] Demetrius announces in this way that Tamora may pattern her behavior on that of Hecuba, but at the same time he suggests that her grief is equal to her Ovidian model. Her emotional state is therefore constructed by her source, setting a precedent for the way emotion will function as something distinctly Ovidian throughout the play.

Although Hecuba is suggested as a model for Tamora at this early point in the play, it is Lavinia who is linked with Hecuba by act 3, when her nephew runs from her, believing her to be mad and therefore in the role of violent revenger:

> *Marc.* Canst thou not guess wherefore she plies thee thus?

> *Boy.* My lord, I know not, I, nor can guess,
> Unless some fit or frenzy do possess her;
> For I have heard my grandsire say full oft,
> Extremity of griefs would make men mad;
> And I have read that Hecuba of Troy
> Ran mad for sorrow. That made me to fear,
> Although, my lord, I know my noble aunt
> Loves me as dear as e'er my mother did.
> (IV.i.15–23).

Lavinia's sorrow, the boy worries, may turn her into another Hecuba, so she, like Tamora, might assume the role of violent revenger like her Ovidian model. The boy has learned from his grandfather, Titus, that extreme grief can lead to violent madness, but his ultimate authority is this Ovidian story, and it is more powerful than the characterization of Lavinia as a nurturing mother figure. She is instead, according to this well-read child, a potentially destructive revenger.

These two allusions to Ovid's Hecuba are especially interesting because they point to two different ways to read this particular Ovidian narrative and suggest the ways *Titus* explores the morality of revenge through Ovidianism. Tamora's son, Demetrius, reads Hecuba's tale as a tale of revenge successfully accomplished. For him the narrative is a model of how to seize an opportunity for power. For Marcus and the younger Lucius, however, the tale is about the madness brought on by extreme grief. For the boy, at least, the possibility that Lavinia might become the revenger is threatening because it means she might be violent and this violence might be indiscriminate. These two Ovidian allusions, read by the male characters from such different perspectives, also point to the dialectical nature of Shakespeare's engagement with this tale in Ovid as well as with the form and ethics of the revenge play. When he alludes to Hecuba, he raises the entire problem of how extreme female emotion might be understood, and by associating both Tamora and Lavinia with the same Ovidian figure of sorrow, he makes clear that Hecuba's grief is also caused by impotence in the face of extreme political circumstances for despair. Ovidian emotion is the generative source of agency, whether it is positively or negatively valued.

Reading Titus' revenge in the context of the play's Ovidianism, finally, it becomes evident that Titus' response to his own impotence in Rome is very like Hecuba's and finally like Procne's. Like Hecuba, he spends most of the play lamenting his losses until in the final moments he takes his revenge. Marcus' repeated worry for Titus, expressed in many of his speeches in the middle acts of the play, is that the excess of his grief might lead to actual madness or death, but although the Andronici voice concerns over the excesses of their expressions of grief, they continue to try new metaphors and modes for expressing it. Titus seems during the scene in which he laments the death of the fly (III.ii) to have gone mad with sorrow, and his family is even more concerned when he decides to shoot arrows to the gods and dig to the underworld in search of justice (IV.iii). Although Marcus asks Titus to control his laments with reason, he participates in the unreasonable and highly wrought behavior of the Andronici right up until the revenge.

Before their revenge is finally accomplished in the last act of the play, therefore, Titus and the Andronici do not conceal their motivations for revenge, but rather enact their extreme grief like many Hecubas on the stage. The play, in fact, investigates how Titus responds to the ghastly wrongs he suffers, and we hear concerns over his ability to survive such affective shocks voiced by Marcus, the character most associated with reasonable and sometimes stoic civic discourse throughout the play:

> *Marc.* O brother, speak with possibility,
> And do not break into these deep extremes.
>
> *Tit.* Is not my sorrow deep, having no bottom?
> Then be my passions bottomless with them!
>
> *Marc.* But yet let reason govern thy lament.
>
> *Tit.* If there were reason for these miseries,
> Then into limits could I bind my woes.
>   (III.i.214–20)

Titus' emotion, because it finds expression in lament on the stage, does not allow for revenge, which, as we have seen in the Ovidian intertext, occurs when grief and rage rise to a level in which they are transformed to the internal picture of revenge.

It is not until act 5, when Titus convinces Tamora that he is mad (she wants to be convinced, as she is disguised as Revenge), that he manipulates his enemies into a position in which he can reciprocate the violence committed against himself and his family. Shakespeare, however, does not represent revenge as the ultimate expression of grief and rage, which in many ways it is in the Ovidian intertext. Rather, having exhausted every means for expressing human suffering, the play represents revenge as the anticlimactic suicide of the revenger. Instead of ending with an Ovidian metamorphosis, which is at least a partial escape from the horror of the situation, *Titus* ends with the bloody banquet, and whatever redemptive force the play achieves is ambiguously consolidated in Lucius, a character who, although he assembles the enemy troops for his own version of revenge, might restore order to Rome. In his final act of violence, Titus marshals Lavinia and becomes the agent for revenge; he tells Chiron and Demetrius,

> This is the feast that I have bid [Tamora] to,
> And this the banket she shall surfeit on,
> For worse than Philomel you us'd my daughter,
> And worse than Progne I will be reveng'd.
>   (V.ii.192–95)

Titus, rather than either Tamora or Lavinia, becomes the revenger condoned by the play, not only because he tells us that his revenge will be "worse" than Procne's, but because he successfully learns that expressions of emotion make revenge impossible. As a character upon whom Shakespeare has piled outrage upon outrage, testing the limits of human suffering, Titus finally learns violence from his female Ovidian models. The difference, however, is that Titus' impotence is a temporary condition of his political situation in Rome, whereas female Ovidian revengers commit acts of violence in the face of more pervasive and permanent social inequalities. Titus tells us that his revenge will be "worse," outdoing his intertextual sources, but in terms of the play's validation of that revenge, it is clearly better. Accomplishing his revenge qua suicide (since he must know killing Tamora will lead to his own death) with Lavinia as an accessory, he restores order to Rome by murdering Tamora and Lavinia, the models of female revenge his own character replaces and exceeds. The Ovidian violence that the play implies may lie within both Tamora and Lavinia is rewritten finally as male. The final image of Tamora's body thrown outside the city walls might serve as an emblem for the way the play has sacrificed the Ovidian gender politics that associated violent action with female figures to a patriarchal order in which a male revenger learns to conceal affect to accomplish revenge. In the end, a masculine revenge is "worse" (meaning better) than Ovid's feminine version, and Philomela's and Hecuba's more gendered griefs about social and political impotence are conspicuously left outside Rome's walls.

Lavinia, however, the other feminine revenger in the play, is quietly buried in the family vault. Shakespeare's Ovidianism in this play raises the possibility that agency, defined as a consequence of the subsuming of emotion, might be the provenance of female characters, allowing the male characters to spend most of the play expressing emotion in extreme and various ways. In this way, the play draws attention to its own exclusions. It also radicalizes its own gender politics by making Titus assume a feminized role—implying that it is impotence in general that is the problem, rather than an explicitly female disenfranchisement.[17] The thematic use of female voices and perspectives in Ovid's *Metamorphoses* to critique from the outside oppressive political systems is embodied in Shakespeare's female characters, and their gendered emotion is a strong threat to the social order and must be excised from the play once Titus can assume this feminized role. While the female characters are killed off at the end of the play, the feminine is not, as it is claimed by Titus as the gender of grief and revenge.

Given that this play was written to be performed, it is difficult not to notice the self-consciousness that such intertextuality produces about the highly wrought behavior of actors on the stage. The extreme and obviously fictional representations of emotion that these actors must enact, and the dissembling that the play depends upon, when set in suspended opposition with these stories that link heightened affect and its concealment with violence, look more and more constructed and more and more threatening. Rather than creating a stylized formality that distances the audience from the characters and does not allow sympathy for their plights (which is how some critics read the play's atmosphere), the Ovidianism of *Titus* suggests that this emotional dissembling itself is a dangerous kind of concealment. It may have the power both to move the audience and accomplish violence. Like Hamlet, Shakespeare's Ovidian play worries out loud about how its players can represent imitated affective states and, more frighteningly, how they can conceal their "true" (rather than fictional) emotion to act their roles. Hecuba and Philomela are to the play the signs of both emotion's power and its danger, and Shakespeare's Ovidianism in the socially powerful theater operates as a commentary on the link between excessive female emotion and a potentially powerful political violence.

CHAPTER 4

OVIDIAN WITCHES IN REGINALD SCOT'S *DISCOVERIE OF WITCHCRAFT*

I have put twenty of these witchmongers to silence with this one question; to wit, whether a witch that can turn a woman into a cat, etc., can also turn a cat into a woman?

—Scot, *Discoverie of Witchcraft* 5.10

Reginald Scot was probably the first English writer to use the term "witchmonger."[1] He used it, in fact, in the title of his work, *The discouerie of witchcraft, Wherein the lewde dealing of witches and witchmongers is notablie detected* (henceforth *Discoverie of Witchcraft*). This neologism suggests the critical heart of his project. He is a skeptic, and he is responding to what he sees as the *selling* of witchcraft by Continental demonologists. Through his often sarcastic and emotive rhetoric, he fashions himself as engaged in an exasperating power struggle with authorities whose motivations are both mysterious and suspect. He is explicitly interested in discovering, or uncovering, the reasons for the witchcraft trials and accusations that circulated around him when he produced his treatise in 1584. The late Elizabethan period, in addition to producing the intensely Ovidian literary works analyzed in previous chapters, also produced this first sustained demonological tract in English, and the simultaneously increased publication of and interest in Ovidian literary texts and demonological writings in England occurred because these two distinct areas of representation were negotiating similar cultural interests. Both Ovidian works and works of demonology explicitly address the fear of the instability of the (usually female) body through figurations or analyses of metamorphosis, both share an interest in the passions of female figures, and both are particularly invested in launching challenges to authority, whether that authority is, in literature, a tradition such as epic or the moral imperatives of heroic literature that accompany it or, in writings on witchcraft, the judicial, academic, or religious authorities perceived to be responsible for dealing with witches. In addition to influencing conceptualizations of metamorphosis throughout the treatise, Ovid's *Metamorphoses* was also instrumental in perpetuating the literary type of the witch—mainly through the figure of Medea—and in that sense this translated classical text directly influenced the constructions of English witches and their fates at the hands of religious and secular authorities.

This construction of the metamorphic witch, however, was never a matter of simple imitation or citation, but was instead the result of a complex intertextual negotiation with the authority of Ovid's literary representations. Ovid's texts are cited in Scot's writings on witchcraft as both what we would consider factual representations of experience and fictional literary imaginings or "feigning," and this is not solely due to the fact that, as a number of scholars have revealed, fact and fiction were not fully recognizable categories in Elizabethan England and were indeed invented over the course of the seventeenth century.[2] Elizabeth Spiller, for example, analyses the ways in which writers and thinkers of the period describe science writing and literary writing as similar acts of "making." Her observations are particularly relevant to writings on witchcraft, although they are further complicated by the claims to fact inherent in the theological and legal discourses that inform these debates.[3] Writings on witchcraft draw upon a number of disciplinary ideas about what is truth—from theology, law, natural philosophy, and science, to name a few—and they participate in the early modern period's reassessment and refiguration of claims of proof and probability.[4] In this context, Ovid's *Metamorphoses* plays a fundamental role both in establishing and in undercutting the truth claims of stories about witches and their emotions.

This chapter will chart Ovid's presence in Reginald Scot's *Discoverie of Witchcraft*, and it will address how this work negotiated the politics of witchcraft in the period, both demonizing and suggesting sympathy for the excessively emotive contemporary witches being constructed as Ovidian figures. Although some excellent scholarly work has been done documenting Ovid's influence on the literary and artistic productions of Renaissance England, considering the roles Ovid's works play in nonliterary as well as imaginative texts gives us a fuller picture of English Renaissance intellectual and social life and helps us avoid the dangers of misreading early modern culture by encountering it only through one representational or cultural lens. While it is true that literary texts always have effects on social and cultural experience, it is rare to be able to trace the way literary constructions—in this case Ovid's metamorphic figures—influence a text that so self-consciously intervenes in social experience. In the highly charged gender context of the male-authored witchcraft debates, allusions to Ovid's texts facilitate imaginative challenges to patriarchal social evaluations of female emotion and the female body. Scot translates Ovid's text into his own and in doing so he negotiates more broadly with the transgressive, excessively emotive figures of metamorphosis that make up Ovid's poem.

There is an overall consensus among scholars that the witchcraft debates and prosecutions were in some way related to cultural fantasies about actual women, although there is still much disagreement about whose fantasies they were and what were their origins.[5] While the practice of witchcraft was made a felony early in Elizabeth's reign in the witchcraft statute of 1563, it was rarely prosecuted and was not accompanied until this later period by what James Sharpe calls "a comprehensive model of satanic witchcraft" constructed by English writers in dialogue with Continental ones in a rash of demonological tracts.[6] By a century later, witchcraft prosecutions had for the most part ended in England, although widespread belief in witchcraft probably continued into the eighteenth century, and in fact beyond and into the present day.[7] What is crucially at stake in most representations of witchcraft in England is anxiety about female anger or jealousy— the kinds of emotions that are excessive enough to incite revenge. Fictional witches in plays like Thomas Middleton's *The Witch* (1613–15) and Ford, Dekker, and Rowley's *The Witch of Edmonton* (1621), for example, are partially modeled on revenge figures with roots in the revenge plays that dominated the English stage at this time. So this is yet another cultural and textual context in which Ovidianism serves to construct and evaluate certain kinds of emotional experience, this time in particularly threatening and embodied female figures.

Reginald Scot's *Discoverie of Witchcraft*, in addition to being the first English demonological text, was also one of only a few strongly skeptical treatises on the power of witches.[8] Stuart Clark, in fact, in *Thinking with Demons*, singles out Scot's treatise as the most famous and most radical skeptical tract of its time, while Sydney Anglo calls Scot an "intellectual iconoclast" because he so thoroughly disbelieves in both devilish and godly supernatural occurrences.[9] Scot's text is fundamentally antiauthoritarian in relation to a number of intellectual traditions, not just other witchcraft treatises, and it shares this characteristic with the most referenced classical author in the treatise—Ovid.

Primary among other poets, Ovid occupies a particularly ambiguous position as an authority in Scot's treatise. Citations from the

Ovidian corpus, usually in Latin with a translation by Abraham Fleming, are repeatedly showcased as examples of the absurdity and untruth of metamorphosis and at the same time as authoritative texts on witches and their behavior. Scot's skepticism about witchcraft, therefore, is matched by a marked skepticism about classical works as records of lived experience. This doubt is cast most vehemently toward *Metamorphoses*. The ambivalence about Ovid's metamorphic figures in the *Discoverie* reveals a larger cultural anxiety about the challenges to patriarchal structures of authority inherent in Ovid's poem, since it represents and values a feminized response to violence and other forms of oppression that complicates the emphasis on reason that is essential to Scot's skepticism. The metamorphic transgressions of the body accomplished by both Ovidian figures and witches, as well as their highlighted emotional states of grief and rage, represent for Scot, and presumably for others, a kind of antiauthoritarian power that is originally theorized in Ovid's epic poem. Ovid's representations contribute, in other words, to the threatening construction of witches as outsiders and powerful threats to civil, judicial, and even natural authority.

Of course, both Ovidianism and English demonism were not natively English but were responding to movements and debates already growing on the Continent. Scot's work is enmeshed in Continental debates from the previous century and relates witchcraft trials in England to movements across Europe. *The Discoverie* engages energetically with Continental writers on witchcraft, especially Jean Bodin and the Catholic inquisitors Jacob Sprenger and Heinrich Kramer. Scot's central argument is that the witches being burned on the Continent and occasionally in English villages are victims of social rather than devilish forces:

> One sort of such as are said to be witches, are women which be commonly old, lame, bleare-eyed, pale, foul, and full of wrinkles; poor, sullen, superstitious, and papists; or such as know no religion; in whose drowsy minds the devil hath gotten a fine seat; so as, what mischief, mischance, calamity, or slaughter is brought to pass, they are easily persuaded the same is done by themselves; imprinting in their minds an earnest and constant imagination thereof. . . . These miserable wretches are so odious unto all their neighbors, and so feared, as few dare offend them, or deny them any thing they ask: whereby they take upon them; yea, and sometimes think, that they can do such things as are beyond the abilities of human nature. (*Discoverie* 1.3)[10]

Outraged by what he sees as blasphemous beliefs in extrabiblical occurrences and powers, Scot is one of the first writers on witchcraft to articulate a view that has dominated witchcraft scholarship into the present day: that witches are silly old women who are victims of their own and their neighbors' errors. As Diane Purkiss has pointed out, Scot's skeptical answer to the problem of witchcraft assumes no power for those women accused, even within the domestic and local spheres.[11] Scot does, however, express apparently genuine concern that these women are being prosecuted, tortured, and killed and that Protestants are engaged in what he considers an ungodly enterprise of witch hunting. His moral and theological outrage is insistently high-lighted in his rhetoric and leads him to write a treatise that mocks the demonizers, sarcastically debunking every accusation and description of witchcraft that has authority in his period. His special targets are Sprenger and Kramer's *Malleus maleficarum* (1486) and Bodin's *De la démonomanie des sorciers* (1580), but he also rails generally against Catholics for their beliefs in what he characterizes as magic, other writers on witchcraft, and, most interestingly, poets. Even granting the point made by some recent scholars of witchcraft that the tracts of the demonologists and those of their skeptics are not so radically differ-ent as was previously assumed (the demonologists share a great deal of skepticism about their topic, and the skeptics often painstakingly rein-scribe an overall belief in spirits and demons), Scot's work is especially rich as a protoanthropological account of beliefs about witchcraft, even if not of real practices.[12] It is also a record of how Ovid's *Metamorphoses* operated outside the realm of literary writings, providing some of the fundamental stereotypical images of witches in the period and offer-ing examples of metamorphic figures to support or refute claims that witches could produce and govern metamorphic transformations.

The published treatise opens by visually announcing in its first his-toriated initial (Figure 4.1) its connection to *Metamorphoses*.[13] This woodcut has most likely been reused from an edition of *Metamorpho-ses*, which would link the book paratextually to Ovid's work even if Ovid did not become one of the central authorities on magical trans-formations in the text itself.[14] There are only two other historiated ini-tials in this edition, and they are both identical depictions of a naked hero (most likely Ulysses or Aeneas) riding the waves with a sea god nearby (Figure 4.2). These two ornamental initials begin the preface to the readers and the treatise itself on page 1, both "T"s. Although they are most likely alluding to the traditional figure of the ship as a metaphor for narrative progression and the circulation of the text, the scene also suggests metamorphic myths, as sea gods are particularly likely to be shape-shifters in *Metamorphoses* and most classical litera-ture. In fact, the illustration may invoke the tale of Glaucus, a sea god,

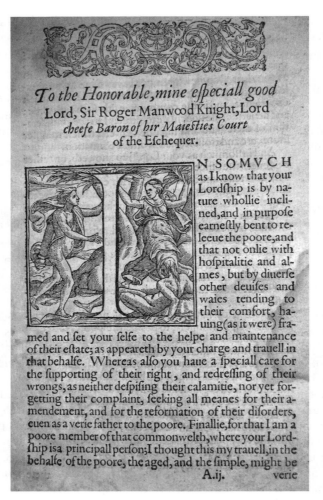

Figure 4.1.   Reginald Scot, *The Discoverie of Witchcraft: wherin the lewde dealing of witches and wotchmongers is notablie detected* . . . William Brome (Henry Denham), 1584. With special thanks to the Masters and Fellows of St. Catharine's College, Cambridge.

and Scylla from books 13 and 14 of *Metamorphoses* (and elsewhere). In this tale of magical transformations that is told during the narration of Aeneas' voyage, Glaucus goes to the witch Circe to look for love charms to seduce Scylla. Circe instead wants Glaucus for herself and uses her magical herbs to turn her competitor, Scylla, into her more familiar form as the metamorphic monster of Homer's *Odyssey*. In addition to the connection with the witch Circe, Glaucus' tale is first alluded to

To the Readers.

O you that are wiſe & diſcreete few words may ſuffice : for ſuch a one iudgeth not at the firſt ſight, nor reprooueth by hereſaie; but patientlie heareth, and thereby increaſeth in vnderſtanding: which patience bringeth foorth experience, whereby true iudgement is directed . I ſhall not need therefore to make anie further ſute to you, but that it would pleaſe you to read my booke, without the preiudice of time, or former conceipt : and hauing obteined this at your hands, I ſubmit my ſelfe vnto your cenſure. But to make a ſolemne ſute to you that are parciall readers, deſiring you to ſet aſide parcialitie, to take in good part my writing, and with indifferent eies to looke vpon my booke, were labour loſt, and time ill imploied. For I ſhould no more preuaile herein, than if a hundred yeares ſince I ſhould haue intreated your predeceſſors to beleeue, that Robin goodfellowe, that great and ancient bulbegger, had beene but a couſening merchant, and no diuell indeed.

If I ſhould go to a papiſt, and ſaie, I praie you beleeue my writings, wherein I will prooue all popiſh charmes, coniurations, exorciſmes, benedictions and curſſes, not onelie to be ridiculous, and of none effect, but alſo to be impious and contrarie to Gods word : I ſhould as hardlie therein win fauour at their hands, as herein obteine credit at yours. Neuertheleſſe, I doubt not, but to

B.ij.   vſe

Iſai.11.
Prouer.1.

Figure 4.2.   Reginald Scot, *The Discoverie of Witchcraft*. With special thanks to the Masters and Fellows of St. Catharine's College, Cambridge.

in the tale of Medea in *Metamorphoses 7*, when Medea goes to find the magical herbs that will be used in this future story by her aunt, Circe. The scene of encounter between human and sea god is freighted, therefore, with complex and multiple associations with metamorphosis and witches, and it may be used here to suggest the world of magical transformations that comes into Scot's treatise through classical texts.

Even more tellingly, the first illustration in the work is quite specifically the scene of Daphne's transformation into a laurel in her flight from Apollo. That this Ovidian metamorphic tale opens the dedica-tion is partly because Scot is seeking patronage and alluding to the laurels he hopes will come with his work's success. The tale of Daphne is also, though, in many respects the paradigmatic tale in Ovid's poem of transformation as a response to rape and is therefore a compelling opening to a book asserting the impossibility of actual physical bodily changes that are not divinely sanctioned miracles. Daphne, the image implies, is shape-shifting in the same manner that witches might be. This illustration of the tale in particular captures the moment of meta-morphosis as both a scene of liminal identity for Daphne and a com-petition between men who have different claims to Daphne's person, since it includes both Apollo and Peneus, her river-god father. In a river-god pose that in this context suggests at least potential submis-sion to Apollo, Peneus and his daughter occupy one side of the "I" while Apollo occupies the other.[15] While Daphne, with hands that have already turned to branches and leaves, turns back toward Apollo and he reaches for her, Peneus appears defeated by his own triumph in saving Daphne from rape. The image self-consciously represents Daphne's removal from the world of masculine desire and rivalry to the realm of metamorphosis and supernatural transformation. While the homosocial competition between lover and father is downplayed in Ovid's version of the tale, its representation of a masculinized desire is a major facet of the story's history in poetry, where it becomes the source tale for poetic achievement and authority. By opening the *Dis-coverie* with this visual allusion to *Metamorphoses* and this particular tale, the publisher links the debate about witches to Ovid's poem and its analyses of the body, as well as the subjection of female metamor-phic figures and their responses to this violence. The illustration sug-gests the similarities between suffering Ovidian figures like Daphne and the witches who are the treatise's subject matter and, perhaps more indirectly, implies that the source of suffering may be a public realm of masculine rivalries and interests.

In addition to these visual connections to Ovid's world of female metamorphoses, the treatise repeatedly draws on Ovid's works for descriptions of witches and witchcraft practices. While Scot enlists a number of classical authors throughout his work, Ovid is often the first author citied, and he is clearly the poet most associated with "poetical" witchcraft throughout the work. Most notable among the Ovidian figures present in Scot's text is, of course, the witch Medea. When listing the evil deeds Continental demonologists have ascribed to witches—that they can cause barrenness, kill children, pass invisibly through the air, alter the minds of judges, and so on—he lists the demonological authors under attack and then adds,

> But because I will in no wise abridge the authority of their power, you shall have also the testimonies of many other grave authors in this behalf; as followeth.
>
> And first Ovid affirmeth, that they can raise and suppress lightning and thunder, rain and hail, clouds and winds, tempests and earthquakes. Others do write that they can pull down the moon and the stars. . . . Some say they can transubstantiate themselves and others, and take the forms and shapes of asses, wolves, ferrets, cows, apes, horses, dogs, & c. (*Discoverie* 1.4)

The beginning of this list is an allusion to Medea's famous incantation in book 7 of *Metamorphoses*, as she gathers magical herbs at night to restore Aeson's youth. The rest of her incantation includes a number of these powers:

> cum volui, ripis mirantibus amnes
> in fontes rediere suos, concussaque sisto,
> stantia concutio cantu freta, nubila pello
> nubilaque induco, ventos abigoque vocoque,
> vipereas rumpo verbis et carmine fauces,
> vivaque saxa sua convulsaque robora terra
> et silvas moveo iubeoque tremescere montis
> et mugire solum manesque exire sepulcris!
> te quoque, Luna, traho, quamvis Temesaea labores
> aera tuos minuant.
> (7.199–208)

And in Arthur Golding's 1567 English translation:

> I have compelled streams to run clean backward to their spring.
> By charms I make the calm Seas rough, and make the rough Seas plain,
> And cover all the Sky with Clouds and chase them thence again;
> By charms I raise and lay the winds and burst the viper's jaw
> And from the bowels of the earth both stones and trees do draw.
> Whole woods and forests I remove; I make the mountains shake
> And even the earth itself to groan and fearfully to quake;
> I call up dead men from their graves; and thee, O lightsome moon,
> I darken oft, though beaten brass abate thy peril soon.
> (Golding, *Met.* 7.268–276)

Jonathan Bate has called this speech Renaissance witchcraft's "great set-piece" and points to the many imitations of it in demonological writings as well as literary productions.[16] The rest of Medea's tale in *Metamorphoses*, in fact, has her practicing many of the habits of Scot's witches—gathering herbs and night-flying, for instance—but Medea does not herself govern over metamorphosis except in the case of Aeson from old age to youth. Metamorphosis, therefore, is an action more generally ascribed to Ovid's characters and his work, and in this sense references to Medea are references to the whole *Metamorphoses* and its most fundamental imagery and structure. *Metamorphoses*, therefore, is implicated in Scot's treatise and in its threatening representations of witchcraft in pervasive ways. Scot implies that the witches he describes are modern Medeas and even Daphnes, aligning them with the female figures of *Metamorphoses* in ways that ostensibly draw attention to the fictionality of witchcraft accusations but that also more surprisingly privilege Ovid's descriptions, making them authoritative in intellectual debates on witchcraft practices. This conflation of witches with Ovid's metamorphic figures draws Ovid's works from the metaphorical realm of poetry into the realm of the everyday. The witch that might be one's neighbor becomes Medea, just as Medea becomes one's neighbor.

Later in his treatise, Scot will emphasize only half of this equation of witches with Ovidian female figures when he sets out to prove that the practices attributed to witches are simply fictive imaginings. The use of Ovid's works as authoritative for witchcraft practices, however, suggests that the link between witches and Ovidian figures has both literary and other cultural consequences. If Scot's witches are like Ovid's metamorphic figures, they have agency beyond his character-ization of them as harmless old women.

Scot's suspicion that witches are too close to Ovid's violent female figures is further expressed in more subtle ways. When attempting to explain why those accused of witchcraft sometimes confess, he anx-iously writes,

> The witch on the other side expecting her neighbor's mischances, and seeing things sometimes come to pass according to her wishes, curses, and incantations . . . being called before a Justice, by due examination of the circumstances is driven to see her imprecations and desires, and her neighbors harms and losses to concur, and as it were to take effect and so confesseth that she (as a goddess) hath brought such things to pass. (*Discoverie* 1.4)

Scot is clearly troubled that these women might think they are pow-erful enough to achieve the magical effects they desire. This worry is registered in his use of the term "goddess," which suggests wider connections between Renaissance witches and the goddesses of classical, and especially Ovidian, poetry. The witch in this passage is also described as cursing, chanting, but also wishing, emphasizing the desire behind her stereotypical behavior and suggesting that when she makes her confession, even if she is wrong, she is admitting the power of her desire to do harm. The witches, like Ovidian goddesses, if they have the powers ascribed to them by the demonologists, also have the potentially destructive emotions that inspire their witchcraft.

Throughout the work and perhaps most famously, Scot also cites Ovid authoritatively to show the ineffectiveness or trickery of much behavior associated with witches. For instance, he uses Ovid, in this case in his guise as preceptor of love, to confute the effectiveness of love potions: "And first you shall hear what Ovid saith, who wrote of the very art of love, and that so cunningly and feelingly, that he is reputed the special doctor in that science" (*Discoverie* 7.7). He goes on to cite book 2 of *Ars amatoria* and then *Remedia*, in both cases as evidence that love potions are ineffectual. According to Ovid, if they worked, Medea could have kept Jason and Circe could have kept Ulysses. While Scot can grant that Ovid is a "special doctor" in the "science" of love, when it comes to *Metamorphoses* and its witches Scot is much more conflicted about how to assess the truth of Ovid's poetry.

In fact, in other places in his text Scot explicitly mocks those who take Ovid's stories for descriptions of real events. When turning his attention specifically to Jean Bodin's *De la démonomanie des sorciers*, which he finds particularly disturbing because it asserts the belief that witches can at least create the illusion of metamorphosis, he mockingly refers to Ovid as "Bodin's poet . . . whose *Metamorphosis* makes so much for him" (*Discoverie* 5.5). Interestingly, Ovid does not occupy a particularly privileged position within Bodin's treatise. When he is cited, it is usually among many other classical authorities who support Bodin's claim that all of these representations in classical literature must constitue historical fact and witchcraft has been practiced for a long time. The fantasy that Bodin has a special relationship with Ovid is therefore a construction of Scot's treatise, indicating that these anxieties about metamorphosis and witches may also in important ways be natively English. Scot further rails, "But lest some poets fables might be thought lies (whereby the witchmongers arguments should quail) he maintaineth for true the most part of Ovids *Metamorphosis*, and the greatest absurdities and impossibilities in all that book: marry he thinketh some one tale therein may be feigned" (*Discoverie* 5.1). Scot ridicules Bodin for misreading all of Ovid's absurdities and impossibilities, but throughout the work Scot vacillates on how to value Ovid's authority. As his use of Ovid to describe witchcraft practices suggests, he is never sure that Ovid can be firmly categorized as fiction, even if we assume a farily loose definition of that category.

In fact, when addressing the widespread stories of metamorphosis in book 5, Scot cites book 1 of *Metamorphoses* to "overthrow" Bodin's "phantastical imagination," reminding him that Ovid states,

> Os homini sublime dedit, caelumque videre
> Jussit, & erectos ad sydera tollere vultus,

for which he provides Abraham Fleming's translation,

> The Lord did set mans face so high
> That he the heavens might behold,
> And look up to the starry sky,
> To see his wonders manifold.
> (*Discoverie* 5.5)[17]

In this particular use of his pagan source, Scot allies Ovid with his Protestant belief in the great chain of being and the superiority of human beings over other creatures and then comfortably invokes Ovid as an authority on this subject.

A final and striking example of Ovid's ambiguous position as an authority in the work occurs when Scot attempts to undercut "the common fabling of lying poets," specifically Ovid and Virgil, by citing other classical authors: "Now let any indifferent man (Christian or heathen) judge, whether the words and minds of the prophets do not directly oppunge these poets words (I will not say minds); for that I am sure they did therein but jest and trifle, according to the common fabling of lying poets." He later continues,

> And that you may see more certainly, that these poets did but jest and deride the credulous and timorous sort of people, I thought good to show you what Ovid says against himself, and such as have written so incredibly and ridiculously of witch's omnipotence:

> Ned media magicis finduntur cantibus angues,
> Nec redit in fontes unda supina suos.

Englished by Abraham Fleming:

Snakes in the middle are not riven
With charms of witches' cunning,
Nor waters to their fountains driven
By force of backward running.
(*Discoverie* 12.15)

Unlike most citations in the work, this one is unattributed and is a rough quotation from Ovid's *Medicamina faciei femineae* (substituting *magicis* for Ovid's *marsis*, 39–40). The fact that Scot must cite this minor poem to prove that Ovid contradicts himself registers his urgent negotiation of poetic authority, especially Ovid's, throughout the text. Unable to search Ovid's mind to determine whether his purposes are "jesting" and "trifling" with the ignorant, Scot cannot decide whose side Ovid is on. Is he Bodin's poet or is he Scot's? At this point in his treatise, the only way to resolve this struggle is to represent Ovid as an authority who undercuts himself.

Later in the work, Scot addresses the difficult problem of poetic authority quite explicitly in a chapter titled "Poetical authorities commonly alleged by witchmongers, for the proof of witches miraculous actions, and for confirmation of their supernatural power." Scot writes that he will "show what authorities are produced to defend and maintain the same [accusations of witchcraft]" (*Discoverie* 12.7). His first two examples are from Virgil's *Eclogue* 8, but he then goes on to cite Ovid three times (*Fasti* 6, and two descriptions of Medea's incantations, from *Metamorphoses* 7 and her epistle in *Heroides* 4), as well as Lucan, Horace, and a few others. Having cited these authorities, he devotes a chapter to "Poetry and popery compared in enchantments, popish witchmongers have more advantage herein than protestants," in which he writes,

You see in these verses, the poets (whether in earnest or in jest I know not), ascribe unto witches & to their charms, more than is to be found in human or diabolical power. I doubt not but the most part of the readers hereof will admit them to be fabulous; although the most learned of mine adversaries (for lack of scripture) are fain to produce these poetries for proofs, and for lack of judgment I am sure do think, that Actaeon's transformation was true. And why not? As well as the metamorphosis or transubstantiation of Ulysses his companions into swine: which S. Augustine, and so many great clarkes credit and report. (*Discoverie* 12.8)

Scot's refutation of his adversaries and their reliance on poets as witnesses is riddled with doubt. Although he begins by mocking them for believing in metamorphosis, he concludes this paragraph by acknowledging that Augustine, an authority par excellence, and "many great clarkes" do in fact credit stories of transformation.

Scot's doubt and his troubled attempt to handle the authority of *Metamorphoses* cannot be only Scot's. What reading this tract reveals is a pervasive cultural anxiety about actual physical metamorphosis and particularly the powers it might suggest for women. This air of actual danger in Ovid's imagery can be easily overlooked if as scholars we focus too narrowly on Ovidianism in literature that we categorize anachronistically as figurative, without direct associations with the real. Scot's tract reminds us that there was not always an easy distinction made in this period between the authority granted to poets and that given to "great clarkes" and more overtly political figures like justices, or kings. Scot exposes metamorphosis as a poetic construction, while at the same time acknowledging that many in his learned community are not so sure that these constructions are not "real." Debates about witchcraft, at least in this instance, are shown to be grounded in more fundamental societal speculation about what counts as fictional and where authority lies.

They are also grounded in what can be identified in *Metamorphoses* as multiple models of the self. The conflict over Ovidian authority that is witnessed in this text reflects a larger dual authority for Ovidianism as a discourse in the period. Ovid here (and everywhere in late sixteenth-century England) is both the poet of metamorphoses and the poet of female grief and rage. Both of these Ovids, however, are handled very carefully in Scot's treatise, suggesting further that the antiauthoritarian politics of Ovid's female figures infects these debates in intimate ways. Katharine Maus has argued that witchcraft believers and skeptics in these debates have fundamentally different conceptions of the self. Believers, Scot's adversaries like Bodin, according to Maus, usually see the self as permeable, subject to demonic possession, or capable of being cursed by the external force of a town witch. Skeptics, on the other hand, tend to see the self as bounded and contained, and they focus on an internalized understanding of human agency and will.[18] Maus' work overall shows how available both of these models of the self were during this period, and Scot actually varies in his descriptions of his witches, employing models of the self and the emotions to suit his varying rhetorical practices. This is not to say that the dualism Maus has pointed to does not exist but instead to reaffirm that the differences between believers and skeptics are not actually so great, their rhetorics interpenetrating in local ways throughout both kinds of texts.

As a pagan discourse for constructing identity, Ovidianism can accommodate both of these models of the self in fascinating ways. As the poet of metamorphosis, Ovid's selves are permeable and shifting. Daphne, for instance, is still Daphne in *Metamorphoses*, even when in the concluding moments of her rape narrative she becomes a laurel tree, but she is also half tree, and Ovid's narrator famously emphasizes our loss of access to her thoughts, emotions, and will, suggesting that she both is and is not present anymore as a bounded self. A better example is Arachne, the famous hubristic weaver who is transformed to a spider in book 4, both continuing and not continuing her selfhood beyond her human form. Her transformation by Minerva is a symbolic replacement for her grief, as the goddess refuses to let her take her own life, revealing her extreme vulnerability to external forces of metamorphosis.

As the poet of excessive emotion, on the other hand, Ovid's selves are often quite bounded, and the moment of metamorphosis emphasizes the ways they are even more fundamentally shut off from interaction with other forces and beings. Narcissus is still Narcissus even after he becomes the flower, so much so that even in the underworld, he is still gazing at himself in the river Styx. In fact, many victims of metamorphosis when it is uninvited, such as Io, who is metamorphosed into a cow to deceive Juno about Jove's adultery, are surprised and saddened by their animal forms. They experience shame and regret that they can no longer speak but are clearly still the same identity within the new form. Io's case is particularly pitiable:

> illa etiam supplex Argo cum bracchia vellet
> tenderet non habuit, quae bracchia tenderet Argo,
> conatoque queri mugitus edidit ore
> pertimuitque sonos propriaque exterrita voce est.
> venit et ad ripas, ubi ludere saepe solebat,
> Inachidas: rictus novaque ut conspexit in unda
> cornua, pertimuit seque exsternata refugit.

[When she strove to stretch out suppliant arms to Argus, she had no arms to stretch; and when she attempted to voice her complaints, she only mooed. She would start with fear at the sound, and was filled with terror at her own voice. She came also to the banks of her father's stream, where she used to play; but when she saw, reflected in the water, her gaping jaws and sprouting horns, she fled in very terror of herself.] (I.635–41)

Io, in fact, is eventually transformed back into herself. So Ovid's poem offers a spectrum of ways to understand the emotional self and the will, and this flexibility also produces the cultural fracturing of authority we see in Scot's skeptical witchcraft treatise.

That Ovid occupies this ambiguous position within Scot's treatise as both "Bodin's poet," the poet of demonic witchcraft and transformation, and the classical authority on artistic renderings of witchcraft, suggests that the *Metamorphoses* was also strongly associated in this different cultural setting with contemporary criminal acts of excessive emotion. All of the nefarious behaviors attributed to witches have their roots in readings of feminine emotion. Witches are said to bring disease, for example, because they are angry when they are denied charity, or curse crops or raise storms as their responses to various kinds of altercations with neighbors. According to historians, these women were usually poor but important members of their villages and had often been considered "wise women," practicing good witchcraft, for a long time before the accusation of witchcraft was made.[19] What seems to be at the root of many of these accusations is a cultural worry (in both men and women) about women in positions of relative social impotence who might respond as Ovidian characters, seizing power to express their emotions through acts of violence. Scot's treatise gives us access to the larger concern in witchcraft debates that contemporary witches might, like Shakespeare's Lavinia, find themselves in Ovid's book.

Afterword

As I suggested in my introduction, while Ovidianism functions in different ways in each of the cultural sites in this book, what is remarkable is the consistency with which Ovid and particularly *Metamorphoses* serve as reference points for representing and evaluating emotion in Elizabethan England. There are many other cultural and textual arenas where Ovidianism plays this definitional role. Most notably missing from this study is a discussion of the minor epics or epyllia, which are insistently Ovidian and also marked by their interest in highly rhetoricized lament and other kinds of emotive discourse. While these poems have recently received some excellent critical attention, they deserve to have a more central place in our readings of Renaissance culture, since they circulated in the influential context of the Inns of Court.[1] What would also complement this study is a broader analysis of Renaissance European Ovidianism cross-culturally, including more attention to the writings of Petrarch, who, as Lynn Enterline has shown, clearly saw the potential for Ovidianism to have powerful emotive effects in his own *Rime Sparse*.[2] Scholarship has largely approached Ovid's greatest work, *Metamorphoses*, the way the title begs for it to be approached, as a poem about changes of form and body, and while this trope is obviously central to understanding an Ovidian aesthetic and its ideological implications, those changes so insistently memorialize the effects of power that the local politics of each tale and its wider repetitions should not be overlooked. Although there is an important strain of European Ovidianism that focuses on Ovid's erotic writings and on Ovid as the preceptor of love, I suspect that this alternate Ovidianism may be read as at least sometimes a response to the potential subversions of Ovid's other works. A broader comparison of these two "Ovids" in Renaissance culture would therefore be particularly relevant and exciting.

It is also enlightening to note the tales from *Metamorphoses* that find their way so insistently into the politicized contexts of this book: Philomela, Hecuba, and Orpheus most repeatedly. This study has focused on these figures because these are tales and tellers where the link between emotion and personal powerlessness or agency is most strongly explored in Ovid's poem. In these violent female figures, and in Orpheus, whose gender is at least called into question when he is described as the founder of a pederastic lifestyle, Renaissance authors met a cultural need to represent complex and often threateningly subversive emotive states and their consequences. Other tales were also central to Renaissance Ovidianism and have come up in this study as well—Apollo and Daphne most frequently, but also Diana and Actaeon, Narcissus, and Medea (although her Ovidian influence is complicated by her prominence in other works of classical literature). Not incidentally, three of these tales (not that of Medea) became the central narratives underlying Petrarch's influential assertions of his emotive self in lyric. While there are many other tales that are cited in Renaissance texts, the frequency with which these tales arise suggests that they answer pressing cultural needs and desires. They might usefully be grouped as tales that consider the extremity and dangers of desire itself, a category of human experience closely linked to emotion in modern thought and even more enmeshed with it in Renaissance writings on the passions or humors. The prominence of these tales in Renaissance Ovidianism further suggests the centrality of this discourse to cultural definitions and evaluations of emotion or desire.

As in all self-conscious intertextual dialogues, in that between Ovidianism and Renaissance writings, the chronologically later writings also influence our readings of the earlier works. Reading *Metamorphoses* as its Renaissance translators and imitators did, it is impossible not to recognize the extreme violence, and usually sexual violence, present in Ovidianism as a discourse, for instance. In some Renaissance writing this association is simply reflexive—it is reflexive for Iachimo and possibly some of his audience when in Shakespeare's *Cymbeline* he approaches the sleeping Imogen and notices that

> She hath been reading, late,
> The tale of Tereus. Here the leaf's turned down
> Where Philomel gave up.
> (2.2.44–46)

An attentive reader or playgoer, however, would find this strange, since Ovid's Philomela never actually gives up. In fact, it is her repeated verbal defiance of Tereus that results in her tongue being cut out and leads to the famous working of her tale into the tapestry. Considering how central Ovid's works were to the Elizabethan educational system (see notes to the introduction), it is hard not to notice this slip, and this Ovidian allusion serves to characterize

Iachimo as not just a potential rapist but an unlearned or selective reader, his reading clouded by his own lust and immorality. Rape and sexual violence in particular are coded again and again as Ovidian, but especially in works like those analyzed in this study, Renaissance writers who respond more fully to the whole of *Metamorphoses* as well as Ovid's other works also acknowledge Ovid's self-conscious theorization of that violence. While Ovid's works do not offer a way out of the confining and dangerous model of love as a hunt, Ovid repeatedly represents its effects, and those repetitions begin to wear away even at the irony of darkly comic descriptions of the victims of desire in *Metamorphoses*, like Io who frightens herself with her mooing. While some of the violent changes in the poem are funny, as are some Renaissance imitations (think, for example, of poor Bottom in *A Midsummer Night's Dream* with the ears of an ass), they become less funny through accretion, perhaps culminating in the seriousness with which most of the tales of transgressive desire in the Orphic book 10 are told (and Bottom does famously become the consort of the fairy queen and may offer the most serious evaluation of the actions of the play). Reading Ovid through the lens of Renaissance Ovidianism highlights the ways Ovid's works interrogate violence and the systems of power (both state and divine) that are never fully invested in controlling its spread or effects.

Other instances of the Renaissance reading Ovid for us might highlight the characterization of desire as a type of emotion, as I have suggested above (in contrast to many contemporary conceptions that firmly separate the two), the feminization of grief, or the concept of the body as ultimately highly unstable and vulnerable, even when the self is not. It is even more revealing to compare the list of central Ovidian tales I just highlighted in this book to the list of tales that populate a different culture, and in particular, our own. While we are obviously not as culturally attuned to classical tales as Renaissance readers and playgoers were, it is notable that the Ovidian tales that still have major cultural currency would probably include Narcissus, Pygmalion, Phaeton, and maybe Midas (at least, those seem to be the ones my students know before they enter my classroom). There are many reasons for the survival of these tales and Freud plays a central role in this particular process of transmission, but it is notable that while some of these tales analyze and represent emotions, they are fundamentally less political in a strict sense than those that are repeated so often in the Renaissance. These figures suffer less from angry forces of absolutist power than from their own misguided or immoral judgments. While the Ovid of the Renaissance maintained a distinctly politicized presence, the Ovid of the twenty-first century is mostly characterized by a group of confused young men.

Another way to approach this comparative question is by narrowing our attention to a contemporary example of our own recent Ovidianism, Mary Zimmerman's critically acclaimed *Metamorphoses: A Play*. Zimmerman's play, while produced earlier by Chicago's Lookingglass Theater (1998) and off-Broadway (2001), arrived on Broadway in 2002, where it earned Zimmerman a Tony for Best Direction in that year. When Ben Brantley reviewed the play for the *New York Times*, he subtitled his piece, "How Ovid Helps Deal with Loss and Suffering." In his praise for the play, he asserts that it is helping New York audiences process their grief after the terrorist attacks of 2001. He writes, "Sorrow is a fugue in Mary Zimmerman's *Metamorphoses*," and "for New Yorkers today who encounter the same recorded visions of terrorist destruction whenever they turn on their televisions, Ms. Zimmerman's portrayal of tragic scenes repeated has an anxious and immediate familiarity. But there is balm in Ovid's world, as Ms. Zimmerman presents it. Those images from television stay the same; metamorphosis occurs in the human imagination. There can be artistry and solace in remembering."[3] Brantley ultimately claims that the play validates a "personal mythology" as solace in the face of communal grief and violence, and although this is only his interpretation of the play (and I think Zimmerman's vision is more social), he is right that the play avoids making statements about strictly political violence and the suffering it causes. Just the selection of tales in comparison to those I have cited previously as central to this study is revealing. Zimmerman includes Midas, Myrrha, Orpheus, Alcyone, Pomona, and Phaethon. She concludes with a final moment of quiet grace in the tale of Baucis and Philemon, who desire nothing more than to serve the gods and are rewarded when they are metamorphosed in old age into two adjacent trees at the same time, to live perpetually together in their metamorphosed forms (a celebration that opens, in book 1, rather than closes, *Metamorphoses*). The play's focus, one that apparently struck a chord with New Yorkers at a painful and confusing moment in history, is ultimately quietist, validating "myth" as an abstracted consolation, rather than personal agency or social movements that address inequalities of power.

The starkness of this contrast between Zimmerman's version of Ovidianism and the Ovidianism in this book helps make the case for the political nature of Renaissance Ovidianism overall, as well as the insistent ways emotion is elevated by the discourse in the service of particular political ends. A review of some of the salient figures of

Elizabethan Ovidianism from the previous chapters makes this point: Lyly's Ceres summons Hunger to punish an insolent ruler, and his Daphne chooses the queen over Apollo; Shakespeare's Lavinia silently reveals that the new empress' sons are rapists and participates in a violent revenge; Titus, in the same play, arrives at a state of mute rage that finally allows his excessively violent reinstatement of his family's political power at the end of the play; Spenser's Adicia attacks the heroic knights of the poem and metamorphoses into a ghostly but still dangerous tiger; the Renaissance Orpheus sings his songs of transgressive loves and links them to normative structures before he suffers extreme violence from which he cannot escape; and Medea uses her magical powers to control her destiny in a hostile and foreign society, even when she is actually an English villager accused of witchcraft who apparently only wants power over her neighbors. Many other Ovidian figures cited throughout this study exhibit extreme and sometimes doomed forms of agency and register their protests of the social systems of power in which they are implicated. As part of the larger discourse of Ovidianism, their emotions are central to their constructions as speakers and agents. They create and participate in a distinctly Ovidian and distinctly Elizabethan politics of emotion.

NOTES

INTRODUCTION

1. Jonathan Bate, for instance, calls this moment, "perhaps the most self-consciously literary moment in all Shakespeare." *Shakespeare and Ovid* (Oxford: Clarendon P, 1993) 103. Leonard Barkan writes that Lavinia "becomes a metonym for the whole history of the book in which Shakespeare found her story." *The Gods Made Flesh: Metamorphosis and the Pursuit of Paganism* (New Haven: Yale UP, 1986) 247. Goran Stanivukovic, in *Ovid and the Renaissance Body* (Toronto: U of Toronto P, 2001), also uses this moment in Shakespeare to introduce the topic of Ovidianism as a defining discourse for the body, and therefore the subject, in the period. He regards the moment as disempowering its female protagonist, calling it "a failed attempt to articulate the pain and fate of femininity at the end of this profoundly Ovidian and misogynistic play" (3).

2. All references to *Titus Andronicus* are to the Arden edition, edited by Jonathan Bate (London: Routledge, 1995).

3. Eve Sanders, in her analysis of the ways educational practices produced male and female subjects in this period, reads Lavinia at this moment as "a figure for the contradictions inherent in humanist recommendations for female reading." She argues that Lavinia's rape is associated in this scene with her transgressive reading of Ovidian erotic poetry and therefore emphasizes Lavinia's victimization rather than her agency at this moment in the play. *Gender and Literacy on Stage in Early Modern England* (Cambridge: Cambridge UP, 1998) 63.

4. Much of the work of Ovidian source study has been carried out by editors of Renaissance texts, and my indebtedness to them is marked at the points where their observations begin my own analysis. A few works, however, take on the subject of Ovid's influence in broader terms. Most important of these works for my purposes is Douglas Bush's *Mythology and the Renaissance Tradition in English Poetry* (New York: Norton, 1963), especially chap. 4, "Ovid Old and New." For examples of later theorizations of especially English Ovidianism in cultural terms see Leonard Barkan's seminal study, *The Gods Made Flesh*, and the work of critics such as Jonathan Bate (cited above), Heather James, and Georgia Brown. Bate's book focuses on Shakespeare's Ovidianism specifically, but his work greatly expands our perspectives on the larger cultural meanings of Ovidianism. Heather James' book *Shakespeare's Troy: Drama, Politics,*

and the Translation of Empire (Cambridge: Cambridge UP, 1997) redefined the study of Ovid and Virgil in Shakespeare, and her recent articles firmly establish English Ovidianism as the site of important political and cultural negotiations. Georgia Brown's book, *Redefining Elizabethan Literature* (Cambridge: Cambridge UP, 2004), which will be discussed below, argues for a central transgressive role for Ovidianism in literary culture in the late Elizabethan period. Stanivukovic's collection, *Ovid and the Renaissance Body* (also cited above), announces itself as marking a critical turning point in approaching Ovidianism as instrumental in defining the self, and Lynn Enterline's book, *The Rhetoric of the Body from Ovid to Shakespeare* (Cambridge: Cambridge UP, 2000), specifically focuses on the ideological negotiations occurring in Ovidianism related to conceptualizing the female body and voice.

5. Emotion occupies a particularly contested space in critiques and debates about poststructuralism itself, although Bartes, as my epigraph suggests, sees no reason not to include emotional codes within other systems of language. For a discussion and possible resolution to the crisis of emotion within poststructuralism, see Rei Terada, *Feeling in Theory: Emotion After the "Death of the Subject"* (Cambridge: Harvard UP, 2001).

6. Barkan 14. Kathryn McKinley, however, has analyzed how female subjectivity is explored in commentaries on the *Metamorphoses* from the period. As McKinley points out, there is also a strong tradition of associating Ovid with misogyny, but, as she explains, this tradition mainly arises from the representation of women in the *Ars Amatoria*. While this treatise on the art of seduction does indeed suggest that women enjoy being physically conquered in love, a disturbing and misogynistic portrayal of female desires, the objective of the treatise is clouded by both its irony and the possibility that it was essentially a political attack on Augustus' legislations of morality. For a discussion of this complex issue, see McKinley, *Reading the Ovidian Heroine: "Metamorphoses" Commentaries 1100–1618* (Leiden: Brill, 2001) xx–xxii.

7. See Heather James, "Ovid and the Question of Politics in Early Modern England," *ELH* 70 (2003): 343–73.

8. Graham Allen makes the argument for the centrality of intertextuality to poststructuralism throughout his book, *Intertextuality* (London: Routledge, 2000).

9. There have been important studies of various Renaissance intertextualities and the nature of the period's classical intertextuality itself—such as Thomas Greene's *The Light in Troy: Imitation and Discovery in Renaissance Poetry* (New Haven: Yale UP), but these earlier analyses, even when they do not limit themselves to the methods of source study, tend not to account for the wider cultural effects of particular intertexts.

10. Mullaney, Plenary Lecture, Shakespeare Association of American Annual Meeting, Philadelphia, PA, 2006.

11. Gail Kern Paster, for instance, has traced the Galenic "psychophysiology" of humoral conceptions of the body in Shakespeare's plays in *Humoring the Body: Emotions and the Shakespearean Stage* (Chicago: U of Chicago P, 2004). Most importantly for this study, she points to the ways the body and in consequence the Renaissance self was considered to be part of the fluid nature of what we would consider the external material world. See also Michael Schoenfeldt's *Bodies and Selves in Early Modern England: Physiology and Inwardness in Spenser, Shakespeare, Herbert and Milton* (Cambridge: Cambridge UP, 1999) for an analysis of how the humoral body encouraged a self-sustaining regulation of the passions in the individual. Finally, a number of essays in *Reading the Early Modern Passions: Essays in the Cultural History of Emotion*, ed. Gail Kern Paster, Katherine Rowe and Mary Floyd-Wilson (Philadelphia: U of Pennsylvania P, 2004), suggest the ways humoralism intersected with various other cultural narratives and discourses.

12. See "The Passions Signified: Imitation and the Construction of Emotions in Sidney and Wroth," *Criticism* 43 (2001): 407–21. As Miller explains, her essay argues for "a different conceptualization [of emotion], one in which the representation precedes and produces the passion" (407). She also notes that "in the Renaissance according to the O.E.D., one meaning of the term emotion was a 'transference from one place to another.' In this sense, perhaps emotion remains a useful term for discussing the Renaissance theory of passions that migrate from one person to another through imitations of the verbal and bodily signifiers that fashion 'within' the 'passion signified'" (419).

13. Lutz, *Unnatural Emotions: Everyday Sentiments on a Micronesian Atoll and Their Challenge to Western Theory* (Chicago: U of Chicago P, 1988) 4.

14. Lutz 56.

15. Juliana Schiesari, *The Gendering of Melancholia: Feminism, Psychoanalysis, and the Symbolics of Loss in Renaissance Literature* (Ithaca, NY: Cornell UP, 1992).

16. A work that does this for Renaissance England is Gwynne Kennedy's *Just Anger: Representing Women's Anger in Early Modern England* (Carbondale: U of Illinois P, 2000).

17. See Elizabeth Spelman, "Anger and Insubordination," *Women, Knowledge, and Reality: Explorations in Feminist Philosophy*, ed. Ann Garry and Marilyn Pearsall (Boston: Unwin Hyman, 1989) 263–74.

18. Gail Kern Paster, *The Body Embarrassed: Drama and the Disciplines of Shame in Early Modern Europe* (Ithaca, NY: Cornell UP, 1993) and *Humoring the Body*. Michael Schoenfeldt, *Bodies and Selves in Early Modern England: Physiology and Inwardness in Spenser, Shakespeare, Herbert, and Milton* (Cambridge: Cambridge UP, 1999). For his discussion of the mind–body dualism and agency, see p. 11 of the Introduction.

19. Two places where these issues are carefully addressed are Lynn Enterline's work and the articles in the recent collection edited by Goran Stanivukovic, *Ovid and the Renaissance Body*. Stanivukovic points out that of all the competing discourses constructing bodily subjectivity in the period, "Ovidian discourse was the most widely available, and the closest to the Renaissance idea that the gender of the body does not determine the erotic nature of that body's desire. No other discourse of subjectivity was so explicitly focused on the terms that constitute the self: body, libido, and agency" (6)

20. Bate, for instance, argues that metamorphosis becomes psychological and metaphorical in Shakespeare's works (28).

21. See Janet Adelman, "Making Defect Perfection: Shakespeare and the One-Sex Model," *Enacting Gender on the English Renaissance Stage*, ed. Viviana Comensoli and Anne Russell (Urbana: U of Illinois P, 1999) 23–52. For the argument for the cultural prevalence of the Galenic one-sex model, see Thomas Laqueur, *Making Sex: Body and Gender from the Greeks to Freud* (Cambridge: Harvard UP, 1990).

22. Grosz's argument is much more complex than can be articulated here. See the Introduction, "Refiguring Bodies," in *Volatile Bodies* (Bloomington: Indiana UP, 1994).

23. See, for example, Georgia Brown's 2004 *Redefining Elizabethan Literature*, in which she notes, "Ovid's role in the English Renaissance is crucial, but is only beginning to receive critical attention" (36n75).

24. Afterword to *Ovid and the Renaissance Body* (Toronto: U of Toronto P, 2001) 261.

25. Alessandro Barchiesi's *The Poet and the Prince: Ovid and Augustan Discourse* (Berkeley: U of California P, 1997) explores in detail the poet's relationship to Augustan culture and politics, and it clarifies the subtleties of Ovid's challenges to Augustus' moralistic political discourse.

26. Recent exceptional treatments of the *Metamorphoses*, especially in relation to its intertextualities, include Dennis Feeney, *The Gods in Epic: Poets and Critics of the Classical Tradition* (Oxford: Clarendon P, 1991) and Stephen Hinds, *The Metamorphoses of Persephone: Ovid and the Self-Conscious Muse* (Cambridge: Cambridge UP, 1987). In addition, two recent books offer especially insightful readings of *Metamorphoses* as well as translations and works in the Ovidian tradition through the Renaissance: Raphael Lynne, *Ovid's Changing Worlds: English Metamorphoses, 1567–1632* (Oxford: Oxford UP, 2001) and Philip Hardie, *Ovid's Poetics of Illusion* (Cambridge: Cambridge UP, 2002). See below (n. 30) for a more comprehensive list of important studies of Ovid's *Metamorphoses*.

27. Almost all current criticism of Virgil's poem acknowledges that its propaganda is internally critiqued by certain aspects of the narrative and moments in the poem. As Philip Hardie puts it in his preface to *The Epic Successors of Virgil*, "one of the greatnesses of this apparently definitive Roman epic is its ability to spawn a vigorous progeny. The successors of

Virgil, at once respectful and rebellious, constructed a space for themselves through a 'creative imitation' that exploited the energies and tensions called up but not finally expended or resolved in the *Aeneid* . . . imitation of Virgil reinforces engagement with contemporary politics inasmuch as the *Aeneid*, written in the very years that Octavian/Augustus was grappling with the definition of the *princeps* and his power, helped both to crystallize and to problematize imperial ideology." *The Epic Successors of Virgil: A Study in the Dynamics of a Tradition* (Cambridge: Cambridge UP, 1993) xi. On this issue, see also David Quint, *Epic and Empire: Politics and Generic Form from Virgil to Milton* (Princeton: Princeton UP, 1993) and Stephen Hinds, *Allusion and Intertext: Dynamics of Appropriation in Roman Poetry* (Cambridge: Cambridge UP, 1998).

28. Leo Curran was among the first to outline the ways Ovid's poem represents an anti-Augustan response to the politics of the *Aeneid*. See "Transformation and Anti-Augustanism in Ovid's *Metamorphoses*." *Arethusa* 5 (1972): 71–91. See also Barchiesi, *The Poet and the Prince*.

29. Dennis Feeney, Introduction to *Metamorphoses*, trans. David Raeburn (London: Penguin, 2004) xxii–xxiii.

30. For examinations of these basic aspects of Ovid's reshaping of epic and other traditions in the *Metamorphoses* see the following: Brooks Otis, *Ovid as an Epic Poet*, 2nd ed. (Cambridge: Cambridge UP, 1970); Karl Galinsky, *Ovid's "Metamorphoses:" An Introduction to the Basic Aspects* (Berkeley: U of California P, 1975); Joseph Solodow, *The World of Ovid's "Metamorphoses"* (Chapel Hill: U of North Carolina P, 1988); Peter Knox, *Ovid's "Metamorphoses" and the Traditions of Augustan Poetry* (Cambridge: Cambridge UP, 1986); Garth Tissol, *The Face of Nature: Wit, Narrative, and Cosmic Origins in Ovid's "Metamorphoses"* (Princeton: Princeton UP, 1997); Phillip Hardie, *Ovid's Poetics of Illusion*. For a discussion of *Metamorphoses* in relation to the neoteric and epic traditions, see Dennis Feeney, *The Gods in Epic: Poets and Critics of the Classical Tradition* (cited above), especially chap. 5.

31. W. R. Johnson, in fact, famously identifies Ovid as the origin of the "counter-classical" tradition in English literature. *California Studies in Classical Antiquity* 3 (1970): 123–51. He also insists on the seriousness of Ovid's political critique of Augustus: "It seems to me not improbable, however, that the *Metamorphoses* is an attack on Augustus' efforts to reform society by means of an artificial religious revival and the imposition of stringent and inhuman moral codes" (147).

32. See *Tristia*, 2.

33. See Amy Richlin, "Reading Ovid's Rapes" *Pornography and Representation in Greece and Rome*, ed. Amy Richlin (Oxford: Oxford UP, 1992).

34. As Kathryn McKinley's study of the representations of female subjectivity in books six through ten of the *Metamorphoses* and later medieval and early modern translations and commentaries suggests, the Ovidian

tradition located much of its theorizing about the nature of the self in female figures. As McKinley argues, especially in the middle books of the *Metamorphoses*, Ovid's "rigorous exploration of a variety of heroines' psychological and emotional struggles, and his provision of a specific discourse for their passion, make an extremely important contribution to the representation of subjectivity in western narrative literature. Ovid's medieval and early modern readers [for her these are only the translators and commentators] show different degrees of willingness to recognize, and capitalize upon, his marked interest in representing the complex forms of this inner landscape." *Reading the Ovidian Heroine*, xxviii.

35. Clark Hulse, in his entry "Ovidian Epic," in *The Spenser Encyclopedia*, ed. A. C. Hamilton (Toronto: U of Toronto P, 1990), remarks on "the Ovidian desire to interweave the private suffering of individuals with grand and impersonal schemes of history" (524).

36. This, it should be noted here, is the essential truth grasped in the Renaissance by Elizabeth and the courtiers promoting or criticizing her individual representation. Much of the success of her monarchy seems to have been based on an Ovidian joining of national to personal politics. Spenser's highly Ovidian *Faerie Queene* is similarly interested in the queen's persona and gender identity as both personal and emphatically political.

37. Enterline 2000. For a very different (and in some ways oppositional) reading of the gender politics surrounding an Ovidian female voice in the case of John Donne, see Elizabeth Harvey's "Ventriloquizing Sappho: Ovid, Donne, and the Erotics of the Feminine Voice," *Criticism* 31 (1989).

38. See "The Natural Tears of Epic," *Epic Traditions in the Contemporary World*, ed. Margaret Beissinger, Jane Tylus, and Susanne Wofford (Berkeley: U of California P, 1999) 195.

39. Douglas Bush writes that in the twelfth century, the "influence of Ovid ranged from the wandering scholars' very practical eulogies of Venus to the idealisms of the *Roman de la Rose*, from mythological romances to allegories of Christ's love for the human soul, from fairy tales to treatises on Amatory etiquette" (8).

40. For studies on the uses of pagan myth in European literature and visual arts, see Jean Seznec, *The Survival of the Pagan Gods: The Mythological Tradition and Its Place in Renaissance Humanism and Art*, trans. Barbara Sessions (New York: Pantheon, 1953); and Edgar Wind, *Pagan Mysteries in the Renaissance*, rev. ed. (New York: Norton, 1968).

41. Barkan 18.

42. Bate 5.

43. Bate 20.

44. *Redefining Elizabethan Literature*, 41.

45. Ezra Pound, *Notes on Elizabethan Classicists* (1915–16), cited in the Introduction to the new edition of the Golding translation, originally edited and introduced by John Frederick Nims (Philadelphia: Paul Dry

Books, 2000) xiii. W. H. Rouse, ed., *Shakespeare's Ovid: being Arthur Golding's Translation of the* Metamorphoses (Carbondale: Southern Illinois UP, 1961).

46. See the new edition of Nims' text cited above. Another recent edition has been published, edited by Madeleine Forey (Baltimore: Johns Hopkins UP, 2002).

47. All references to Golding's translation of the *Metamorphoses* are to the edition edited by John Frederick Nims and cited above.

48. *Responsive Readings: Versions of Echo in Pastoral, Epic and Jonsonian Masque* (New Haven: Yale UP, 1984) 35.

CHAPTER 1

1. *The Political Writings of John Knox: The First Blast of the Trumpet against the Monstrous Regiment of Women and Other Selected Works,* ed. Marvin A. Breslow (Cranbury, NJ: Associated University Presses, 1985) 43–44.

2. Knox was a central figure in the radical Scottish Reformist movement. His treatise was directed not against Elizabeth but against the Catholic female rulers who headed England, Scotland, and France in the period just before Elizabeth took the throne. Knox saw Catholicism entrenched in these countries by a tribe of unnatural women rulers—Mary Tudor, Mary Stuart, and Catherine De Medici. When Elizabeth took the throne, she promptly had him banished from the realm, and he later had to seek her good graces as a supporter of European, and most importantly, Scottish, Protestantism.

3. Leah Marcus analyzes this same passage in her analysis of Elizabeth's androgynous self-representation: "Where could the blurring of sexual identities be expected to stop: if the queen, a woman, was also a man, did that mean, according to the fears of contemporary moralists about the effects of cross-dressing, that men were turned into women?" *Puzzling Shakespeare: Local Reading and its Discontents* (Berkeley: U of California P, 1988) 66.

4. See Reginald Scott, *The Discovery of Witchcraft* (London, 1584) bk. 5, chap. 4–5.

5. Scott, bk. 5, chap. 5.

6. Marie Axton's *The Queen's Two Bodies: Drama and the Elizabethan Succession* (London: Royal Historical Society, 1977) outlines the earlier work of Ernst Kantorowicz, *The King's Two Bodies* (Princeton: Princeton UP, 1957), and then argues that cultural debates and anxiety about the Elizabethan succession were met with a legal reframing of this theological premise. She explains, "The concept of the king's two bodies was an attempt to deal with a paradox: men died and the land endured; kings died, the crown survived; individual subjects died but subjects always remained to be governed . . . for the purposes of law it was found necessary by 1561 to endow the Queen with two bodies" (12). Susan Frye

also addresses the utilization of this premise by Parliamentary decree in *Elizabeth I*, 12–13.

7. "Queen Elizabeth's Armada Speech to the troops at Tilbury, August 9, 1588," *Elizabeth I: Collected Works*, ed. Leah S. Marcus, Janel Mueller, and Mary Beth Rose (Chicago; U of Chicago P, 2000). 326.

8. "Speech 17, Version 2," *Collected Works*, 193.

9. "Speech 23, Version 1," *Collected Works*, 340. As Marcus, Mueller, and Rose explain in their notes to the various surviving versions of this speech, the differences in these versions probably reflect the fact that it was printed from the notes of more than one person present. None of the surviving texts is, therefore, authoritatively Elizabeth's own words, but the reactions of her parliament that may be preserved in these transcripts are just as culturally valuable.

10. Leah Marcus argues this point most persuasively in her section on Elizabeth in *Puzzling Shakespeare*, 53–66. See also Frye 13–16, and Carole Levin, *"The Heart and Stomach of a King": Elizabeth I and the Politics of Sex and Power* (Philadelphia: U of Pennsylvania P, 1994). Continuing and retheorizing this strain of analysis, Stephen Cohen describes her "radical destabilization of identity" in this way: "Through a rhetoric of political masculinity deployed throughout her reign, Elizabeth assured her subjects that they were not being ruled by a 'mere' woman. At the same time, her manipulation of the evolving early modern understanding of interiority and exteriority complicated antagonistic constructions of the queen as a woman behaving like or usurping the position of a man; if anything, her presentation of the masculine body politic as more fundamental than and concealed within a conventional femininity whose 'naturalness' was mitigated by its conspicuous externalization, suggested that the queen was—if not quite a man—a *male*, disguised as or acting as a woman. Neither a naïve reversion to a medieval conception of the socially defined self nor a surrender to the modern interiorization of subjectivity, Elizabeth's rhetorical self-fashioning instead exploited the early modern transitional juxtapositioning of the two ideologies of identity, offering not a model of the successful containment of the individual by ideology, but of opportunistic resistance from a subject-position uniquely situated to understand and manipulate the forces of containment" (28–29). "(Post)modern Elizabeth: Gender, Politics, and the Emergence of Modern Subjectivity," *Shakespeare and Modernity: Early Modern to Millennium*, ed. Hugh Grady (London: Routledge, 2000) 20–39.

11. Frances Yates, *Astrea: The Imperial Theme in the Sixteenth Century* (London: Routledge, 1975). Roy Strong, *The Cult of Elizabeth: Elizabethan Portraiture and Pageantry* (London: Thames and Hudson, 1977). See also Helen Hackett, *Virgin Mother, Maiden Queen: Elizabeth I and the Cult of the Virgin Mary* (London: Macmillan, 1995). Hackett revises the previous critical commonplace that Elizabethan representation adopted the iconography of the Virgin Mary to fill the void left by the replacement of Catholicism by

Protestantism. She traces the complex changes in Elizabeth's Marian iconography over the course of her rule and suggests that her cult benefits from
earlier venerations of virgins as much as Christian ones.

12. See Philippa Berry, *Of Chastity and Power: Elizabethan Literature and
    the Unmarried Queen* (London: Routledge, 1989).

13. John King, "Queen Elizabeth I; Representations of the Virgin Queen,"
    Renaissance Quarterly 43 (1990): 30–74.

14. Susan Frye, *Elizabeth I: The Competition for Representation* (Oxford:
    Oxford UP, 1993).

15. Montrose, "Idols of the Queen: Policy, Gender and the Picturing of
    Elizabeth I," *Representations* 68 (1999): 133.

16. The entertainments were performed before Elizabeth during her pro-
    gresses to visit the country estates and major counties of her reign, and
    they constitute a unique genre of writing that requires some explanation.
    Elizabeth spent most of her summers on the move, traveling from place
    to place and visiting the homes of courtiers and local governors. In order
    to do so, she created a movable court with at least a hundred nobles and
    servants of assorted varieties and functions. In her early reign, for most
    of the 1560s and 1570s, she traveled every summer, often leaving Lon-
    don for as many as seventy-five days and making as many as forty-two
    stops. In 1575, in fact, she traveled for an unprecedented 139 days and
    made an astounding forty-four stops. Then, for reasons that have only
    been speculated about, she stayed put for most of the 1580s, using tilts
    instead of progresses as public appearances. She ventured out again in the
    early 1590s, but after 1591 and 1592 she did not really spend the whole
    summer in these travels again, leaving for between thirteen and thirty-
    four days only in 1597, 1601, and 1602. Mary Hill Cole, in *The Por-
    table Queen*, argues that these peregrinations served a vital political role
    and are essential for understanding the success of Elizabeth's rule. They
    united the country under a ruler they had actually seen in person, and
    they allowed the queen herself to gauge the conditions of her country.
    Until recently, scholars have focused on the entertainments performed
    before the queen at the estates of her closest courtiers, because some
    (approximately fifteen) of these entertainments survive in pamphlets
    published after the entertainments themselves. This focus, however, has
    obscured the fact that Elizabeth visited many types of people on these
    progresses, including certainly the local nobility, but also the clergy and
    more bourgeois local officials, such as sheriffs and mayors. These were
    decidedly public and even democratic events, and the grand entertain-
    ments that we have records of at the homes of her wealthiest nobles, even
    if they were performed for a select audience, would certainly have been
    village gossip before many of them were published. The entertainments,
    therefore, are not, as some have seen them, purely an aristocratic genre,
    or the product of a closed court society. They are part of Elizabeth's
    deliberate attempt to keep herself in the public eye.

17. John Nichols, "The Princely Pleasures at the Courte at Kenelwoorth," *The Progresses and Processions of Queen Elizabeth*, vol. 1 (New York: Burt Franklin, 1823) 485–523. For this episode, see pp. 515–23. Future references to this work will be cited parenthetically in the text.

18. Philippa Berry, for instance, reads the entertainment as presenting a conditional celebration of Elizabeth's chastity, whereas Susan Frye focuses on this entertainment as the site of a public struggle between the queen and her courtier for control of her representations and hence her political power. Philippa Berry, *Of Chastity and Power: Elizabethan Literature and the Unmarried Queen* (London: Routledge, 1989) 95–100. Susan Frye, *Elizabeth I: The Competition for Representation* (Oxford: Oxford UP, 1993) 56–96.

19. Berry reads the metamorphosed figures in this entertainment as allusions to the myth of Diana and Actaeon, but this Ovidian tale is not directly alluded to, and it is more useful to approach this issue in the context of a broader Ovidianism.

20. Michael Leslie, in "'Something Nasty in the Wilderness': Entertaining Queen Elizabeth on Her Progresses," points out that the queen is in a position of increased vulnerability when these entertainments take her outside the structural safety of court or palace and into the unpredictable landscape. While this is certainly true at the event, this moment in the entertainment as published points to the way the absence of the queen's figure in print can in fact make her powerfully present, as readers would certainly speculate about her reactions. *Medieval and Renaissance Drama in England* 10 (1998): 47–72.

21. Although Lyly is not identified on this pamphlet, the thematic and stylistic similarities between these three entertainments and Lyly's plays are striking. Bond makes a very persuasive case for Lyly's authorship and includes the entertainment in his *Complete Works of John Lyly*.

22. Nichols, 3: 137. For this entertainment, see pages 130–43. All further references to this entertainment will be cited parenthetically. For the translation of Ovid's text, see *Metamorphoses*, trans. Frank Justus Miller and G. P. Goold, 2 vols. (1916; Cambridge, MA: Harvard UP, 1984). All future citations of Latin and translations will be taken from these volumes in the Loeb Classical Library series and will be cited parenthetically by book and line number in Latin.

23. The tale of Apollo and Daphne is arguably the most pervasive Ovidian tale in Elizabethan literature, second only, perhaps, to the tales of Actaeon and Orpheus. This fact is largely due to the centrality of this narrative to Petrarch's *Rime Sparse* and is also related to its importance as the etiological myth of the laurel, the tree associated with military and poetic achievement in classical as well as early modern times. It also takes on the significances of its history as a commonly and variously moralized tale in the Middle Ages. The original Ovidian tale is familiar, but its emphases, obscured for modern readers by the tale's numerous

retellings, deserve repeating. In bk. 1 of *Metamorphoses*, Apollo has just defeated the python, and in his pride he insults Cupid, suggesting that he carry a torch rather than a bow, as he is clearly the inferior power. Cupid responds by shooting two arrows: one golden, which inflames Apollo with desire for Daphne; the other lead, which inspires Daphne to take a vow of chastity and to beg to live like Diana, hunting and avoiding the company of men. The tale dilates, in fact, on her desire for independence: "Multi illam petiere, illa aversata petentes / impatiens expersque viri nemora avia lustrat / nec, quid Hymen, quid Amor, quid sint conubia curat [Many sought her, but she, averse to all suitors, impatient of control and without thought for man, roamed the pathless woods, nor cared at all that Hymen, love, or wedlock might be]" (I.478–80). The emphasis on Daphne's chastity as directly related to her independence from traditional feminine roles makes this tale an especially relevant one to perform before the Virgin Queen. The entertainments from 1591 and 1592 are filled with celebration of the queen's perfect chastity, so introducing a tale about a chaste nymph who is, at least to some degree, the victim of Apollo, might be a risky proposition. In fact, in Ovid's version of the tale, Daphne begs her father by appealing to Diana, who is the goddess repeatedly associated with Elizabeth, especially in her later reign. The nymph pleads, "Da mihi perpetua, genitor carissime, dixit / virginitate frui! Dedit hoc pater ante Dianae [O father, dearest, grant me to enjoy perpetual virginity. Her father has already granted this to Diana]" (I.81–82). There is no doubt that the retelling of this tale in the entertainment asks the audience (both Elizabeth herself, and the larger audience of courtiers, servants, and possibly villagers) to associate Daphne with the Virgin Queen. This risky association, however, leads to a surprising twist in the retold Ovidian tale.

24. Louis Montrose uses this moment in "Shaping Fantasies" as an example of celebrations of the queen's virginal power, but he argues that it makes Ovid's story into "an emblem of Constancy" (92). Rather than constancy, my analysis suggests a celebration of, if not bodily inconstancy, at least bodily flexibility.

25. See prefatory notes to the play in R. W. Bond's edition, *The Complete Works of John Lyly* (Oxford: Clarendon, 1902) 3: 295–98.

26. Most analyses of Lyly's Ovidianism have been done cursorily in the service of studying Shakespeare's. Jonathan Bate, for instance, implies that Lyly's engagement with Ovid, while more obvious, is less creative than Shakespeare's. Speaking of the ways the Ovidianism of *Gallathea* influences Shakespeare's Ovidianism, he writes, "[Shakespeare] always resolves the apparent need for a sex-change naturalistically, he does not resort [like Lyly] to direct divine intervention in the Ovidian manner. Shakespearean metamorphosis takes place within the mind: even when they are imposed from without, as with the love-juice in *A Midsummer Night's Dream*, the change is psychologically purposeful" (*Shakespeare*

and Ovid, 37). Before him, Leonard Barkan noted that Shakespeare seems to have received some of his sense that metamorphosis is linked to theatricality from Lyly, but Barkan does not analyze the plays (*The Gods Made Flesh*, 282). A more complex analysis, but one that at times takes this mythic approach, is offered in the work of Jeff Shulman, who argues that Ovidianism appealed to Lyly because it figured the dangers of psychological stasis that might befall Elizabeth if she chose a life of chastity. "Ovidian Myth in Lyly's Courtship Comedies," *Studies in English Literature 1500–1900* 25 (1985): 249–69. While Shulman is attentive to one way of reading *Metamorphoses*, as psychological allegory, he depoliticizes the poem and thus simplifies Lyly's complexly political intertextuality. Ellen Caldwell, writing about *Gallathea*, reads the play as a subtle celebration of androgynous marriage, and her reading of the political resonances of that play is similar to my own reading of *Love's Metamorphosis*. She argues that while Lyly followed the Ovidian story of Iphis, who is granted metamorphosis into a male in order to be with Ianthe, he downplayed actual sexual change: "Constancy, not metamorphosis or transformation, is celebrated, and the love of Gallathea and Phyllida seems to remain at the same pitch, no matter under what physical guise they are allowed to express it" (24). She asserts that the play offered Elizabeth a new way of conceptualizing marriage as "a marriage of minds, not bodies; as marriage of women, not of man and woman; and as a way to satisfy both the duties of one's kingdom and the conflicting urges of the heart" (40). "John Lyly's *Gallathea*: A New Rhetoric of Love for the Virgin Queen," *English Literary Renaissance* 17 (1987): 22–40. My reading of the political allegiances of *Love's Metamorphosis* differs in that it reads the mutable, sometimes androgynous Ovidian body as central to the play's analysis of Elizabethan chastity.

27. G. K. Hunter began this political analysis when he described Lyly as a wavering propagandist in what was for many years the only book-length study of his works, *John Lyly: the Humanist as Courtier* (Cambridge: Harvard UP, 1962). He sees Lyly as a great compiler and synthesizer of materials, including myths, and traces a struggle in him between the critical demands of humanism and the political demands of courtier ship. Philippa Berry also analyzes the complexities of Lyly's political representations in chap. 5 of *Of Chastity and Power*. She argues that Lyly's early plays helped remake Elizabeth into a mystical, Neoplatonic figure of contemplation in her final decade, but that they became increasingly misogynistic and satiric, as the poet replaced worship of his queen with his own self-fashioning (111–13).

28. The play was the subject of an article by Theodora Jankowski in 1993, but her reading of it as revealing cultural anxieties about virginity (and hence, about the virginity of the queen), does not take into account the variable meaning of metamorphosis for both Ovid and, therefore, Lyly and his audience. She sees metamorphosis as nothing but violence and

reification, a way of objectifying the female figures in the play, but as I hope my reading demonstrates, the play, in dialogue with Ovid, actually thematizes metamorphosis in many complex ways. See "'The scorne of Savage people': Virginity as 'Forbidden Sexuality' in John Lyly's *Love's Metamorphosis*," *Renaissance Drama* 24 (1993): 123–53. Bond links *Love's Metamorphosis* with *Gallathea* as plays that privilege love over an unwedded chastity (294).

29. Quotations from Lyly's play are taken from the edition of his complete works by R. Warwick Bond. See note 25.

30. Mark Dooley's "The Healthy Body: Desire and Sustenance in John Lyly's *Love's Metamorphosis*," [*Early Modern Literary Studies* 6 (2000): 1–19] argues that the play celebrates a "social body" that is fertile and socially interrelated over the sterile virginal body associated with the queen. He writes, "Lyly effects a metamorphosis of several bodies from a closed, virginal, autoerotic and sterile state to one which is open to possibilities, fruitful, a site of pleasure and exchange; a social body, which is replicated at both levels of the plot" (1). He reads the play as supporting the interrelatedness of Ceres and Cupid, mind and body, and offers an analysis of the play's pervasive bodily imagery. While the play is certainly, as he argues, a celebration of the permeable and interconnected body, it is not necessarily as hostile to its virgin queen as this reading assumes.

31. For one reading of the ways Ovid both signals gender difference and then disrupts such difference, see Lynn Enterline's discussion of rape narratives in *Metamorphoses*. She describes the way the accretion of tales about different kinds of desire ends up destabilizing the gender of the object, making it not just the female body but the male body, animals, inanimate objects, and sometimes no objects at all. In addition, she points out that "when the poem ostentatiously engenders its own important distinction between *anima* and *form* in the story of rape, it requires us to pay attention to the *process of conferring* gender—to the way that its various poetic tropes and genres impose meaning on bodily forms" (*Rhetoric*, 84–85).

Chapter 2

1. See David Lee Miller's seminal discussion of the relationship between Elizabethan politics and Spenserian poetics in *The Poem's Two Bodies: The Poetics of the 1590 Faerie Queene* (Princeton: Princeton UP, 1988).

2. Clark Hulse, in fact, calls Ovid the "presiding genius" of *The Faerie Queene Metamorphic Verse: The Elizabethan Minor Epic* (Princeton, NJ: Princeton UP, 1981) 253. Although many have pointed to the pervasiveness of Ovid's influence on *The Faerie Queene*, the depths of Ovidian intertextuality are still being sounded. Important work has been done analyzing some of Spenser's most Ovidian moments from widely

varied perspectives. See Harry Berger, "Busirane and the War between the Sexes: An Interpretation of *The Faerie Queene* III.xi–xii," *ELR* 1 (1971): 99–121; "Actaeon at the Hinder Gate: The Stag Party in Spenser's Gardens of Adonis," *Desire in the Renaissance: Psychoanalysis and Literature*, ed. Valeria Finucci and Regina Schwartz (Princeton: Princeton UP, 1994); Lauren Silberman, "The Hermaphrodite and the Metamorphosis of Spenserian Allegory" *ELR* 17 (1987): 207–23; Collin Burrow, "Original Fictions: Metamorphoses in *The Faerie Queene*," *Ovid Renewed: Ovidian Influences on Literature and Art from the Middle Ages to the Twentieth Century*, ed. Charles Martindale (Cambridge: Cambridge UP, 1988); Mihoko Suzuki, *The Metamorphoses of Helen: Authority, Difference and the Epic* (Ithaca: Cornell UP, 1989), chap. 4; Theresa Krier, *Gazing on Secret Sights: Spenser, Classical Imitation, and Decorums of Vision* (Ithaca: Cornell UP, 1990); Julia Walker, *Medusa's Mirrors: Spenser, Shakespeare, Milton, and the Metamorphosis of the Female Self* (Newark: U of Delaware P, 1998), chap. 3. More recently, Syrithe Pugh, *Spenser and Ovid* (Ashgate, 2005), has provided the systematic analysis of the poem's Ovidianism in explicit dialogue with Virgil that had been lacking in studies of the poem to date. It is a testament to the huge project of trying to account for Ovid in the poem that Pugh does not provide readings of many of what I consider the most important Ovidian moments in the poem.

3. See Harry Berger, Jr., "'Kidnapped Romance': Discourse in *The Faerie Queene*," in *Unfolded Tales: Essays on Renaissance Romance*, ed. George Logan and Gordon Teskey (Ithaca, NY: Cornell UP, 1989).

4. See Miller, *The Poem's Two Bodies*. On daemonic allegory, see Angus Fletcher, *Allegory: The Theory of a Symbolic Mode* (Ithaca: Cornell UP, 1964).

5. All citations of *The Faerie Queene* are from the edition by A. C. Hamilton, 2nd ed. (London: Longman, 1977).

6. Although most commentaries agree that the transgressive loves in this book are granted considerable sympathy, William Anderson, in his notes to his edition of bks. 6–10 of *Metamorphoses*, argues that the grief in this book is not meant to be genuine and that even Orpheus' grief is parodied in this retelling: "Ovid . . . avoids any convincing sympathy and exploits almost every opportunity to circumvent pathos. The death of Eurydice comes abruptly, and the decision to plead with the powers of the Underworld . . . sounds more like flamboyance than serious mourning." *Ovid's Metamorphoses: Books 6–10* (Norman: U of Oklahoma P, 1972) 475. The controversy about Ovid's tone will continue, but I interpret the irony of the book working in the opposite way. While Orpheus claims to be telling "lighter" tales, a typically Ovidian reversal of hierarchies grants legitimacy and weight to these tales of thwarted desire. Renaissance readings of the book, in fact, especially readings of Orpheus, display a great deal of sympathy with, rather than mockery of, its figures. Thanks to Lynn

Enterline for her particularly insightful comments on Anderson's reading of Ovid's tone.

7. Hamilton, notes to stanza 17.

8. A. C. Hamilton provides the beginnings of a comparison between Spenser's tapestries and Arachne's when he lists the similarities of the tales told in the weaving (note to stanzas 29–46). According to the variorum edition, both Upton (1758) and Jortin (1734) make the comparison, and since then a great many commentators have focused on Spenser's "inaccuracies" in the narratives he chooses to depict from Arachne's tapestry.

9. The central critical controversy about this canto is whether the mind or imagination being allegorized is male (e.g., as Harry Berger would have it) or female (as Thomas Roche and many critics after him have argued)—the demonic magician poet, Busirane, or one of the female characters, Britomart or Amoret. In addition to the previously cited studies by Harry Berger, see Roche, *The Kindly Flame: A Study of the Third and Fourth Books of Spenser's* Faerie Queene (Princeton: Princeton UP, 1964). For a review of this criticism and the additional argument that Busirane's House is an allegory of Elizabeth's privy chamber, see Frye, *Elizabeth I: The Competition for Representation*, 68–69, 124. Frye argues that this section of the poem enacts a metaphorical rape of Elizabeth in her article, "Of Chastity and Rape: Edmund Spenser Confronts Elizabeth I in *The Faerie Queene*," *Representing Rape in Medieval and Early Modern Literature* (New York: Palgrave 2001). See Susanne Wofford's "Gendering Allegory" or Lauren Silberman's analysis of this episode in *Transforming Desire* for two very different readings that both focus on the house as related to methods of artistic production.

10. "majesty n." *OED Online*, Mar. 2009, Oxford University Press, 15 Jul. 2009. http://dictionary.oed.com.ezproxy1.lib.asu.edu/cgi/entry/00299999.

11. For a version of this reading, see Karl Galinsky's *Ovid's Metamorphoses*, 82–83.

12. Barkan 242. Barkan notes this, but then goes on to argue differently about the significance of the tapestries in the House, seeing them as a negative representation of metamorphosis that Spenser corrects elsewhere in the poem: "For in [his poem] Spenser builds a hierarchy of types of transformation. Though he classifies amorous self-metamorphoses as quintessentially empty and immoral, he places them among other types of transformation in such a way as to suggest the shifting nature of the moral categories themselves. . . . The whole poem is a sequence of images, tapestries, pageants, triumphs, masques, changing aesthetic shapes. The narrative motion is not linear but metamorphic, each subject flowing into the next with its own internal logic. Spenser has with the whole poem fulfilled the terms of Arachne's web: and the ultimate chain of changes is that which takes us from the literal Arachne's web of Busyrane's house, at the moral nadir of transformation, to the larger web of *The Faerie Queene*, which attempts to contain the cosmos of metamorphosis" (242).

13. As Judith Anderson puts it in *The Spenser Encyclopedia*, ed. A. C. Hamilton (Toronto: U of Toronto P, 1990), "Britomart is a character in an allegorical romance, but she is less simply a metaphor and more simply herself than are the heroes of earlier books . . . Her person has a history and, at least in these two books [3 and 4], a future; like Arthur, she is involved in historical time" (114).

14. For a discussion of this allegory, see Donald Stump, "The Two Deaths of Mary Stuart: Historical Allegory in Spenser's Book of Justice," *Spenser Studies* 9 (1991): 81–106.

15. "Adicia" is a transliteration of the Greek word for injustice.

16. Some time ago, Jane Aptekar in *Icons of Justice* noted that "[Spenser's] justice is seen to be a more complex and contradictory virtue than one might have assumed." *Icons of Justice: Iconography and Thematic Imagery in Book V of the Faerie Queene* (New York: Columbia UP, 1969) 6. Many more recent critics have stressed Spenser's complex treatment of justice in this book. For example, Michael Dixon argues that bk. 5 is a rhetorical examination and "persuasion" or "courtship" of justice, which implies all of the complexity that such a genre entails. Michael Dixon, *The Polliticke Courtier: Spenser's the Faerie Queene as a Rhetoric of Justice* (Montreal, Canada: McGill-Queens UP, 1996).

17. "wreak. v." *The Oxford English Dictionary*, 2nd ed, 1989, *OED Online*, Oxford University Press, 15 Jul. 2009 http://dictionary.oed.com .ezproxy1.lib.asu.edu/cgi/entry/50287713.

18. According to the variorum edition, John Upton, in his 1758 edition of *The Faerie Queene*, was the first to cite Ovid as the source of this episode, but there has been no further commentary on the subtext's significance. He also cites Euripides' *Hecuba* and Plauttus' *Menaechmus* as other possible sources. Edmund Spenser, *The Faerie Queene*, bk. 5, ed. Edwin Greenlaw et al., *The Works of Edmund Spenser: A Variorum Edition*, vol. 5 (Baltimore, MD: Johns Hopkins UP, 1936). There is a significant tradition of Hecuba's metamorphosis into a dog in Greek and later Roman narrative, found most notably in a prophecy at the end of Euripides' *Hecuba*, and at least one Renaissance writer, Boccaccio, recounts the basic plot of this narrative (*De Muleribus Claris* XXXIV). Ovid's Troy story is also in dialogue with Homer's and Virgil's, but Spenser's emphasis on Hecuba's transformation as a result of her excessive emotion and right after her attempted revenge shows him to be most closely engaged with Ovid's version of this tale.

19. Giovanni Boccaccio, *Famous Women*, ed. and trans. Virginia Brown, I Tatti Renaissance Library (Cambridge: Harvard UP, 2001) 34:1–2.

20. The Latin more literally says Ulysses' hands dragged her away: "Dulchichiae traxere manus" (*Met.* XIII.425).

21. In *The Limits of Eroticism in Post-Petrarchan Narrative* (Cambridge: Cambridge Univ. Press, 1998), Stephens argues that Spenser "positively courts gender confusion—and real confusion, at that, rather than

a carefully engineered cross-dressing that ultimately reinscribes standard gender differences between the sexes. But this is not a happy comfort with androgyny or fluidity; it is a risky venture into territory not yet mapped or anatomized" (14). Her analysis of Spenser's narrative method describes well the operations of his intertextuality in both this episode and more generally.

22. Critics have only begun to explore the complexity of Spenser's engagements with questions of female authority and agency in this section of the poem. See, for example, Katherine Eggert, "'Changing All That Forme of Common Weale': Genre and the Repeal of Queenship in *The Faerie Queene*, Book 5," *English Literary Renaissance* 26 (1996).

23. Eggert 276.

24. Mihoko Suzuki, for example, analyzes Radigund, Britomart, and Mercilla as anxious and often politically oppositional representations of Elizabeth in *The Metamorphoses of Helen* (Ithaca, NY: Cornell UP, 1989) 190–93. See also Eggert, "Changing."

25. Eggert, "Changing" 278.

26. Eggert, "Changing" 282.

27. A. C. Hamilton provides an excellent summary of this strain of criticism, along with some appropriate correctives, in his preface to bk. 5 in his edition of the poem.

28. Upton, as cited in the variorum edition of *The Faerie Queene*, is the first to outline this historical allegory.

29. Richard Mallett argues that this section of bk. 5 "is constructed as an apocalyptic exegesis of contemporary history and is inseparable from a variety of post-Armada apocalyptic texts" in "Book Five of *the Faerie Queene*: An Elizabethan Apocalypse," *Spenser Studies* 11 (1994): 129.

30. Additional evidence that this canto is specifically "about" Phillip II is outlined by René Graziani, who explores the iconography of the King of Spain's *impresa* in relation to the Souldan's representation. According to Graziani, the *impresa* was invented for Phillip sometime before 1566 and was published in Girolamo Ruscelli's *Le imprese illustri con espositioni et discorsi* in 1566, 1572, 1580, and 1584. Analyzing the pictorial allegory of the impresa, Graziani suggests the ways in which Spenser exploited the irony inherent in the impresa's implied claims for naval dominance and Christian empire, both areas that, he is right to suggest, would provoke Spenser greatly. Rene Graziani, "Phillip II's Impresa and Spenser's Souldan," *Journal of the Warburg and Courtauld Institutes* 27 (1964): 322.

31. Judith Anderson, "'Nor Man It Is': The Knight of Justice in Book V of Spenser's *Faerie Queene*," *PMLA* 85 (1970): 76.

32. Spenser, Edmund. *The Works of Edmund Spenser: A Variorum Edition*. Ed. Edwin Greenlaw, Charles Grosvenor Osgood, Frederick Morgan Padelford, and Ray Heffner. 5 vols. (Baltimore: Johns Hopkins UP, 1936) 225. According to *The Spenser Encyclopedia*, Adicia is the "idea" of injustice, whereas the Souldan is its "practical consequences." A. C.

Hamilton, ed., *The Spenser Encyclopedia* (Toronto: U of Toronto P, 1990). T. K. Dunsheath writes of the "marriage of convenience" between Adicia and the Souldan and says that it "quite obviously, reveals similarities of temperament, as both are proud and irascible, despiteful and malicious. A difference in manner of execution, however, exists between husband and wife. It is Adicia, as her name implies, who 'counsels' her husband to perform the acts of injustice so dear to her heart . . . He is in effect her physical manifestation and carries out her policies; or, to put it in other terms, Adicia is theory and Soldan is practice." T. K. Dunseath, *Spenser's Allegory of Justice in Book V of "The Faerie Queene"* (Princeton, NJ: Princeton UP, 1968) 195. James Norhnberg comments only that "injustice is joined to cruelty, as Spenser's Adicia is joined to the Souldan." After this, he refers to Adicia only as "the Souldan's consort." *The Analogy of "The Faerie Queene"* (Princeton, NJ: Princeton UP, 1976) 362, 74.

33. Mallett, "Book Five" 138.
34. Sheila Cavanaugh, "Ideal and Practical Justice: Artegall and Arthur in *Faerie Queene* V," *Renaissance Papers* (1984): 27. Cavanaugh assumes Adicia's straightforwardly negative characterization in her analysis of Britomart, Radigund, Malbecco, and Adicia as a "confederacy of cows" whose virtue is called into question by the poem. Sheila T. Cavanaugh, *Wanton Eyes and Chaste Desires: Female Sexuality in "The Faerie Queene"* (Bloomington: Indiana UP, 1994) 163–72. The episode has received slightly more extensive commentary by Michael Dixon in his recent book on bk. 5, *The Polliticke Courtier: Spenser's "The Faerie Queene" as a Rhetoric of Justice* (Montreal, Canada: McGill-Queens UP, 1996). Most importantly, Dixon offers a corrective to dismissing it as a dry or simplistic historical allegory: "As exempla of injustice the Souldan and Adicia thus resonate with narrative precedents and homologous patterns, and this episode surely functions as something more than an enabling allegorical gloss on the external, topical exemplum of the Spanish Armada" (139). Even he, however, is quick to read Adicia as an abstraction in relation to the Souldan, arguing that she is the personification of his appetitive motives, since she "counsels him through confidence of might / To breake all bonds of law, and rules of right" (20.4–5) (138). While his reading is sensitive to the ways in which her metamorphosis marks Adicia as an important figure for reading the meaning of the episode, Dixon's analysis of the pathos of this section does not account for the fact that she is compared to Hecuba, the noble Trojan Queen. Although the text may be, as Dixon argues, attempting to value differently the motivations of its protagonist and its villains, these distinctions become confused by Adicia's representation. The "thin line" Dixon draws between celebration of Arthur and Artegall and condemnation of the Souldan and Adicia becomes impossibly blurred.
35. Cesare Ripa, *Iconologia*, ed. Stephen Orgel (Padua, 1611; New York: Garland, 1976).

36. James Nohrnberg describes Malbecco's trajectory as the movement from man to demonic allegory in *The Analogy of The Faerie Queene*, 99. Susanne Wofford reads the "genealogy" of Malbecco, "the man Malbecco being transformed before our eyes into the figure," as a representation of the cost of personification and "the operations of allegorical representation itself." Susanne Wofford, *The Choice of Achilles: The Ideology of Figure in the Epic* (Stanford, CA: Stanford UP, 1992) 298. Linda Gregerson argues that in representing Malbecco's metamorphosis, Spenser is "anatomizing his own symbolic method" (23) and shows how this allegorical trajectory is simultaneously the result of Malbecco's inabilities as a Christian reader and lover. He is "an admonitory exemplum" (24), guilty of concupiscence and the inability to distinguish between letter and spirit, and his figure embodies the dangers of misreading the icons of Spenser's own text. Linda Gregerson, "Protestant Erotics: Idolatry and Interpretation in Spenser's *Faerie Queene*," *ELH* 58 (1991): 1–34.

CHAPTER 3

1. All quotations from Shakespeare's plays are taken from the Arden Shakespeare editions (Thomas Nelson and Sons Ltd, United Kingdom): *Hamlet* edited by Harold Jenkins (1982, reprinted 1997) and *Titus Andronicus* by Jonathan Bate (1995).
2. In *Aeneid*, Hecuba's laments are part of the pathos of the description of the fall of Troy itself, as they are in the player's play. Ovid, however, in *Metamorphoses*, focuses on Hecuba's subsequent losses of her daughter and remaining son, her revenge on Polymnestor, and her metamorphosis. See my discussion of Ovid's tale below.
3. As Heather Dubrow has pointed out in *Shakespeare and Domestic Loss: Forms of Deprivation, Mourning, and Recuperation*, Shakespeare was invested throughout his career in negotiating the cultural significance of various kinds of loss and grief. Dubrow notes that the Troy story, like the Edenic fall, served as a central cultural narrative of loss—be it physical or literal, emotional, social, or often all of these at once. *Shakespeare and Domestic Loss: Forms of Deprivation, Mourning, and Recuperation* (Cambridge: Cambridge UP, 1999). 10.
4. See, for example, Clark Hulse, in "Wresting the Alphabet: Oratory and Action in *Titus Andronicus*." Hulse writes, "As a first experiment with the shifting levels of dramatic action, Titus is a worthy predecessor to Hamlet" (118).
5. Jonathan Bate, in his introduction to the Arden edition of the play, explains, "Shakespeare is interrogating Rome, asking what kind of an example it provides for Elizabethan English; in so doing, he collapses the whole of Roman history, known to him from Plutarch and Livy, into a single action" (17). Andrew Ettin argues that in this play Shakespeare

critiques the "idea" of Rome by pointing to the violence and lack of heroism exemplified in the Roman works of literature that serve as Elizabethan models: "We cannot ignore a central fact which Shakespeare takes pains to call to our attention in the early play: the literary sources for the most shocking images of 'unregenerate barbarism' in the play are in fact products of the Roman imagination, Ovid's *Metamorphoses* and Seneca's *Thyestes*." "Shakespeare's First Roman Tragedy," *ELH* 37 (1970): 326. Responding to Eugene Waith's earlier argument about the play (see below), he points to the "emotional and therefore moral inadequacy of the Ovidian stance" (339). Similarly, Grace Starry West argues that Shakespeare is criticizing the immorality of Roman education, especially through Ovid, in the play. She writes that the "juxtaposition of delicately allusive speech and villainous action in a play about Rome at the twilight of its greatness suggests that Shakespeare is exploring the relationship between Roman education—the source of all the bookish allusions—and the disintegration of the magnificent city which produced that education." "Going by the Book: Classical Allusion in Shakespeare's *Titus Andronicus*," *Studies in Philology* 79 (1982): 65. Such readings do not fully take into account the self-conscious and self-critical representation of violence in the works of either Ovid or Seneca. In contrast, in an early defense of the play, Albert Tricomi, in "The Aesthetics of Mutilation in *Titus Andronicus*," offers an influential and illuminating analysis of the way horrific metaphors are literalized throughout the play, and he links this strategy to the play's Ovidianism and its Senecanism. *Shakespeare Survey* 27 (1974): 11–19.

6. See Bate's introduction to the Arden edition (29) and his *Shakespeare and Ovid* for a full discussion of the tale of Philomela as a pattern for the play's action. Ann Thompson also explores the play's reliance on the narrative of Philomela's rape, and its revisions, in "Philomel in *Titus Andronicus* and *Cymbeline*," *Shakespeare Survey* 19 (1978): 23. This overdetermined intertextuality has not always been considered a strength of the play. Robert Miola, for instance, calls the play "a vile hash of Ovid, Seneca, Plutarch, and Virgil, made more unpalatable by the self-consciousness of the various imitations and allusions." Such a reading of the aesthetic value of Shakespeare's insistent intertextuality reveals our historical distance from a culture in which self-conscious imitation legitimated, rather than debased, artistic production. There is considerable debate about whether there is enough evidence to suggest that the play is based on a source that does not survive. Frank Kermode, in his introduction to the play in *The Riverside Shakespeare*, summarizes the arguments that have been made that an Italian tale, for which we have an eighteenth-century chapbook translation, is the primary source for *Titus* (1020). Jonathan Bate, in the Arden edition, argues persuasively that the chapbook does not necessarily indicate a lost source for the play.

7. Leonard Barkan in *The Gods Made Flesh* and then Jonathan Bate in *Shakespeare and Ovid*, in addition to offering structural analyses of this intertext, also offer insightful readings of the ways Ovidianism comments especially on Humanism and rhetoric throughout the play. Bate argues that the play is Shakespeare's critique of the humanist educational practice of *imitatio*, because in the play the only thing the characters seem to have learned from their educations in Roman literature is violence. The characters do repeatedly cite their literary precedents when they commit acts of extreme violence, but Bate's condemnation of these acts is often stronger than the play's. Titus' revenge, for example, which Bate reads as excessively violent and immoral, is in fact much more ambiguously validated by the play. Another most important contribution to our understanding of the function of Ovidianism in the play is Heather James' argument that the Ovidian intertext serves to dismember the Virgilian, deconstructing Virgilian codes of Roman honor and thereby complicating the Elizabethan "translation of empire" that made London into Troynouvant. Like Bate, James sees the Ovidianism of the play operating to critique Roman values. While the play certainly critiques the violence of the precedents it cites, however, it also refers more positively to these precedents to define and open possibilities for expression and agency for its characters.

8. Close to my own concerns with the Ovidian constructions of emotion in *Titus* is perhaps the most influential article on the play before the last period of increased interest, that is Eugene Waith's 1957 article, "The Metamorphosis of Violence in *Titus Andronicus*." *Shakespeare Survey* 10 (1957): 39–49. In this seminal piece, Waith outlines how "psychic metamorphosis"—his term for the way in which human beings experiencing "unendurable emotion" are robbed of their humanity in *Metamorphoses*—is at stake in both Ovid and Shakespeare. He argues, ultimately, that while Ovid's narrative form can make use of the device of metamorphosis, Shakespeare is attempting to do the impossible, because when he imitates Ovid's interest in a man whose emotions force him to "transcend the normal limits of humanity" (39), he cannot represent the results of this moment on the stage. Although I disagree with Waith's characterization of the play as a failure, I think he begins to articulate some of the most compelling cultural work the play does in politicizing and gendering certain types of emotion.

9. Julie Taymor's filmic production of this scene, in fact, exploits this allusion by representing Lavinia standing on the stump of a tree in a field with branches protruding from her wrists. This representation of Lavinia as an emblem not just of mutilation but also of metamorphosis contributes to the repeated visual representations of violent metamorphosis in *Titus*.

10. Tricomi, for example, argues that Lavinia's violation is identified with "the violation of Rome and of all civilized virtue" (17).

11. This play has been especially important as a text for feminist investi-
gations of representations of violence, female language, and the body
on the stage, and these analyses often equate silence with powerlessness. See Marion Wynne-Davies, "'The Swallowing Womb': Consumed
and Consuming Women in *Titus Andronicus*," *The Matter of Difference: Materialist Feminist Criticism of Shakespeare*, ed. Valerie Wayne
(Ithaca: Cornell UP, 1991); Caroline Asp, "Upon her Wit Doth Earthly
Honor Wait': Female Agency in *Titus Andronicus*," *"Titus Andronicus": Critical Essays* (New York: Garland, 1995); Cynthia Marshall, "'I
can interpret all her martyr'd signs': *Titus Andronicus*, Feminism and
the Limits of Interpretation," *Sexuality and Politics in Renaissance
Drama*, ed. C. L. and Karen Robertson (Lewiston, NY: Edwin Mellen,
1991); R. L. Kesler, "Subjectivity, Time and Gender in *Titus Andronicus, Hamlet*, and *Othello*," *Enacting Gender on the English Renaissance
Stage*, ed. V. C. Russell (Urbana: U of Illinois P, 1999). Karen Robertson and Robin Bott have contributed articles on the representation
of rape in the play to the collection, *Representing Rape in Medieval
and Early Modern Literature*, ed. Elizabeth Robertson and Christine M. Rose (New York: Palgrave, 2001); Bott, "'O, Keep Me From
Their Worse than Killing Lust': Ideologies of Rape and Mutilation in
Chaucer's *Physician's Tale* and Shakespeare's *Titus Andronicus*"; Robertson, "Rape and the Appropriation of Progne's Revenge in Shakespeare's *Titus Andronicus*, Or, 'Who Cooks the Thyestean Banquet?'"
Although Robertson's observations about the play are very similar to
my own, our overall interpretations of the play's gender politics differ
widely, as will be discussed below.

12. My reading of Lavinia as an agent involved in the Andronici revenge has
been most influenced by Katherine Rowe's work on the iconography of
hands and the moment in the play in which Titus asks Lavinia to carry
his hand in her mouth. Rowe argues that although it is tempting to
read Lavinia with Titus' hand in her mouth as a symbol of her, and by
extension the family's, extreme powerlessness, this "sentimental" (300)
reading is undercut by the fact that the hand could stand for political
power in itself and could therefore mark their agency rather than their
lack of it. As a fetish, she argues, the hand operates to hide the memory
of their helplessness to facilitate their revenge and agency. She asserts
that "we can read Lavinia as an intending agent who deploys manual
icons to powerful effect. In taking up Titus' hand, she assumes the iconography of agency to herself. She deploys the emblematic conventions
of empowerment less as a kind of walking *main de justice* than as a *non
sine casus*. Thus the function of the stick-writing scene is not to tell us
what we already know has happened but to reintroduce Lavinia into the
sequence of revenge that leads to the reinstatement of the Andronici in
the Roman polis." "Dismembering and Forgetting in *Titus Andronicus*,"
Shakespeare Quarterly 45 (1994): 300–301.

13. A number of critics have pointed to the way the play's characters are self-conscious about their implications in pagan narratives. See, for example, Mary Fawcett, "Arms/Words/Tears: Language and the Body in *Titus Andronicus*," *ELH* 50 (1983): 261–77; Maurice Hunt, "Compelling Art in *Titus Andronicus*," *Studies in English Literature* 28 (1988): 197–218.

14. On this absence of the maternal presence, especially in Shakespeare's early plays, see Janet Adelman, *Suffocating Mothers: Fantasies of Maternal Origin in Shakespeare's Plays, "Hamlet" to "The Tempest"* (New York: Routledge, 1992).

15. I am indebted to Professor James McKeown at the University of Wisconsin–Madison for help with reading this Latin phrase and also for pointing out that its repetition is a reflection of Ovid's quasi-formulaic style.

16. Marion Wynne-Davies argues that this allusion generates at least confused sympathy for Tamora (145). I think this sympathy is presented as possible and then intentionally withdrawn.

17. Robertson reads the final scene of Titus' regendering as a violent exclusion of the rape victim and her female revengers, as it is not Philomela's sister but her father who cooks the banquet. The text's exclusions are, however, highlighted and incomplete.

Chapter 4

1. "witchmonger n." *The Oxford English Dictionary*, 2nd ed. 1989, *OED Online*, Oxford University Press, 15 Jul. 2009 http://dictionary.oed .com.ezproxy1.lib.asu.edu/cgi/entry/50286256.

2. Elizabeth Spiller, *Science, Reading, and Renaissance Literature: The Art of Making Knowledge* (Cambridge: Cambridge UP, 2004) 1. See also B. J. Shapiro, *Probability and Certainty in Seventeenth-Century England: A Study of the Relationships Between Natural Science, Religion, History, Law and Literature* (Princeton: Princeton UP, 1983).

3. For an analysis of the transitions in legal discourse related to conceptualizing evidence that mark witchcraft debates, see Frances Dolan, "'Ridiculous Fictions: Making Distinctions in the Discourses of Witchcraft," *Differences: A Journal of Feminist Cultural Studies* 7 (1995): 82–110.

4. Shapiro, *Probability and Certainty*, especially chap. 6, "Witchcraft."

5. For an extensive discussion and analysis of these issues in historical studies of witchcraft, see Diane Purkiss, *The Witch in History: Early Modern and Twentieth-Century Representations* (London: Routledge, 1996).

6. James Sharpe, *Witchcraft in Early Modern England* (Harlow: Pearson Education, 2001) 16–17. For a fuller discussion, see Sharpe, *Instruments of Darkness: Witchcraft in England 1550–1750* (London: Hamish Hamilton, 1996).

7. Sharpe, *Witchcraft* 70–88.

8. Sharpe (*Instruments of Darkness*, 50) notes, "It is one of the great peculiarities of the history of witchcraft in England that the first major theoretical work on the subject published by an English writer, Reginald Scots' *Discoverie of Witchcraft* of 1584, was unrelentingly skeptical."

9. See Stuart Clark, *Thinking with Demons: The Idea of Witchcraft in Early Modern England* (Oxford: Clarendon, 1997). Sydney Anglo, "Reginald Scot's Discoverie of Witchcraft: Scepticism and Sadduceeism," *The Damned Art: Essays in the Literature of Witchcraft*, ed. Sydney Anglo (London: Routledge, 1977).

10. *The Discoverie of Witchcraft* is currently available in a few mostly facsimile editions. The Bodleian Library's copy is reprinted as number 299 in the series The English Experience published by Da Capo Press. The most accessible is the paperback Dover edition, which reprints Montague Summers' condensed edition of 1930. I have used both of these editions, but my main source for citations is a 1584 edition in the collection of St. Catharine's College, Cambridge. In the material for this essay, no serious variances among these editions were found. I have silently modernized Scot's spelling whenever an obvious modern variant was available.

11. As Purkiss points out, "though historians distinguish Scot sharply from demonologists like his opponent Jean Bodin, his argument has a lot in common with theirs. Both skeptics and demonologists created elaborate cosmological theses in order to deny that strange old women in villages had any real power. For demonologists, real power lay with the devils summoned by the witch, and by the beginning of the seventeenth century most argued that even the power to summon devils was illusory. While demonologists displaced the witches' power onto male demons or refused her even this much authority, Scot saw the witch as completely powerless, since in a providential universe divine power could brook no competition from demons or witches" (64).

12. In this chapter, I assume that skeptical writing is a subgenre or antigenre of demonological writing and part of the same discourse. For a discussion of how similar mainstream demonological writing can be to skeptical writing, see Clark, *Thinking with Demons*, chap. 13, "Believers and Skeptics."

13. Because this woodcut is a historiated initial, it is not noted in Luborsky and Ingram's entry on *The Discoverie* in *A Guide to English Illustrated Books*. The woodcuts depicting the "juggling tricks" attributed to witchcraft are described.

14. A cursory analysis of the surviving works printed by the publishers associated with *The Discoverie*, William Brome and Henry Denham, did not reveal the origins of this initial. Although Henry Denham did publish at least two editions of *Heroides*, neither contains such elaborately illustrated initials.

15. I would like to thank the many art historians (whose names I did not record) who rushed to my assistance to identify the typical pose of a river god when I presented this illustration as a handout in my talk at the

conference, *Metamorphosis: The Changing Face of Ovid in Medieval and Early Modern Europe* (University of Toronto; March 2005).

16. Bate, *Shakespeare and Ovid* 252. Bate also cites Carroll's more extensive treatment of this passage in *The Tempest*, in *Metamorphoses of Shakespearean Comedy* (Princeton: Princeton UP, 1985).

17. Reference is to *Met.* 1.85–86.

18. Katharine Eisaman Maus, "Sorcery and Subjectivity in Early Modern Discourses of Witchcraft," *Historicism, Psychoanalysis, and Early Modern Culture*, ed. Carla Mazzio and Douglas Trevor (New York: Routledge, 2000).

19. See Sharpe, *Witchcraft* 32–44.

Afterword

1. See Jim Ellis, *Sexuality and Citizenship: Metamorphosis in Elizabethan Erotic Verse* (Toronto: U of Toronto P, 2003).

2. See Lynn Enterline, *Rhetoric of the Body* (Cambridge: Cambridge UP, 2000), especially chap. 3, "Embodied Voices: Autobiography and Fetishism in the *Rime Sparse.*"

3. Ben Brantley, "Theater Review: How Ovid Helps Deal with Loss and Suffering," *New York Times* 10 Oct. 2001, 22 Jul. 2008 http://query.nytimes.com/gst/fullpage.html?res=9B06E3DE1E3CF933A25753C1A9679C8B63&scp=1&sq=brantley%20ovid&st=cse.

WORKS CITED

Adelman, Janet. "Making Defect Perfection: Shakespeare and the One-Sex Model." *Enacting Gender on the Renaissance Stage*. Ed. Viviana Comensoli and Anne Russell. Urbana: U of Illinois P, 1999. 23–52.

———. *Suffocating Mothers: Fantasies of Maternal Origin in Shakespeare's Plays*, Hamlet *to* The Tempest. New York: Routledge, 1992.

Allen, Graham. *Intertextuality*. London: Routledge, 2000.

Anderson, Judith. "'Nor Man It Is': The Knight of Justice in Book V of Spenser's *Faerie Queene*." *PMLA* 85 (1970): 65–77.

———. "Artegall" and "Britomart." *The Spenser Encyclopedia*. Ed. A. C. Hamilton. Toronto: U of Toronto P, 1990. 62–4, 113–115.

Anglo, Sydney. "Reginald Scot's *Discoverie of Witchcraft*: Scepticism and Sadduceeism." *The Damned Art: Essays in the Literature of Witchcraft*. Ed. Sydney Anglo. London: Routledge, 1977. 106–39.

Aptekar, Jane. *Icons of Justice: Iconography and Thematic Imagery in Book V of* The Faerie Queene. New York: Columbia UP, 1969.

Asp, Carolyn. "'Upon Her Wit Doth Earthly Honor Wait': Female Agency in *Titus Andronicus*." *Titus Andronicus: Critical Essays*. New York: Garland, 1995.

Axton, Marie. *The Queen's Two Bodies: Drama and the Elizabethan Succession*. London: Royal Historical Society, 1977.

Barchiesi, Alessandro. *The Poet and the Prince: Ovid and Augustan Discourse*. Berkeley: U of California P, 1997.

Barkan, Leonard. *The Gods Made Flesh: Metamorphosis and the Pursuit of Paganism*. New Haven: Yale UP, 1986.

Barnard, Mary. *The Myth of Apollo and Daphne from Ovid to Quevedo: Love, Agon and the Grotesque*. Durham, NC: Duke UP, 1987.

Barthes, Roland. *S/Z*. New York: Hill and Wang, 1974.

Bate, Jonathan. *Shakespeare and Ovid*. Oxford: Clarendon, 1993.

Berger, Harry, Jr. "Actaeon at the Hinder Gate: The Stag Party in Spenser's Garden of Adonis." *Desire in the Renaissance: Psychoanalysis and Literature*. Ed. Valeria Finucci and Regina Schwartz. Princeton: Princeton UP, 1994. 91–119.

———. "Busirane and the War Between the Sexes: An Interpretation of *The Faerie Queene* III.xi–xii." *Revisionary Play: Studies in the Spenserian Dynamics*. Berkeley: U of California P, 1988. 172–94.

———. "'Kidnapped Romance': Discourse in *The Faerie Queene.*" *Unfolded Tales: Essays on Renaissance Romance.* Ed. George Logan and Gordon Teskey. Ithaca: Cornell UP, 1989. 208–56.

Berry, Philippa. *Of Chastity and Power: Elizabethan Literature and the Unmarried Queen.* London: Routledge, 1989.

Boccaccio, Giovanni. *Famous Women.* Ed. and trans. Virginia Brown. Cambridge: Harvard UP, 2001.

Bott, Robin. "'O, Keep Me from Their Worse Than Killing Lust': Ideologies of Rape and Mutilation in Chaucer's 'Physician's Tale' and Shakespeare's *Titus Andronicus.*" *Representing Rape in Medieval and Early Modern Literature.* Ed. Elizabeth Robertson and Christine M. Rose. New York: Palgrave, 2001. 189–211.

Brown, Georgia. *Redefining Elizabethan Literature.* Cambridge: Cambridge UP, 2004.

Burrow, Collin. "Original Fictions: Metamorphoses in *The Faerie Queene.*" *Ovid Renewed: Ovidian Influences on Literature and Art from the Middle Ages to the Twentieth Century.* Ed. Charles Martindale. Cambridge: Cambridge UP, 1988. 99–119.

Bush, Douglas. *Mythology and the Renaissance Tradition in English Poetry.* New York: Norton, 1963.

Caldwell, Ellen. "John Lyly's *Gallathea*: A New Rhetoric of Love for the Virgin Queen." *English Literary Renaissance* 17 (1987): 22–40.

Carroll, William C. *The Metamorphoses of Shakespearean Comedy.* Princeton: Princeton UP, 1985.

Cavanaugh, Shiela. "Ideal and Practical Justice: Artegall and Arthur in *Faerie Queene V.*" *Renaissance Papers* (1984): 19–28.

———. *Wanton Eyes and Chaste Desires: Female Sexuality in* The Faerie Queene. Bloomington: Indiana UP, 1994.

Clark, Stuart. *Thinking With Demons: The Idea of Witchcraft in Early Modern England.* Oxford: Clarendon, 1997.

Cohen, Stephen. "(Post)modern Elizabeth: Gender, Politics, and the Emergence of Modern Subjectivity." *Shakespeare and Modernity: Early Modern to Millennium.* Ed. Hugh Grady. London: Routledge, 2000. 20–39.

Cole, Mary Hill. *The Portable Queen: Elizabeth I and the Politics of Ceremony.* Amherst: U of Massachusetts P, 1999.

Curran, Leo. "Transformation and Anti-Augustanism in Ovid's *Metamorphoses.*" *Arethusa* 5 (1972): 71–92.

Dixon, Michael. *The Polliticke Courtier: Spenser's* The Faerie Queene *as a Rhetoric of Justice.* Montreal: McGill-Queens UP, 1996.

Dolan, Frances. "Ridiculous Fictions: Making Distinctions in the Discourses of Witchcraft." *Differences: A Journal of Feminist Cultural Studies* 7 (1995): 82–110.

Dooley, Mark. "The Healthy Body: Desire and Sustenance in John Lyly's *Love's Metamorphosis.*" *Early Modern Literary Studies* 6 (2000): 1–19.

Dubrow, Heather. *Shakespeare and Domestic Loss: Forms of Deprivation, Mourning, and Recuperation*. Cambridge: Cambridge UP, 1999.

Dunseath, T. K. *Spenser's Allegory of Justice in Book V of* The Faerie Queene. Princeton: Princeton UP, 1968.

Eggert, Katherine. "'Changing All That Forme of Common Weale': Genre and the Repeal of Queenship in *The Faerie Queene*, Book 5." *English Literary Renaissance* 26 (1996): 259–90.

———. *Showing Like a Queen: Female Authority and Literary Experiment in Spenser, Shakespeare, and Milton*. Philadelphia: U of Pennsylvania P, 2000.

Ellis, Jim. *Sexuality and Citizenship: Metamorphosis in Elizabethan Erotic Verse*. Toronto: U of Toronto P, 2003.

Elizabeth I. *Elizabeth I: Collected Works*. Ed. Leah Marcus, Janel Mueller, and Mary Beth Rose. Chicago: U of Chicago P, 2000.

Enterline, Lynn. *The Rhetoric of the Body from Ovid to Shakespeare*. Cambridge: Cambridge UP, 2000.

Ettin, Andrew. "Shakespeare's First Roman Tragedy." *English Literary History* 37 (1970): 325–41.

Fawcett, Mary Laughlin. "Arms/Words/Tears: Language and the Body in *Titus Andronicus*." *English Literary History* 50 (1983): 261–77.

Feeney, Dennis. *The Gods in Epic: Poets and Critics of the Classical Tradition*. Oxford: Clarendon, 1991.

Fletcher, Angus. *Allegory: The Theory of a Symbolic Mode*. Ithaca: Cornell UP, 1964.

Frye, Susan. *Elizabeth I: The Competition for Representation*. Oxford: Oxford UP, 1993.

———. "Of Chastity and Rape: Edmund Spenser Confronts Elizabeth I in *The Faerie Queene*." *Representing Rape in Medieval and Early Modern Literature*. New York: Palgrave, 2001. 353–79.

———. "Of Chastity and Violence: Elizabeth I and Edmund Spenser in the House of Busirane." *Signs* 20 (1994): 49–78.

Galinsky, Karl. *Ovid's* Metamorphoses*: An Introduction to the Basic Aspects*. Berkeley: U of California P, 1975.

Graziani, Rene. "Phillip II's Impresa and Spenser's Souldan." *Journal of the Warburg and Courtauld Institutes* 27 (1964): 322–24.

Greene, Thomas M. *The Light in Troy: Imitation and Discovery in Renaissance Poetry*. New Haven: Yale UP, 1982.

———. "The Natural Tears of Epic." *Epic Traditions in the Contemporary World: The Poetics of Community*. Ed. Margaret Beissinger, Jane Tylus, and Susanne Wofford. Berkeley: U of California P, 1999. 189–202.

Gregerson, Linda. "Protestant Erotics: Idolatry and Interpretation in Spenser's *Faerie Queene*." *English Literary History* 58 (1991): 1–34.

Grosz, Elizabeth. *Volatile Bodies: Toward a Corporeal Feminism*. Bloomington: Indiana UP, 1994.

Guy, John, ed. and introd. *The Reign of Elizabeth I: Court and Culture in the Last Decade*. Cambridge: Cambridge UP, 1995.

————. *Tudor England*. Oxford: Oxford UP, 1988.

Hackett, Helen. *Virgin Mother, Maiden Queen: Elizabeth I and the Cult of the Virgin Mary*. London: Macmillan, 1995.

Hardie, Philip. *The Epic Successors of Virgil: A Study in the Dynamics of a Tradition*. Cambridge: Cambridge UP, 1993.

————. *Ovid's Poetics of Illusion*. Cambridge: Cambridge UP, 2002.

Harvey, Elizabeth. "Ventriloquizing Sappho: Ovid, Donne, and the Erotics of the Feminine Voice." *Criticism* 31 (1989): 115–38.

Hamilton, A. C., ed. *The Spenser Encyclopedia*. Toronto: U of Toronto P, 1990.

Hinds, Stephen. *Allusion and Intertext: Dynamics of Appropriation in Roman Poetry*. Cambridge: Cambridge UP, 1998.

————. *The Metamorphoses of Persephone: Ovid and the Self-Conscious Muse*. Cambridge: Cambridge UP, 1987.

Hulse, Clark. *Metamorphic Verse: The Elizabethan Minor Epic*. Princeton: Princeton UP, 1981.

————. "Wresting the Alphabet: Oratory and Action in *Titus Andronicus*." *Criticism* 19 (1979): 106–18.

Hunt, Maurice. "Compelling Art in *Titus Androncius*." *Studies in English Literature* 28 (1988): 197–218.

Hunter, G. K. *John Lyly: The Humanist as Courtier*. Cambridge: Harvard UP, 1962.

James, Heather. "Ovid and the Question of Politics in Early Modern England." *ELH* 70 (2003): 343–73.

————. *Shakespeare's Troy: Drama, Politics, and the Translation of Empire*. Cambridge: Cambridge UP, 1997.

Jankowski, Theodora. "'The Scorne of Savage People': Virginity as 'Forbidden Sexuality' in John Lyly's *Love's Metamorphosis*." *Renaissance Drama* 24 (1993): 123–53.

Johnson, W. R. "The Problem of the Counterclassical Sensibility and Its Critics." *California Studies in Classical Antiquity* 3 (1970): 123–51.

Johnson-Haddad, Miranda. "A Time for Titus: An Interview with Julie Taymor." *Shakespeare Bulletin* 18 (2000). 10 Jul. 2002 http://www.shakespeare-bulletin.org/issues/fall00/interview-johnson-haddad.html.

Kantorowicz, Ernst. *The King's Two Bodies*. Princeton: Princeton UP, 1957.

Kennedy, Gwynne. *Just Anger: Representing Women's Anger in Early Modern England*. Carbondale: U of Illinois P, 2000.

Kesler, R. L. "Subjectivity, Time and Gender in *Titus Andronicus*, *Hamlet*, and *Othello*." *Enacting Gender on the English Renaissance Stage*. Ed. V. C. Russell. Urbana: U of Illinois P, 1999. 114–32.

King, John. "Queen Elizabeth I: Representations of the Virgin Queen." *Renaissance Quarterly* 43 (1990): 30–74.

Knox, John. *The Political Writings of John Knox: The First Blast of the Trumpet Against the Monstrous Regiment of Women and Other Selected Writings*. Ed. Marvin A. Breslow. Cranbury, NJ: Associated University Presses, 1985.

Knox, Peter. *Ovid's* Metamorphoses *and the Traditions of Augustan Poetry.* Cambridge, Cambridge UP, 1986.

Krier, Theresa. *Gazing on Secret Sights: Spenser, Classical Imitation and the Decorums of Vision.* Ithaca: Cornell UP, 1990.

Laquer, Thomas. *Making Sex: Body and Gender from the Greeks to Freud.* Cambridge: Harvard UP, 1990.

Leslie, Michael. "'Something Nasty in the Wilderness': Entertaining Queen Elizabeth on Her Progresses." *Medieval and Renaissance Drama in England* 10 (1998): 47–72.

Levin, Carole. *"The Heart and Stomach of a King": Elizabeth I and the Politics of Sex and Power.* Philadelphia: U of Pennsylvania P, 1994.

Loewenstein, Joseph. *Responsive Readings: Versions of Echo in Pastoral, Epic and Jonsonian Masque.* New Haven: Yale UP, 1984.

Lutz, Catherine. *Unnatural Emotions: Everyday Sentiments on a Micronesian Atoll and Their Challenge to Western Theory.* Chicago: U of Chicago P, 1988.

Lyly, John. *The Complete Works of John Lyly.* Ed. R. W. Bond. 3 vols. Oxford: Clarendon, 1902.

Lyne, Raphael. *Ovid's Changing Worlds: English Metamorphoses, 1567–1632.* Oxford: Oxford UP, 2001.

MacCaffrey, Wallace T. *Elizabeth I: War and Politics, 1558–1603.* Princeton: Princeton UP, 1992.

Mallett, Richard. "Book Five of *The Faerie Queene*: An Elizabethan Apocalypse." *Spenser Studies* 11 (1994): 129–59.

Marcus, Leah. *Puzzling Shakespeare: Local Reading and Its Discontents.* Berkeley: U of California P, 1988.

Marshall, Cynthia. "'I Can Interpret All Her Martyr'd Signs': *Titus Andronicus*, Feminism and the Limits of Interpretation." *Sexuality and Politics in Renaissance Drama.* Ed. Carole Levin and Karen Robertson. Lewiston, NY: Edwin Mellen, 1991. 193–213.

McKinley, Kathryn L. *Reading the Ovidian Heroine:* Metamorphoses *Commentaries 1100–1618. Leiden: Brill, 2001.*

Miller, David Lee. *The Poem's Two Bodies: The Poetics of the 1590* Faerie Queene. Princeton: Princeton UP, 1988.

Miller, Jacqueline. "The Passions Signified: Imitation and the Construction of Emotions in Sidney and Wroth." *Criticism* 43 (2001): 407–21.

Miola, Robert. "*Titus Andronicus* and the Mythos of Shakespeare's Rome." *Shakespeare Studies* 14 (1981): 85–98.

Montrose, Louis Adrian. "Idols of the Queen: Policy, Gender and the Picturing of Elizabeth I." *Representations* 68 (1999): 108–61.

———. "'Shaping Fantasies': Figurations of Gender and Power in Elizabethan Culture." *Representations* 1 (1983): 61–94.

Mullaney, Steven. "Mourning and Misogyny: *Hamlet, The Revenger's Tragedy,* and the Final Progress of Elizabeth I, 1600–1607." *Shakespeare Quarterly* 45 (1994): 139–62.

Nichols, John, ed. *The Progresses and Public Processions of Queen Elizabeth.* 1823. 3 vols. New York: Burt Franklin, 1965.

Nohrnberg, James. *The Analogy of* The Faerie Queene. Princeton: Princeton UP, 1976.

Otis, Brooks. *Ovid as an Epic Poet.* 2nd ed. Cambridge: Cambridge UP, 1970.

Ovid. *Metamorphoses.* 1916. Trans. Frank Justus Miller. Loeb Classical Library. 3rd ed. Cambridge: Harvard UP, 1984.

———. *Metamorphoses.* Trans. David Raeburn. Introd. Dennis Feeney. London: Penguin, 2004.

———. *Metamorphoses.* 1567. Trans. Arthur Golding. Ed. Madeline Forey. Baltimore: Johns Hopkins UP, 2002.

———. *Ovid's Metamorphoses: The Arthur Golding Translation of 1567.* Ed. John Frederick Nims. Introd. Jonathan Bate. Philadelphia: Paul Dry, 2000.

———. *Shakespeare's Ovid: Being Arthur Golding's Translation of "The Metamorphoses."* Ed. W. H. D. Rouse. London: De La More, 1904.

———. *Ovid's "Metamorphoses": Books 6–10.* Ed. William Anderson. Norman: U of Oklahoma P, 1972.

Paster, Gail Kern. *The Body Embarrassed: Drama and the Disciplines of Shame in Early Modern England.* Ithaca: Cornell UP, 1993.

———. *Humoring the Body: Emotions and the Shakespearean Stage.* Chicago: U of Chicago P, 2004.

Paster, Gail Kern, Katherine Rowe, and Mary Floyd-Wilson, eds. *Reading the Early Modern Passions: Essays in the Cultural History of Emotion.* Philadelphia: U of Pennsylvania P, 2004.

Paster, Gail Kern, and Skiles Howard, eds. *A Midsummer Night's Dream: Texts and Contexts.* Boston: Bedford/St. Martin's, 1999.

Pugh, Syrithe. *Spenser and Ovid.* Aldershot, Hants, England: Ashgate, 2005.

Purkiss, Diane. *The Witch in History: Early Modern and Twentieth-Century Representations.* London: Routledge, 1996.

Puttenham, George. *The Arte of English Poesie.* 1589. Kent, OH: Kent State UP, 1970.

Quint, David. *Epic and Empire: Politics and Generic Form from Virgil to Milton.* Princeton: Princeton UP, 1993.

Richlin, Amy. "Reading Ovid's Rapes." *Pornography and Representation in Greece and Rome.* Ed. Amy Richlin. Oxford: Oxford UP, 1992. 158–79.

Ripa, Cesare. *Iconologia.* 1611. Ed. Stephen Orgel. New York: Garland, 1976.

Robertson, Karen. "Rape and the Appropriation of Progne's Revenge in Shakespeare's *Titus Andronicus,* Or, 'Who Cooks the Thyestean Banquet?'" *Representing Rape in Medieval and Early Modern Literature.* Ed. Elizabeth Robertson and Christine M. Rose. New York: Palgrave, 2001. 213–37.

Roche, Thomas. *The Kindly Flame: A Study of the Third and Fourth Books of Spenser's* Faerie Queene. Princeton: Princeton UP, 1964.

Rose, Mary Beth. "The Gendering of Authority in the Public Speeches of Elizabeth I." *PMLA* 115 (2000): 1077–82.

Rowe, Katherine. "Dismembering and Forgetting in *Titus Andronicus*." *Shakespeare Quarterly* 45 (1994): 279–303.

Sanders, Eve Rachele. *Gender and Literacy on Stage in Early Modern England*. Cambridge: Cambridge UP, 1998.

Schiesari, Juliana. *The Gendering of Melancholia: Feminism, Psychoanalysis, and the Symbolics of Loss in Renaissance Literature*. Ithaca: Cornell UP, 1992.

Schoenfeldt, Michael. *Bodies and Selves in Early Modern England: Physiology and Inwardness in Spenser, Shakespeare, Herbert, and Milton*. Cambridge: Cambridge UP, 1999.

Scot, Reginald. *The Discouerie of Witchcraft wherein the Lewde Dealing of Witches and Witchmongers Is Notablie Detected . . .* London: William Brome, 1584.

———. *The Discoverie of Witchcraft.* "The English Experience." Amsteram: Da Capo, 1971. Facsimile of Bodleian Library, Shelfmarks: Douce S.216 and 4_.S.53Th.

———. *The Discoverie of Witchcraft.* Ed. M. Summers. 1930. Mineola, NY: Dover, 1972.

Seznec, Jean. *The Survival of the Pagan Gods.* New York: Pantheon, 1953.

Shakespeare, William. *Titus Andronicus.* Ed. Jonathan Bate. London: Routledge, 1995.

Shapiro, B. J. *Probability and Certainty in Seventeenth-Century England: A Study of the Relationships Between Natural Science, Religion, History, Law and Literature*. Princeton: Princeton UP, 1983.

Sharpe, James. *Instruments of Darkness: Witchcraft in England 1550–1750.* London: Hamish Hamilton, 1996.

———. *Witchcraft in Early Modern England.* Harlow: Pearson Education, 2001.

Shulman, Jeff. "Ovidian Myth in Lyly's Courtship Comedies." *Studies in English Literature 1500–1900* 25 (1985): 249–69.

Silberman, Lauren. "The Hermaphrodite and the Metamorphosis of Spenserian Allegory." *English Literary Renaissance* 17 (1987): 207–23.

———. *Transforming Desire: Erotic Knowledge in Books III and II of* The Faerie Queene. Berkeley: U of California P, 1995.

Solodow, Joseph. *The World of Ovid's* Metamorphoses. Chapel Hill: U of North Carolina P, 1988.

Spelman, Elizabeth. "Anger and Insubordination." *Women, Knowledge, and Reality: Explorations in Feminist Philosophy*. Ed. Ann Garry and Marilyn Pearsall. Boston: Unwin Hyman, 1989. 263–74.

Spenser, Edmund. *The Faerie Queene.* Ed. A. C. Hamilton. London: Longman, 1977.

———. *The Works of Edmund Spenser: A Variorum Edition.* Ed. Edwin Greenlaw, Charles Grosvenor Osgood, Frederick Morgan Padelford, and Ray Heffner. 5 vols. Baltimore: Johns Hopkins UP, 1936.

Spiller, Elizabeth. *Science, Reading and Renaissance Literature: The Art of Making Knowledge*. Cambridge: Cambridge UP, 2004.

Stanivukovic, Goran, ed. *Ovid and the Renaissance Body*. Toronto: U of Toronto P, 2001.

Stephens, Dorothy. *The Limits of Eroticism in Post-Petrarchan Narrative*. Cambridge: Cambridge UP, 1998.

Strong, Roy. *The Cult of Elizabeth: Elizabethan Portraiture and Pageantry*. London: Thames and Hudson, 1977.

Stump, Donald. "The Two Deaths of Mary Stuart: Historical Allegory in Spenser's Book of Justice." *Spenser Studies* 9 (1991): 81–106.

Suzuki, Mihoko. *The Metamorphoses of Helen*. Ithaca: Cornell UP, 1989.

Terada, Rei. *Feeling in Theory: Emotion After the "Death of the Subject."* Cambridge: Harvard UP, 2001.

Teskey, Gordon. *Allegory and Violence*. Ithaca: Cornell UP, 1996.

Thompson, Ann. "Philomel in *Titus Andronicus* and *Cymbeline*." *Shakespeare Survey* 19 (1978): 23–32.

Tissol, Garth. *The Face of Nature: Wit, Narrative, and Cosmic Origins in Ovid's* Metamorphoses. Princeton: Princeton UP, 1997.

Tricomi, Albert. "The Aesthetics of Mutilation in *Titus Andronicus*." *Shakespeare Survey* 27 (1974): 11–19.

Waith, Eugene. "The Metamorphosis of Violence in *Titus Andronicus*." *Shakespeare Survey* 10 (1957): 39–49.

Walker, Julia. *Medusa's Mirrors: Spenser, Shakespeare, Milton, and the Metamorphosis of the Female Self*. Newark: U of Delaware P, 1998.

West, Grace Starry. "Going by the Book: Classical Allusion in Shakespeare's *Titus Andronicus*." *Studies in Philology* 79 (1989): 62–77.

Wind, Edgar. *Pagan Mysteries in the Renaissance*. 1958. New York: Norton, 1968.

Wofford, Susanne. *The Choice of Achilles: The Ideology of Figure in the Epic*. Stanford: Stanford UP, 1992.

———. "Epics and the Politics of the Origin Tale: Virgil, Ovid, Spenser, and Native American Aetiology." *Epic Traditions in the Contemporary World: The Poetics of Community*. Ed. Margaret Beissnger, Jane Tylus, and Susanne Wofford. Berkeley: U of California P, 1999. 239–69.

———. "Gendering Allegory: Spenser's Bold Reader and the Emergence of Character in *The Faerie Queene* III." *Criticism* 30 (1988): 1–21.

Wynne-Davies, Marion. "'The Swallowing Womb': Consumed and Consuming Women in *Titus Andronicus*." *The Matter of Difference: Materialist Feminist Criticism of Shakespeare*. Ed. Valerie Wayne. Ithaca: Cornell UP, 1991. 129–51.

Yates, Frances. *Astraea: The Imperial Theme in the Sixteenth Century*. London: Routledge, 1975.

Index

Burrow, Collin, 160n2
Bush, Douglas, 152n39
Busirane, 60, 67, 72–75, 77, 84–85,
    160n2, 161n9

Caldwell, Ellen, 158n26
Castle Joyeous, 77, 80, 83–84
Cavanaugh, Sheila, 102
Celia, 47, 52, 54
Cerberus, 111
Ceres, 14, 46–47, 49, 51–55,
    57–58, 159n30
characterization, 76–77, 102, 108,
    115, 120, 134, 143
chastity, 44, 47, 50, 52, 75,
    156n18, 157n23, 158n26,
    161n9
Cinyras, 49
Circe, 28, 30, 56, 130–31, 135
Clark, Stuart, 127
Cohen, Stephen, 33, 154n10
commentaries, Ovidian, 25, 148n6,
    151n34, 160n6
concealment, 117, 124
Cupid, 46–47, 49, 51–55, 57–58,
    70–71, 74, 157n23, 159n30
Curran, Leo, 151n28
Cynthia, 31, 33, 83–84
Cyparissus, 60–67, 104

Daphne, 8, 14–15, 42–45, 48–50,
    52, 110, 132, 139, 142, 145,
    156–57n23
death, 15, 23, 37–38, 50–51, 66,
    79–80, 82, 84, 87–88, 90, 92,
    118, 121, 123, 160n6, 162n14
Deepedesire, 36, 39
Demetrius, 109, 113, 119–22
demons, 129
Denham, Henry, 130
Diana, 13, 31, 61–62, 78, 142,
    156n19, 157n23
Dido, 15–16

Discoverie of Witchcraft, 25, 30,
    125–37, 139, 153n4
divine, 17, 22, 31, 66, 69–70, 143
Donne, John, 152n37

Eggert, Katherine, 99–100
ekphrasis, 71, 81–82
Elizabeth I, 1, 23–24, 27–37, 39,
    41, 43–47, 49–51, 53, 55,
    57, 72, 74, 84–87, 100–101,
    152n36, 153n2
emblem, 103, 111–12, 123
entertainments, Elizabethan, 24, 28,
    31, 34–42, 44–45, 155n16,
    156nn20–21, 157n23
Enterline, Lynn, 15, 18, 148n4,
    150n19, 152n37, 159n31,
    161n6, 174n2
Erysichthon, 49, 51, 55, 57

Faerie Queene, The, 59–61, 63, 65,
    67–69, 71, 73, 75, 77, 79,
    81, 83–85, 87–89, 91, 93, 95,
    99–101
Feeney, Dennis, 150n26,
    151nn29–30
Finucci, Valeria, 160n2
Floyd-Wilson, Mary, 149n11
Fradubio, 50, 52
Frye, Susan, 34, 153n6, 154n10,
    155n14, 156n18, 161n9

Galinsky, Karl, 151n30, 161n11
Gallathea, 159
Ganymede, 39, 63–64, 72
Gardante, 75, 84–85
Garry, Ann, 149n17
Gascoigne, George, 35–36
Geertz, Clifford, 5
gender, 9, 14, 24, 27, 29, 31–34,
    40–41, 45–46, 49, 54–55,
    57–58, 60, 68, 77–80, 83–85,
    123